Praise for *Managing Ge...*

"Robin and Kat have created a book that is as fun to read as it is impactful. This book is way more than a how-to manual for leading Gen Z employees . . . it is an inspiring book that gave me new leadership and business insights. *Managing Generation Z* is a must-read for all aspiring leaders!"
—**Jim Damian**, founder and CEO, Stria

"A great resource, not just for those dealing with Gen Z, but for anyone who wants or needs a good introduction to or review of the best practices in human resources management."
—**John B. Stark**, PhD, Professor of Management, Organizational Consultant, and Director of the Program in Educational Leadership at California State University, Bakersfield

"A must-read for owners and managers of any organization that recruits on a regular basis. My hat is off to the authors for providing such practical advice."
—**Nancy C. Belton**, CPA, managing partner, Daniells Phillips Vaughan & Bock

"*Managing Generation Z*'s pragmatic, realistic approach will appeal to HR professionals and general managers."
—*Library Journal*

"*Managing Generation Z* is a must-read for business professionals. Paggi and Clowes provide a fresh perspective as to how one can recruit, engage and retain the newest members of our workforce."
—**John McFarland**, SHRM-CP, Senior Vice President, Worklogic HR

"Paggi and Clowes offer informative and practical insight into dealing with Generation Z and other generations in the workplace. The book is easy to read but packed with information and advice on a multitude of human resources issues and effective communication among colleagues. Every manager and human resources professional will take away important tips from *Managing Generation Z*."
—**Daniel K. Klingenberger**, Esq., employment law attorney and president of the Kern County Society for Human Resource Management

"*Managing Generation Z* provides practical advice—infused with real-life examples and knowledge of the law—to inspire leaders to facilitate a successful environment for the newest generation in the workplace."
—**Christine L. Peterson**, executive editor, *The Bakersfield Californian*

"An insightful, generous, and most of all, practical guide about how to success-fully hire, work, and achieve alongside Gen Z workers. *Managing Generation Z* is essential reading for anyone interested in what is unique and special about America's next work force."
—**Jeremy Adams**, author of *The Secrets of Timeless Teachers*

"Exceptional informative, impressively well written, thoroughly reader friendly in organization and presentation, *Managing Generation Z* is a comprehensive course of insightful instruction and essential reading for anyone with a man-agement responsibility for this new and on-coming generation of employees."
—*Midwest Book Review*

"By the time I had read to page 9, I had already started a mental checklist for things our managers and HR team needed to do. *Managing Generation Z* is a great manual for anyone who manages employees of any age."
—**Zane Smith**, executive director, Boys & Girls Clubs of Kern County

"*Managing Generation Z* should be part of any manager or HR leader's read-ing . . . . From their tech-savvy abilities which might supersede those of their superiors to their naivety over professional interactions and office politics, this management guide is key to understanding this generation and tapping their inherent skills."
—*The Bookwatch*

"A timely, practical, and immediately implementable game plan to successfully welcome Gen Z into your organization."
—**Michael Russo**, entrepreneurship instructor

Managing Generation Z

How to Recruit, Onboard, Develop, and Retain the Newest Generation in the Workplace

Robin Paggi and Kat Clowes

Fresno, California

Published by Quill Driver Books
An imprint of Linden Publishing
2006 South Mary Street, Fresno, California 93721
(559) 233-6633 / (800) 345-4447
QuillDriverBooks.com

Quill Driver Books and Colophon are trademarks of
Linden Publishing, Inc.

ISBN 978-1-61035-400-4

35798642

Printed in the United States of America
on acid-free paper.

Library of Congress Cataloging-in-Publication Data

Names: Paggi, Robin, author. | Clowes, Kat, author.
Title: Managing Generation Z : how to recruit, onboard, develop, and retain
    the newest generation in the workplace / Robin Paggi and Kat Clowes.
Identifiers: LCCN 2021011580 (print) | LCCN 2021011581 (ebook) | ISBN
    9781610354004 (paperback ; alk. paper) | ISBN 9781610353809 (epub)
Subjects: LCSH: Generation Z--Employment--United States. | Conflict of
    generations in the workplace--United States. | Intergenerational
    relations--United States.
Classification: LCC HF5549.5.C75 P44 2021 (print) | LCC HF5549.5.C75
    (ebook) | DDC 658.300973--dc23
LC record available at https://lccn.loc.gov/2021011580
LC ebook record available at https://lccn.loc.gov/2021011581

To Michayla and Victoria—my two favorite Gen Zers.
—Robin

To all of my students past, present, and future.
—Kat

TABLE OF CONTENTS

INTRODUCTION

I n 2018, my (Robin's) seventeen-year-old granddaughter asked her grandfather if his accounting firm might have a part-time position for her. He told her that she would need to apply and interview with the firm's administrator, and I advised that she must dress professionally for an interview rather than wear one of her usual outfits. The firm had no openings, so there was no interview.

Shortly thereafter, the human resources outsourcing company where I work needed a part-time temporary employee, and my granddaughter was hired based on my recommendation. Because I had already advised her on appropriate work attire, I assumed she would arrive at the office in a business-like outfit. Instead, she arrived in leggings, a long T-shirt, and sandals. (Note to self: never assume!)

I sent her a text after work that day to let her know her outfit had not complied with the company's dress code. She asked what she should wear instead, so I sent her several pictures of appropriate apparel. The next time she came to work, she was wearing this outfit.

I told her she looked great and took this picture to send to her grandfather. ("Look how cute our girl is!")

Then she wore the same outfit every time she came to the office!

I didn't ask her why she always wore the same thing, but I did ask Kat Clowes, who works with people my granddaughter's age.

This is what Kat said: "This generation grew up with metrics, benchmarks at school, and extensive standardized testing. Wanting specific instructions, your granddaughter knew that you had approved this outfit; therefore, that was the one to go with when showing up for work."

According to Kat, my granddaughter is a member of Generation Z. Sixty-one million strong, this generation already outnumbers Generation X and is almost as big as the Baby Boomer generation. Born shortly before or after 9/11, most of this generation has always had a smartphone, the internet, and social media. Gen Zers have never lived in a world with privacy, security, or stability.

Over the past fifteen years or so, thousands of articles and books have sought to explain the Millennials as they traveled through school and began their careers, but now the world needs to get ready for Gen Zers. They are not just younger Millennials—they are from a different world. The only world that Gen Zers have ever known looks far different from the world that Millennials or Boomers or any other generation has known.

Mostly because of technology, Gen Zers grew up with a different set of common experiences than earlier generations. They also missed some of the lessons most previous generations learned. Only 19 percent of them gained any job experience as teenagers—whereas almost half of Baby Boomers had jobs when they were teens.[1] As a result, much of Gen Z lacks some of the general know-how that hiring managers assume is common knowledge. And if a manager displays frustration, a Gen Zer is likely to simply quit, leaving managers confused and bewildered—and shorthanded.

As a training and development specialist at Worklogic HR, I work with hundreds of employers, human resources professionals, managers, and supervisors, and I know all of them could benefit from a better

---

[1] Knowledge@Wharton, "Make Way for Generation Z in the Workplace," Wharton School, University of Pennsylvania, January 22, 2019, https://knowledge.wharton. upenn.edu/article/make-room-generation-z-workplace/.

understanding of Gen Z. Kat Clowes has worked with hundreds of young people as they get ready for colleges and careers and knows that these young workers can bring a wealth of skills and insights into your workplace. This book will help you make sense of Gen Zers and maximize their potential.

About the Authors

Robin Paggi is a training and development specialist at Worklogic HR, a human resources outsourcing company in Bakersfield, California. She has more than twenty-five years of experience in creating and delivering training to employees in supervisory positions on topics such as effective communication, performance management, conflict resolution, and harassment prevention. She also coaches employees who need individual assistance with their interpersonal skills and mediates conflicts between coworkers. She has been a human resources manager and college instructor.

With a master's degree in interdisciplinary studies and a master's degree in communication studies, Robin is currently pursuing a master's degree in industrial and organizational psychology. She also has earned professional certifications in human resources (SHRM-SCP and SPHR-CA), training (CPLP), coaching (CPC), and in administering the MBTI, DiSC, and EQ-I assessments.

Robin is active in her community and has served as the president of Bakersfield Twilight Rotary, board president of the Kern County Society for Human Resource Management, chair of the Greater Bakersfield Employment and Labor Law Forum, legislative director of the Human Resources Association of Central California, and member of the Youth Leadership Bakersfield advisory committee. She is also a graduate of the San Joaquin Valley Civic Leadership and Leadership Bakersfield programs.

Robin frequently speaks at conferences, writes articles for local publications, and appears on local radio and television shows to discuss human resources (HR) issues. Throughout the book, "I" and "me" refer to Robin, unless the text is specifically attributed to Kat Clowes.

Kat Clowes is the founder and CEO of March Consulting and author of *Put College to Work: How to Use College to the Fullest to Discover Your Strengths and Find a Job You Love Before You Graduate.* She created March Consulting to help prepare high school students for college and beyond, offering advice on college applications and career paths. Around 2017, Kat began to recognize a definite change in her students' questions, learning styles, and preparedness for adulthood, giving her an early look at the unique skills and challenges Generation Z will bring to the workplace.

Kat earned a bachelor's degree in communications with an emphasis in digital film and broadcast from Santa Clara University, a master's degree in business administration with an emphasis in entrepreneurship from Mount Saint Mary's University, and a certificate in educational consulting from the University of California, Irvine. In addition to her book *Put College to Work,* which was published by Quill Driver Books in 2015, she has authored various miniguides for her clients, including *A Beginner's Guide to LinkedIn, How to Rock Your Job Fair,* and *A Complete Guide to Interviewing.*

Kat has offered workshops or keynote talks to various organizations, including the Boys & Girls Clubs of Kern County and the Distinguished Young Women of California, and has been featured in *U.S. News and World Report, Her Campus, Bakersfield Life,* and *Bakersfield Magazine,* discussing various topics related to college admissions and early career advice. She is an professional member of the Independent Educational Consultants Association, a member of the Western Association for College Admission Counseling, and a member of the Higher Educational Consultants Association.

Kat is also heavily involved in Rotary, serving as president of the Bakersfield Twilight Rotary in 2016–2017. She is currently working with District 5240, which includes seventy-four clubs in California, to make Rotary more attractive to young professionals.

Together, the authors have your bases covered. Robin understands the needs of HR and hiring managers and employee trainers and supervisors. Kat has seen the inner workings of the minds of hundreds of Gen Zers and can help explain who they are and what they value. In this book, we provide practical tips on how to manage this newest generation in the workforce so you will get the best work from them.

About This Book

This book is divided into seven sections addressing multiple aspects related to finding, hiring, and training Gen Z workers, getting the best results from your employees, avoiding workplace problems, and promoting health and security in your organization. At the beginning of each section, you will find a list of key takeaways from the chapters that follow. Chapters are short and self-contained, allowing you to dip into the sections that are most relevant to you at any moment. Throughout the book, you will find sections labeled "Kat's Take," which are thoughts from Kat Clowes regarding some of the unique characteristics of Gen Z.

You will also see boxes labeled "Employers React to Gen Z," which are quotes that Robin collected from employers, HR professionals, managers, and supervisors regarding their experiences with Gen Z workers. Robin has given presentations on the different generations in the workplace for over a decade, talking to hundreds of training participants about their experiences working with younger people, and has utilized some of that anecdotal information in this book. In addition, while writing this book, she contacted select clients to ask specifically about their experiences with Gen Z employees. Most of these clients are from the Central Valley of California, where Robin lives, and work in oil, agriculture, finance, health care, various service industries, and nonprofit industries.

About twenty-five clients responded directly to these questions about Gen Z workers:

- In general, what are their strengths?
- What challenges have you encountered with them?
- How have you addressed those challenges?
- What do you still need help with?

Also included throughout the book and in several appendices are examples from court cases and legal proceedings related to employer-employee relations.

About the Generations

For the first time in history, there are five generations in the workplace, which can make for some interesting meetings! Even while acknowledging that individuals rarely fit neatly into predetermined categories, many managers agree that employees from similar age ranges and similar backgrounds tend to share characteristics that were likely developed in their formative years. Recognizing common experiences of the various generations and how those experiences helped promote certain traits can help us understand each other better and work together better.

As Jacques May writes in his article "Generation Z: Understanding a Generation and Culture," "If you understand culture you can understand a generation and if you understand a generation you can bridge the gap that can so easily divide us."[2]

Although there are no "official" dividing lines or definitions for the various generations, this book generally follows these boundaries and descriptions offered by the Center for Generational Kinetics.[3]

Traditionalists or the Silent Generation, born before 1946

Members of this generation lived through the aftermath of the Great Depression and World War II; they are described as patient, dedicated, hardworking conformists.

Baby Boomers (1946-1964)

The sheer number of births in the years following World War II meant that this generation grew up vying for limited resources; Baby Boomers are typically described as competitive and driven.

---

[2] Jacques May, "Generation Z: Understanding a Generation and Culture," Info Pilgrims, July 24, 2018, https://infopilgrims.com/blog/2018/7/23/generation-z-understanding-a-generation-and-culture.

[3] Center for Generational Kinetics, "Generational Breakdown: Info About All of the Generations," accessed on March 30, 2020, https://genhq.com/FAQ-info-about-generations/.

Gen X (1965-1976)

Because many of this generation grew up with working parents, Gen Xers are often described as "latch-key kids" who came home to empty houses after school. They did their chores and took care of themselves (and sometimes younger siblings) until a parent returned home. This generation learned to be independent but also sensitive to work-life balance.

Gen Y or Millennials (1977-1995)

Members of this generation are referred to as both Gen Y and Millennials because they grew up near the turn of the century. Many of them grew up with more technology than earlier generations and under the sometimes-too-watchful eye of "helicopter" parents. They are described as wanting quick results and needing lots of guidance.

Gen Z (1996-TBD)

One device sets this generation apart from every other: the smartphone. Although smartphones are now ubiquitous in the US population, no previous generation had this technology so widely available throughout its formative years. Ninety-five percent of people in this age group have a smartphone, and 55 percent use it five or more hours daily. Twenty-six percent use a smartphone ten or more hours daily.[4] Thus, Gen Zers value technology and also independence to work on their own. However, they may lack skills and experiences most older people picked up early in life, such as the ability to use a map or locate information from nondigital sources.

Bonnie Monych, in "3 No-Nonsense Tips for Effectively Managing Gen Z," says that "Gen Zers value and expect independence, creativity, freedom to work when and where they want, diversity and, of course, technology. But while millennials introduced many of these expectations to the workforce, Gen Zers now demand them, and they won't

---

[4]Center for Generational Kinetics, "Top 10 Gen Z Statistics From 2018," accessed on May 29, 2020, https://genhq.com/top-10-ways-gen-z-is-shaping-the-future/.

settle for anything less."[5]

Some managers and researchers warn that generalizing about people based on their age can foster inaccurate beliefs and lead to stereotyping.[6] And it's certainly true that not all Baby Boomers are competitive and not all Millennials want lots of guidance. However, many employers find that being aware of generational differences can enhance their understanding of individuals and help them plan for the reactions of various groups.

And even if you disagree with the generalizations about the generations, you cannot deny that Gen Z is young. Young people rarely have the knowledge and experience they need to meet the expectations of their older managers, who too often forget they didn't know everything when they started working either.

Because you're reading this book, chances are you understand that Gen Z will need to be successful at your workplace in order for your organization to remain successful in the long run. And you may be worried about how you're going to incorporate these young workers into your company. Don't fret! Hiring Gen Z workers and helping them become valuable employees is not that complicated.

You don't need to reinvent the wheel—many tried-and-true management practices still work for Gen Z; this book will help you brush up on some of those techniques. And we'll also tell you what practices should be adjusted for Gen Z workers and which adjustments will help the most.

Employers, supervisors, HR managers, and survey respondents say that working with this tech-savvy, practical, and young generation has many benefits—but also many challenges. This book is designed to help you meet those challenges and get the best work from your Gen Z employees.

Because when Gen Z is happy and working productively, your workplace will be in a better position to thrive.

---

[5]Bonnie Monych, "3 No-Nonsense Tips for Effectively Managing Gen Z," Insperity, n.d., accessed March 30, 2020, https://www.insperity.com/blog/managing-gen-z/.

[6]Eden King, Lisa Finkelstein, Courtney Thomas, and Abby Corrington, "Generational Differences at Work Are Small. Thinking They're Big Affects Our Behavior," *Harvard Business Review*, August 1, 2019, https://store.hbr.org/product/generational-differences-at-work-are-small-thinking-they-re-big-affects-our-behavior/ H0520T.

OPEN THE DOOR TO GEN Z

Section 1 Takeaways

- Recognize the Gen Z gems.
- Find the Gen Zers who will help your company.
- Perfect your hiring process.
- Know what you want: experience or talent.
- Choose your interview questions carefully.
- Test—legally—to finalize the process.

CHAPTER 1

WHY SHOULD YOU HIRE GEN Z?

Some of you may be thinking that hiring and training Gen Z workers sounds like it could be a lot of trouble. It could force you to learn new techniques and think about your employees from a new point of view. Is that really necessary? Maybe you don't expect to have any trouble filling vacancies for a while and you assume that anyone you hire will be happy just to have a job—any job.

This book was written in the spring and early summer of 2020 as millions of people were losing jobs because of the COVID-19 pandemic and lockdowns. In that climate, employers might be tempted to think it won't be too difficult to find workers or replacement workers if their new hire doesn't work out. But your company could soon regret not having some enthusiastic Gen Zers on board, for a number of reasons.

They're Techies

For starters, Gen Z has skills your company needs. Hundreds of employers, HR professionals, managers, and supervisors whom I've talked to overwhelmingly say that being tech savvy is this generation's greatest strength.

Do you understand the differences between Snapchat, Instagram, and Twitter and how all of them can be used to reach your potential customers? Has your company struggled during the pandemic to adapt to virtual meetings or find long-distance substitutes for in-person sales and marketing efforts? Would you like to have an employee who seems to intuitively grasp all the finer points of Zoom? Or one who could tell you where all the young people went when they left Facebook? Then you need some Gen Zers in your office.

" Employers React to Gen Z

They are able to do research on the internet—they google every-thing or YouTube it so they can find an answer or how to fix some-thing. So, they have the answer in a matter of minutes instead of the old-fashioned way of going to the library, checking out a book, and then reading it; or they find an expert in that field to tell them or teach them.

"

As we get older, we tend to resist change—especially new technol-ogy, although once we learn it, we usually can't live without it. Gen Z can help you plug into the latest programs and gadgets, and you might be surprised by how quickly you come to rely on an app or tech device once you've seen how helpful it can be. According to a *Forbes* article by Robert Glazer, "A 2019 Pew Research study found that 68% of Baby Boomers own smartphones and 52% own tablets. That technology use is about to leap upward (because of the coronavirus)."[7]

Employing Gen Z workers and helping them feel empowered and engaged can help your company make the most from rising technology use—for both your employees and your customers.

---

[7]Robert Glazer, "COVID-19 Will Permanently Change the Way Every Gen-eration Lives—Here's How," *Forbes*, April 1, 2020, https://www.forbes.com/sites/robertglazer/2020/04/01/covid-19-will-permanently-change-the-way-every-genera-tion-lives-heres-how/#7edee67e493b.

They're Younger

According to "Marist Mindset List for the Entering College Class of 2023":

- The primary use of a phone has always been to take pictures.
- PayPal has always been an online option for purchasers.
- YouTube has become the video version of Wikipedia.
- There have always been "smartwatches."[8]

There are 61 million Gen Zers, so you are not going to be able to ignore them for long. And they're coming along at just the right time to help replace all the Boomers who are hitting retirement age. In fact, you may soon discover that a number of your Gen X employees are also looking to retire or find a new career path, especially with the global pandemic upending so much of "normal" life.

"Many Gen-Xers will likely come out of all this thinking long and hard about what they really want to be doing for the remaining few chapters of their life," according to Glazer. "I expect a lot of voluntary and involuntary career changes."[9]

So, who will replace all the Boomer and Gen X employees who are deciding to step away from your company? The Gen Z wave is coming.

They Can Be Practical

Gen Zers were children and adolescents during the recession of 2008. Many of them saw parents and family members lose their jobs, their houses, their retirement accounts, and their sense of security. So, Gen Zers tend to be more risk averse and to seek more stability, which means we're less likely to see them bounce around from company to company as Millennials have tended to do. Gen Zers tend to look at jobs more practically.

In addition, Gen Zers are used to testing and metrics because they grew up participating in high-stakes testing at their schools, which

---

[8]Marist College, "Marist Mindset List for the Entering College Class of 2023," accessed June 1, 2020, https://www.marist.edu/mindset-list.

[9]Glazer, "COVID-19."

needed to hit certain benchmarks to avoid funding cuts. So workers from this generation are likely to meet or exceed expectations—as long as those expectations are clearly communicated and documented.

They're Magnets

If you make your Gen Z employees feel valuable and engaged, they are likely to attract other qualified Gen Zers who want to work at your company. One of the best ways to attract highly qualified applicants of all ages is to build a great reputation as an employer. Your employees are living advertisements for your business, and you can ensure that they say good things about your company if you make your organization a great place to work.

How can you make sure your company is a great place to work? Of course, it never hurts to offer higher pay and better benefits than your competition. But it requires more than that. Companies that made *Fortune* magazine's "100 Best Companies to Work For" list in 2020

- demonstrate they care about their employees and put them first;
- give employees autonomy and support;
- are transparent;
- provide a work-life balance and flexible work schedule;
- cultivate an inclusive and diverse culture;
- provide opportunities to learn and grow; and
- are philanthropic.[10]

Having happy Gen Z employees will attract more Gen Zers who will be valuable additions to your firm. The next chapter offers other tips for finding great Gen Z workers.

---

[10] *Fortune*, "Fortune 100 Best Companies to Work For 2020," accessed May 29, 2020, https://www.greatplacetowork.com/best-workplaces/100-best/2020.

CHAPTER 2

HOW DO YOU FIND GEN Z WORKERS?

E ven when millions of people are looking for a job, it's not always easy to find just the right person for your company. And Gen Z workers may be harder to find because their job searches may not be following the "traditional" paths.

It is highly unlikely that Gen Zers will ever answer your classified ad in the newspaper, and not many of them will stop in and ask about the Help Wanted sign in your window. If you want to find great Gen Z candidates—or have them find you—you're going to have to get in the social media game.

Consider this: in the first quarter of 2020, more than 2.6 billion people logged on to Facebook every month,[11] more than 166 million people actively used Twitter every day,[12] and 690 million people had a LinkedIn membership.[13] So, you're doing yourself a disservice if you dis-

---

[11]Zephoria Digital Marketing, "The Top 20 Valuable Facebook Statistics—Updated May 2020," May 2020, https://zephoria.com/top-15-valuable-facebook-statistics/.

[12]Zephoria Digital Marketing, "Top 10 Twitter Statistics—Updated May 2020," May 2020, https://zephoria.com/twitter-statistics-top-ten/.

[13]LinkedIn, "About Us," accessed May 29, 2020, https://news.linkedin.com/about-us#1.

count the impact social media can play in employee recruitment—even if you think Facebook is silly, have no idea how to tweet, and have not looked at your LinkedIn account in years.

Social media is especially important if you are trying to attract Gen Z workers. The Center for Generational Kinetics calls social media a carefully curated lifeline to and for Gen Z.

According to Laura Hill, CEO and executive recruiter of Pinnacle Recruitment Services, social media isn't just for Gen Z. "Social media has become a go-to resource for us in almost every candidate search. We continue to see our business rely heavily on it as all generations become more technologically advanced."[14]

Here are some tips for setting up a Gen Z–friendly application process:

- Allow applicants to apply on their mobile device. Although about 95 percent of Gen Z members have a smartphone, fewer of them have access to computers.
- Make the application process quick—it should take less than fifteen minutes.
- Make sure applicants can save the form and return to it later if necessary.
- Allow applicants to express interest in a job online before beginning the formal application process. If you do that, you can connect with the ones you want to apply.
- Promptly notify applicants that their application was received and let them know about the next steps in the process.

Online Attraction

Your company's website is one of your most powerful tools for finding job candidates. Post job openings there, but do more than that—use your website to make people *want* to work at your business. Post pictures of company events, positive employee testimonies, your mission statement and company values, and other messages that communicate your company culture.

---

[14]Laura Hill, interview by Robin Paggi, April 17, 2018.

Job boards are another powerful tool to reach Gen Z workers. You can advertise openings on a variety of generalized online job boards, such as Monster and Indeed. But look for the more specialized job boards to get the best results. For example, I'm a member of the Kern County Society for Human Resource Management, so the society's job board is the perfect place to post when I'm looking for HR candidates.

If your firm has a Facebook page, you can always post your job opening there. However, you will probably get better results if you buy a targeted ad so you can ensure that more of the right people will see it. Facebook will allow you to choose your exact audience and then offer different options and price levels.

When posting on Twitter, use hashtags such as #jobpost so your tweet will be instantly searchable. You'll need to be concise—no more than 280 characters—and interesting to attract attention.

Most people consider LinkedIn a more professional social media platform, especially if you are advertising a job opening. You can post available positions for free on your profile or sign up for LinkedIn Talent Advantage to pay for recruiting on the site. Additionally, you should use LinkedIn to search for prospective candidates and invite them to apply.

Develop Relationships with Local Schools

Remember that many Gen Zers are still in college or high school, so a great way of attracting the cream of the crop is to develop relationships with them there. Volunteer to speak to a high school or college class about careers in your field, get involved in career day, participate in on-campus interviews, or offer internships to students. All are great ways to introduce your business to future job candidates.

In addition, campus job counselors can help you by steering qualified candidates your way. Beyond job postings and job fairs, many colleges and vocational schools look to partner with particular companies to create employment pipelines for their graduates.

Hungry for employer involvement, many college departments and career centers will hold workshops, create pathways, and develop programs to better provide students with the skill sets employers are looking for. They will host interview days and invite recruiters to speak in classes and in student organizations. Some will even give companies their own space on campus: Columbia University has its own Goldman Sachs office in the career center.

The Ivy League schools have been wildly successful in creating partnerships with high-level consulting firms and in steering their graduates into those firms. Top consulting firms like McKinsey & Company begin aggressively recruiting students for internships early in their college careers, building the foundation to hire a large number of graduates. Through interviews hosted on campus, recruiting events, and coveted internships, consulting companies have created a pipeline of talented, constant new candidates.

Know the Law!

Although internships can be a great way to develop relationships with Gen Z workers, beware of using them simply to provide free labor. In times of high unemployment rates, people of all ages and skill levels might be willing to take an intern position if they think it can help them transition to a full-time job. And many employers might think this situation is a good way to get free labor.

However, if you are a for-profit employer with unpaid interns, you need to know that six criteria established by the US Department of Labor must be met in order to legally not pay them:

1. The internship, even though it includes actual operation of the employer's facilities, is similar to training that would be given in an educational environment.
2. The internship experience is for the benefit of the intern.

3. The intern does not displace regular employees but works under close supervision of existing staff.

4. The employer that provides the training derives no immediate advantage from the activities of the intern, and on occasion its operations may actually be impeded.

5. The intern is not necessarily entitled to a job at the conclusion of the internship.

6. The employer and the intern understand that the intern is not entitled to wages for the time spent in the internship.

Historically, it has been easier to demonstrate that the internship is for educational purposes when the intern is receiving school credit for it, so employers are encouraged to coordinate internships through colleges and high schools.

Unpaid interns have filed suit against several high-profile employers, including the Hearst Corporation, Fox Searchlight Pictures, and Charlie Rose, Inc., according to numerous news sources.

Even paid internships can lead to problems if the intern is not paid properly. A former paid intern sued Hamilton College for intentionally misclassifying him and other interns as being exempt from minimum wage and overtime pay. In her article "Revenge of the Intern: Wage and Hour Class Actions Keep Employers on Their Toes," Alicia M. Feichtmeir writes, "The complaint asserted that the college lacked funds to hire full-time assistant coaches and used interns instead, requiring them to work up to 100 hours per week below minimum wage."[15]

Internships are intended to be learning experiences that benefit the intern, not free or poorly paid labor that benefits the employer. Failing to comply with this labor law could result in a lawsuit, which is no laughing matter.

Unpaid internships will also disproportionately favor wealthy students—particularly over the summers—because many low- and

---

[15] Alicia M. Feichtmeir, "Revenge of the Intern: Wage and Hour Class Actions Keep Employers on Their Toes," May 2013. (website now defunct)

middle-class students cannot afford to take unpaid work. This will immediately eliminate a number of candidates who work really hard and often have more work experience.

If your organization can afford to offer paid internships, you could open up a wider base of candidates from all backgrounds and income levels. And you may end up finding a terrific candidate for your next full-time opening.

An Indirect Pipeline

The majority of Gen Zers get their information about job openings from family and friends, so spreading the word on social media is a way to get to Gen Zers *through* their personal contacts, according to the Center for Generational Kinetics.[16]

Gen Zers do use social media to find out about employment—not to find out where the openings are but to determine whether they want to work for a company or not. And they don't tend to use the same platforms that their parents and older cousins use. According to a national survey conducted by the Center for Generational Kinetics, "40% of Gen Z says they would use YouTube to determine if they want to work for a company while 37% would use Instagram and 36% would use Snapchat."[17] So, if you really want to reach this youngest generation of workers, you'll want to become adept at using their preferred channels.

Hill emphasizes that "any social media recruitment campaign is only as good as its reach to your target audience. Focusing on identifying the correct outlets and style that match your desired candidates' skill set is necessary with every position you advertise. Name branding and recognition also play a role in attracting quality candidates and should be consistent through all media outlets."

---

[16]Center for Generational Kinetics, *The State of Gen Z 2018*, accessed May 20, 2020, https://genhq.com/wp-content/uploads/2019/11/State-of-Gen-Z-2018.pdf.
[17]Ibid.

CHAPTER 3

NARROW THE LIST

Posting your job opening to multiple locations—especially in a time of high unemployment—will undoubtedly bring a deluge of unqualified candidates. Experts say that hiring the wrong candidate can cost up to three times the employee's salary. Therefore, the "hire-them-and-fire-them-if-they-don't-work-out" strategy is expensive.

And Gen Z applicants are too young to provide a long work history, so how can you find the one who is going to fit best in your firm?

Start by requiring all applicants to answer a few questions about the position they just applied for. The truly unqualified will not answer or will give such inadequate answers that they can be easily spotted and eliminated even before an interview.

For example, if you are advertising a position in your human resources department, ask applicants these questions:

- What is the purpose of an HR department?
- What steps are critical in the hiring process?
- What does at-will employment mean?
- What are the steps in the progressive discipline process?
- What role does HR play in keeping employers in compliance?

Create or Update Your Hiring Process

You can take a variety of steps to help ensure that the people you hire are the right people for the job. These steps are especially important when you are hiring younger workers who may have unrealistic expectations—or no expectations at all—about being an employee in your company.

Create a Job Description

Develop a list of the key responsibilities of the job and the knowledge, skills, and abilities needed to be successful. A well-written job description

- provides a general overview of the job ;
- lists the essential job duties (these are the duties that employees must be able to perform with or without a reasonable accommodation);
- describes the work environment; and
- states the minimum qualifications (such as high school diploma or GED).

Know the Law!

Employers can legally set minimum educational requirements for all positions. However, you must be able to demonstrate that employees need the education in order to perform the job. Numerous employers have lost discrimination lawsuits because they could not prove their educational requirements were related to the duties of the job.

I've found that smaller businesses, with their informal atmospheres, tend not to establish job descriptions. Larger businesses usually have them, but they are often vague or outdated.

Recruitment specialist Andrena Clark says, "When hiring new people, understanding the skills and attributes you require for the position will help you to streamline the process and achieve your organizational goals. Once an applicant is employed, staff retention should be better as the parameters are clearer and there are not false expectations from either party."[18]

Review Your Application

Review your employment application to ensure that it does not contain any inappropriate questions. The Equal Employment Opportunity Commission prohibits any inquiries—whether verbal or in writing—about an applicant's race, color, religion, sex (including gender identity, sexual orientation, and pregnancy), national origin, age (though employers may ask if an applicant is at least 18 or 21), disability, or genetic information. These are called protected classes, and employers may not make employment decisions about people because of their protected-class status.

States also have their own protected classes; therefore, check with your state government to ensure that you're in compliance with its anti-discrimination laws.

Require an Application

Be sure that every potential employee completes an employment application before you grant an interview. In a 2018 survey by CareerBuilder, 75 percent of the human resources managers surveyed reported noticing lies on applicants' resumes. That's surprising because the survey also found that "2 in 5 hiring managers spend less than a minute looking

---

[18]Andrena Clark, "The Importance of Job Descriptions," Event Recruitment, accessed May 29, 2020, http://www.eventrecruitment.com.au/articles/1203JobDescriptionsMICE.pdf.

at a resume, and 1 in 4 spend less than 30 seconds," according to Mary Lorenz in her article "The Truth about Lying on Resumes."[19]

It's easier for prospects to massage the truth in resumes than on applications that ask for specific dates of employment, job duties, reasons for leaving, and so on. For example, an applicant could say on a resume that she was a customer service representative from 2018 to 2019 and provide no reason for leaving the position. However, when faced with the more specific questions on your company's job application, she reveals that her job duties consisted of being a cashier from December 20, 2018, to January 2, 2019, and she left the position when she was terminated.

Employment applications are legal documents, signed by the applicant, verifying that the information provided is true. Employees who are discovered lying on their applications can be lawfully terminated at any time. You can fire people for lying on resumes too; however, half-truths and exaggerations on resumes are easier to wiggle out of.

Who is most likely to lie on their resumes? According to a survey by *GOBankingRates*, the biggest offenders are Millennials, who are five times more likely to lie on their resumes than are Baby Boomers, but Gen Zers are most likely to *consider* lying.[20] If you're the one who reviews resumes at your workplace, you should probably spend more than a minute doing so.

Although applicants should be able to apply online, you should not require them to do so, because not everyone has access to technology or is tech savvy.

Kat's Take

Because I work with Gen Z on a daily basis, I want to point out that it's often not the young applicants who are willing to consider lying on their resumes—it's their parents. You might have heard about "helicopter parents" who tend to "hover" a little too close

[19]Mary Lorenz, "The Truth about Lying on Resumes," CareerBuilder, August 24, 2018, https://www.careerbuilder.com/advice/the-truth-about-lying-on-resumes.

[20]Erica Corbin, "Millennials Lie Twice as Much as Everyone Else on Resumes—Here's What They Lie About," GOBankingRates, August 6, 2019, https://www.gobankingrates.com/money/jobs/why-americans-lie-on-resumes/.

over their children. But about the time the class of 2016 was graduating from high school, I began to witness a new type of parent:
"snowplow parents."

In a society where parents increasingly see their children as a
reflection of themselves, more and more of them are attempting to
obliterate any barrier or struggle for their children, plowing away
any obstacle.

From what I have witnessed, this parenting style reflects the
rising cost of raising children and sending them to college, which
often leads to a decrease in free time as parents struggle to keep up
with those rising costs. Parents simply lack the time to teach their
children some of the more important lessons that would facilitate
their transition into adulthood.

When I give presentations about Generation Z, I ask parents
in the room whether they would drop everything to take lunch to
their teenager who had forgotten their lunch money. Most hands
in the room go up. Then I ask if their parents would have done the
same. No hands. Although this is a small example, it illustrates
how much contemporary parents tend do for their children, often
to the detriment of their children's development.

I've seen parents try to step in to complete college application
essays or job applications and develop their teenagers' plans for the
future. College professors tell me they have seen a drastic increase
in calls from parents about grades in college-level courses.

I have advised parents not to call their kids' employers or
professors. Convinced them the college admissions office wants
to hear from their teenagers, not them. Gently explained why
they should not write their teenager's college application essays.
Encouraged them to allow their teenagers to order their own food
at a restaurant and make their own doctor appointments.

Being an educational consultant in the college admissions
field, I was not surprised when the US Department of Justice
announced arrests in a college admissions scam dubbed Operation

Varsity Blues in March 2019.[21] Rick Singer, the owner of a college preparation firm, was charged along with dozens of parents, test administrators, and college coaches in a scheme that resulted in parents paying thousands of dollars and falsifying entrance applications so their children would be admitted into some of the most elite colleges in the country. Some parents falsely claimed their children were elite athletes while others paid test administrators to change students' answers on college entrance exams to boost scores.

The investigation revealed that dozens of parents chose to lie, commit fraud, and pay thousands of extra dollars to get their students into their preferred schools. As a consultant who works with teenagers daily, I was both fascinated and saddened to see many parents explain that their children had known nothing about their schemes. The ultimate snowplow parents.

Experience or Talent?

This book is about Gen Z in the workplace, so most of our advice is geared to help you find, hire, and keep the best workers from that age cohort. Of course, you know that limiting your job search to people from one age group is not only illegal but also unwise. This book is not advising you to hire Gen Z *only*. But we are encouraging you to give Gen Z a chance.

When you have a pile of applications on your desk, you may need to decide whether it's better to hire people because of their job experience or their natural talent.

In his article "When to Hire Raw Talent vs. Job Experience," Joel Trammell, CEO and founder of Khorus Software, says that hiring based on experience is best when filling a leadership position because "if this person has no experience managing others, it will be difficult for

---

[21]US Attorney's Office for the District of Massachusetts, "Arrests Made in Nationwide College Admissions Scam: Alleged Exam Cheating & Athletic Recruitment Scheme," press release, March 12, 2019, https://www.justice.gov/usao-ma/pr/arrests-made-nationwide-college-admissions-scam-alleged-exam-cheating-athletic.

him or her to build and guide a team." He also suggests hiring someone with experience when you need specialized knowledge for things your organization doesn't know how to do or doesn't do well.[22] Makes sense.

But for just about any other job, especially if the new employee will be one of several performing the same job following clear processes and procedures, you will be better off to hire based on talent.

Zane Smith, the executive director of the Boys & Girls Clubs of Kern County, says hiring based on talent is best for most of the positions in his organization. When he became the executive director more than twenty years ago, Smith managed seven employees at one location. Now he employs hundreds at sixty-three locations throughout the county. Much of the organization's success relies on the quality of the employees who work closely with members, so Smith and his managers are choosy about whom they hire. While education and experience are important, Smith said being talented more often tips the scale in the applicant's favor:

Applicants for hip-hop instructor should be able to impressively "bust a move" at the interview; applicants for art instructor should be able to pick up a drawing element and create an inspiring work of art; and, applicants for resource development staff should be able to role-play a major gift ask with finesse. Although we value work experience when it comes to making decisions that will directly impact our children, we tend to place a higher priority on talent that can be developed and expanded with training.[23]

According to Claudio Fernandez-Araoz, senior adviser at the executive search firm Egon Zehnder, a person's ability to be developed and expanded through training is called "potential" and that is most important when making hiring decisions.

Author of the book *It's Not the How or the What but the Who: Succeed by Surrounding Yourself with the Best*, Fernandez-Araoz says in a *Harvard Business Review* article that "organizations and their leaders must transition to what I think of as a new era of talent spotting—one in which our evaluations of one another are based not on brawn, brains, experience, or competencies, but on potential."

---

[22]Joel Trammell, "When to Hire Raw Talent vs. Job Experience," *Entrepreneur*, September 13, 2016, https://www.entrepreneur.com/article/281329.

[23]Zane Smith, interview by Robin Paggi, March 30, 2019.

After spending thirty years tracking and studying executive performance, Fernandez-Araoz concludes, "The question is not whether your company's employees and leaders have the right skills; it's whether they have the potential to learn new ones."

How can you tell if applicants have potential? Assess whether they are motivated, curious, insightful, engaging, and determined during the interview process. Here's an important clue: "High potentials . . . show deep personal humility and invest in getting better at everything they do," says Fernandez-Araoz.[24]

I've trained hundreds of people over the last twenty years, and I think that wanting to learn and improve is critical to success, regardless of the job being filled. Experience is more important for some positions and talent for others; however, the desire to grow must be prevalent in both cases.

---

[24]Claudio Fernandez-Araoz, "It's Not the How or the What but the Who: Succeed by Surrounding Yourself with the Best," *Harvard Business Review*, September 5, 2014, https://hbr.org/2014/09/its-not-the-how-or-the-what-but-the-who-succeed-by-surrounding-yourself-with-the-best.

CHAPTER 4

TALKING AND TESTING

A fter you've determined your priorities for this position and pre-screened your applicants, it's time to choose a select few for an interview. Depending on the position, you may choose to bring applicants into your workplace or meet them in a neutral site. Or you may decide to interview them by Zoom or FaceTime or on an old-fashioned phone call.

Whatever method you choose, interviews can be time consuming and energy depleting. So, take the time to create a process that will provide you with the most beneficial information about your prospective employees. This process may involve some job-specific tests, in addition to your conversations.

When you are looking to hire Gen Z workers, keep in mind their age and experience. This is very possibly their first real interview. Being green doesn't mean they are incapable of performing well during this process, but don't be surprised if they are more nervous than older job candidates would be. It's possible that you have been interviewing and hiring for more years than Gen Zers have been alive.

The Importance of Interviews

Before you begin your interviews, create a list of open-ended questions that should elicit specific examples of past behavior. For example, instead of asking, "Do you know how to handle difficult customers?" (which can be answered with a yes or no), say, "Tell me about a difficult customer you had and how you handled the situation." When you're looking to hire Gen Z workers, remember that many of them may not have a lot of workplace experience, so make your questions less "job specific." Allow them to answer by describing something that happened at school or while they were doing volunteer work.

Ask all applicants for the position the same question, write a short summary of their answers on the list of interview questions, and attach the list to their employment application. Keep applications and interview notes on applicants you do not hire for three years in case you need to defend yourself against discrimination claims. (Yes, you can be sued for discrimination by people you don't hire.)

Most of your interview questions should be based on the position's essential duties for the position. For example, if you're hiring a person who will be responsible for recruiting, interviewing, and evaluating candidates, say, "Tell me about your experience recruiting, interviewing, and evaluating candidates." Or if you're talking to a Gen Z applicant who has no previous experience, say, "Tell me what you know about recruiting, interviewing, and evaluating candidates."

Also consider involving current employees in the interviewing process. They can help by providing job-related questions or even sitting in on interviews. For example, an experienced legal secretary helped me interview secretarial candidates when I was the human resources manager at a law firm. Her input in the hiring process was invaluable as I had no prior experience in law or in selecting legal secretaries!

Kat's Take

Past generations have had the benefit of walking into a shop and getting a job by asking if the owner is hiring. Or getting a paper route by asking the town's newspaper if they can deliver. These first jobs helped teens and young adults get interview experience and work experience. They might have gained confidence in classes like home economics, which taught them how to dress, act, and talk in a professional setting.

But in the past couple of decades, young people have been steered away from vocational training or after-school jobs as parents and schools focus on college admissions instead. Thus, Generation Zers have not had the opportunity to learn firsthand how to present themselves professionally in interviews. Teens are given few opportunities in the school system to learn how to interview, while busy parents are relying on the school system to teach such skills. The lack of education or chances to practice puts an entire generation at a significant disadvantage.

Many students I work with simply do not know how to describe their responsibilities and achievements on a resume, as they don't think they "count." They are unsure how to talk about themselves or present themselves.

In many meetings to prepare for admissions or employment interviews, I have explained how interviewers would love to know more about the responsibilities young people have taken on to help support their families. As an employer myself, I'm attracted to potential employees who have been taking care of siblings while their parents work, or mowing yards or washing windows to help support the family, or shouldering other such responsibilities. Such responsible behavior demonstrates how independent, reliant, and responsible they are. But many young people don't think to list such activities on a resume, which they think should be reserved for "official" jobs.

Therefore, I would highly encourage employers to add interview questions that will allow entry-level employees to give context to their experience, such as:

- Are there responsibilities you might have at home or school that give you more experience in this area?
- Do you have any volunteer experience or hobbies that give you more experience in this field? (For example, did they recruit other student members for a club or get the entire neighborhood to work on a volunteer project?)

Preemployment Testing

A variety of preemployment tests can also help you determine which applicants are most qualified. Although their use has declined since the legalization of marijuana in many states,[25] drug tests are still probably the most common type of preemployment test used by employers. Depending on your state's law and company policy, drug tests may be administered before a conditional job offer is made; in fact, they may be the first step in the entire hiring process. Because much legislation has been passed recently regarding workplace drug testing, it's critical for you to determine what your state's laws say about the issue before you begin testing.

Quest Diagnostics, one of the nation's largest clinical laboratory testing company, reported in 2019 that the number of positives for drugs in the workforce reached a fourteen-year high, which was 25 percent higher than a decade earlier.[26]

Unlike drug tests, employers may not require an applicant to agree to a medical exam until after a conditional job offer is made. After an offer is made, employers can require medical exams as long as they do so for all individuals applying for the same job and the exam is related to the job.

Functional capacity tests commonly measure applicants' strength, stamina, range of motion, and physical ability to do the job they applied for. If this kind of test is job related, employers can require it before a conditional job offer has been made. However, because there is some danger of a functional capacity test turning into a medical exam, I suggest you utilize this test only after you have made a conditional offer.

Employers may refuse to hire applicants who demonstrate that they are not physically capable of performing the essential functions of the

---

[25]Janet Macdaniel, "The Coming Decline of the Employment Drug Test," *Pre-Employment, Inc., April 20,* 2018, https://pre-employment.com/2018/04/20/coming-decline-employment-drug-test-2/.

[26]Valentina Sanchez, "Is Cannabis Use the Same as Off-duty Drinking by Workers? Many Companies Still Say No," *CNBC,* July 27, 2019, https://www.cnbc.com/2019/07/27/will-cannabis-use-soon-be-the-same-as-off-duty-drinking-by-workers.html.

job. However, the Americans with Disabilities Act (ADA) makes it unlawful to

- use employment tests to screen out individuals with disabilities unless the test is shown to be job related and consistent with business necessity;
- fail to select or administer tests in the most effective manner to ensure that they accurately reflect skills that the tests purport to measure; and
- fail to make a reasonable accommodation, including in the administration of the tests.

Additionally, the Age Discrimination in Employment Act forbids employers from giving a medical exam, functional capacity test, or any other type of test only to applicants over the age of forty.

Employers may utilize a variety of other preemployment tests, including cognitive, personality, integrity, English proficiency, and job sample tasks.[27] Tests are permitted as long as they are not designed, intended, or used to discriminate against applicants because of their race, sex, age, or other protected characteristic. According to the Equal Employment Opportunity Commission (EEOC), use of tests can violate antidiscrimination laws if they disproportionately exclude people in a protected class, unless the employer can justify the test or procedure under law.[28] Employers who use employment tests need to comply with the Uniform Guidelines on Employee Selection Procedures, which identifies ways that employers can show that their tests are job related and consistent with business necessity.

---

[27]Although I use the Myers-Briggs Type Indicator and the DiSC personality profile in training and coaching, I'm not a fan of using personality assessments in the hiring process because the results tend to be based on how people *want* to see themselves. Frequently in training, they will identify themselves as one style while their coworkers identify them as a different style. How we see ourselves is not necessarily how other people see us.

[28]A client told me her company was requiring all applicants to complete a test on a computer even though most employees did not use a computer for their jobs. The company thought the practice would result in better hires. I told her it would probably result in a discrimination claim instead.

Background Checks

Before you make a job offer, conduct a background check of the applicant. Although there are no laws requiring employers to conduct background checks, employers who don't conduct them run the risk of being sued for negligent hiring. According to *USLegal,* "negligent hiring is a claim made by an injured party against an employer based on the theory that the employer knew or should have known about the employee's background which, if known, indicates a dangerous or untrustworthy character."[29]

Background checks can be as simple as contacting previous employers to verify employment or as elaborate as thorough checks of criminal history, credit history, and a variety of other inquiries. I strongly recommend that you use the services of a professional agency to check the backgrounds of job applicants. You may check public records for tax liens, judgments, convictions, and indictments; however, certain disclosures must be made to applicants with respect to these searches. A reputable outside agency will ensure that you comply with all the authorization, notification, and disclosure requirements of state and federal law.

Can you google applicants' names or check their Facebook page? Public internet searches of applicants are generally viewed as lawful; however, unauthorized use of private sites is not. More importantly, you may not consider any information revealed on social media about an applicant's protected class—such as pictures or posts that reveal the applicant is pregnant—in the hiring process.

Following a carefully planned hiring strategy can help you hire the right people the first time. As Jim Collins, author of *Good to Great,* emphasizes, "People are not your most important asset. The *right* people are."[30]

[29]USLegal, "Negligent Hiring Law and Legal Definition," accessed May 29, 2020, https://definitions.uslegal.com/n/negligent-hiring/.

[30]Jim Collins, *Good to Great: Why Some Companies Make the Leap and Others Don't* (New York: HarperCollins, 2001).

SECTION 2

HIRE THEM

Section 2 Takeaways

- Find a good fit for your position.
- Be realistic and honest about the job.
- Match employees' strengths to appropriate jobs.
- Consider your workplace culture.
- Recognize that culture and diversity are not mutually exclusive.
- Gather useful information about your prospects.

CHAPTER 5

FIND A GOOD FIT

O nce upon a time, I was a secretary. I was really good at answering the phone and interacting with customers, but I was really bad at filing and just about everything else a secretary is supposed to do. As a result of being inept, I became burned out.

According to the authors of the article "You Can Conquer Burnout" published in *Scientific American Mind*, the term "burnout" became popular in the 1970s as a way to describe the discouragement young health care professionals and social workers were experiencing because they had insufficient resources to do their jobs well. Today the term can be applied to any employee in any industry who is experiencing exhaustion or cynicism or feeling inadequate. Burnout can be caused by any number of things; however, the article authors say that "the true culprit is a mismatch between a person and a job."[31]

A mismatch can be caused by many things; however, I think the fundamental cause is an employee who does not have the right skill set for a job (like putting a person who is lousy at filing in charge of filing) or is not working in the right environment. For example, in my secretarial job, I usually sat at a desk for eight hours a day in a quiet office completing the same tasks over and over. I now know that I work best

---

[31]Michael Leiter and Christina Maslach, "You Can Conquer Burnout," *Scientific American*, January 2015, https://www.scientificamerican.com/article/you-can-conquer-burnout/.

when I'm moving from place to place, when I have some music playing in the background, and when I'm completing a variety of tasks.

Burned-out employees of any age or skill set will not perform well, so it's imperative that you screen job applicants carefully to try to make the best match possible between a person and the job.

Check Skill Sets and Interests

First, find out if their skill set is a match by asking questions about their experience with the tasks that they will be required to do for you. For example, secretarial applicants could be asked, "What filing management techniques do you use?" If a candidate's eyes start to shine when talking about color-coded files, you have probably found a good match. On the other hand, if the prospect has been a secretary for a while but doesn't recognize the term "filing management techniques," you should probably keep looking.

In addition to asking applicants about their knowledge, skills, and experience, try to determine their preferred work environment by asking them to describe what they liked about previous jobs, work environments, and supervisors. It's probably a mismatch when

- the applicant tells you she liked working with lots of different people, and your job will require her to work alone in an isolated office;
- the applicant tells you he liked the variety and fast pace at his last job, and your job is slow and monotonous; or
- the applicant tells you her favorite supervisor was very supportive and nurturing, and you're not.

It might be a little harder to determine whether Generation Z applicants will be a good match in your environment because they may not have enough work experience to know how they will react in a given setting. However, if an applicant tells you her favorite activities are skydiving and rock climbing and the job you're offering requires hours and hours of desk work in a quiet office, you might think twice about the fit. Or if your idea of a good public relations rep is someone who will handle TV and radio interviews, you probably don't want to hire an applicant who admits to a fear of public speaking—even if she is a wizard at social media.

" Employers React to Gen Z

They believe they are capable of doing anything without experience.

"

Finding the right match doesn't mean burnout will never happen. However, it does mean that employees have a fighting chance to be good at their jobs, which can help prevent it.

Be Honest about the Job

According to a survey by Jobvite, one in four employees quit their jobs within the first ninety days, and 43 percent of them said they quit because the day-to-day role wasn't what they had expected.[32] When you have done all the work to attract qualified candidates, screen them, interview them, test them, and train them, the last thing you want is to have to replace them within a few months!

To stop the new employee merry-go-round at your workplace, it's imperative that you provide a realistic preview of what the job entails. This is especially important with Gen Z candidates. Because they tend to be young, idealistic, and new to the working world, Gen Zers may have little idea of what to expect from a job. If the job is not what they envisioned, they are likely to feel you tricked them, which means they don't believe they owe you their best effort or their loyalty.

Don't oversell a position's positives and neglect its negatives. If workers are going to get dirty on the job, don't just tell candidates about it—show them pictures of employees after a day's work. If they are going to work in a noisy environment, take them there so they can experience the noise. Encourage candidates to talk to current employees to see what it's really like to work at your organization. Do whatever it takes to ensure that applicants know exactly what they're getting themselves

---

[32]Jobvite, *2018 Job Seeker Nation Study: Researching the Candidate-Recruiter Relationship*, 2018, https://www.jobvite.com/wp-content/uploads/2018/04/2018_Job_Seeker_Nation_Study.pdf.

into. Otherwise, you might lose them within a few weeks and have to start the process all over again. (Remember, it costs three times what you pay employees to replace them.)

The Peace Corps is an excellent example of a realistic job preview that can actually entice people to apply for a hard job. Television commercials depicted both the hardships—living thousands of miles away from home, sometimes without running water, toilet facilities, or heat—and the rewarding personal experiences, proclaiming that the Peace Corps is "The Toughest Job You'll Ever Love." Thousands of people signed up as a result of this truth in advertising.[33]

Don't be afraid to be honest—even if you wouldn't want to do a particular job, there are others who will find it suits them very well.

Understand Strengths

Being a secretary was the wrong job for me, and now I know why: my brain is not wired to be a secretary. Sound like a cop-out? Numerous neuroscientists would agree with me.

Dario Nardi, an award-winning UCLA professor, has been studying the neuroscience of personality types using electroencephalogram (EEG) technology, which measures brain waves. Nardi records the brain activity of students and participants while they perform tasks such as math or storytelling, and he reports that students who shared the same personality type show similar brain activity while performing the tasks. Different brain regions light up when students with different personality types complete the same tasks, leading Nardi to conclude that people with different personality types use their brains in fundamentally different ways. "Truly, brain activity varies by type," he says.[34]

Our brains have four sections, and we are born hardwired to use or favor one section more than the others, explains clinical psychotherapist Anne Dranitsaris, who cocreated an assessment and developmental program called the Striving Styles Personality System (SSPS). The section of the brain we favor provides us with our sense of identity and

---

[33]Ad Council, "The Classics," accessed May 30, 2020, https://www.adcouncil.org/our-story/our-history/the-classics.

[34]Dario Nardi, *Neuroscience of Personality: Brain Savvy Insights for All Types of People* (Radiance House, 2009).

strengths.[35]

According to the SSPS, I favor the upper right section of my brain, where foresight, insight, conceptualizing, and synthesizing take place. This means that one of my strengths or talents is the ability to creatively solve problems. This makes sense because I'm frequently told I come up with good ideas, and I'm happiest when I'm finding a unique answer to a thorny problem.

"The reality is that each person has unique talents that are strongly wired into the neural network of the brain through the building of dense synaptic structures," says Paul O'Keefe in his article "How Successful Organizations Maximize Employee Strengths." "These areas of strength present as behaviors that are performed well and with ease. Conversely, each person has certain behaviors that are weakly wired into the neural network with fewer, thinner synaptic structures—areas of weakness."[36]

The weakest section of my brain is the lower left, which inspires behavior that is precise, mechanical, sequencing, and following. No wonder I was a lousy secretary!

Take Advantage of Aptitudes

You don't have to know all the details of all of your employees' personalities or preferences. But becoming aware of their strengths and skill sets will help you to create a more efficient and enjoyable work atmosphere. And you should especially focus on strengths when filling positions, communicating with workers, and encouraging your employees. Of course, this advice applies to workers of all stages and ages, but it is especially important to help Gen Z employees determine their strengths and weaknesses—before they burn out from trying to succeed in a mismatched job.

---

[35]Anne Dranitsaris, "Striving Styles Personality System," Striving Styles, accessed May 30, 2020, https://strivingstyles.com/ssps/striving-styles-personality-system.

[36]Paul O'Keefe, "How Successful Organizations Maximize Employee Strengths," *Edge Training Systems*, accessed May 30, 2020, https://www.edgetrainingsystems.com/how-successful-organizations-maximize-employee-strengths/.

Filling Positions

According to O'Keefe,

> So often in companies, management puts people in positions that draw upon their weaknesses. Why do they do this? One common reason is that management is simply filling vacant positions, rather than waiting for the right fit. Another reason is that they misjudge their workers' strengths and put them in positions that draw on their weaknesses and neglect their strengths, thereby setting them up for failure.[37]

Can you determine an applicant's strengths during a job interview? Interviewers often try to do this by asking, "What are your strengths?" However, according to *National Geographic*'s *Your Personality Explained: Exploring the Science of Identity*, "Only one worker in three can name her strengths."[38]

When people answer a question about strengths, they tend to mention what they do well. But our strengths are what we do well *and* enjoy doing. If we do something well but don't enjoy it, it's not a strength. So, stop asking, "What are your strengths?" Instead, ask, "What do you do well and enjoy doing?"

Communicating with Workers

According to a Gallup poll, 61 percent of employees who agreed that "My supervisor focuses on my strengths or positive characteristics" were engaged in the workplace. The same survey found that 22 percent of people who agreed that "My supervisor focuses on my weaknesses or negative characteristics" and 40 percent of employees who felt ignored by their supervisor were actively *disengaged* at work.[39]

---

[37]Ibid.

[38]*National Geographic, Your Personality Explained: Exploring the Science of Identity*, (Washington, DC: *National Geographic* Society, June 2017.

[39]Susan Sorenson, "How Employees' Strengths Make Your Company Stronger," *Gallup*, February 20, 2014, accessed June 20, 2020, https://www.gallup.com/workplace/231605/employees-strengths-company-stronger.aspx.

How do you communicate with your workers about their strengths? Catch them when they do something right. Take advantage of opportunities to praise employees when you see or hear about them doing something well. For example, if an employee does a great job handling an irate customer, tell her so, and be as specific as possible: "Great job in taking care of that customer. You really know how to calm people down and help solve their problems."

" Employers React to Gen Z

A common characteristic I see in Gen Zers is a lack of confidence.

"

Encouraging Employees

Says, O'Keefe, "Employees who are encouraged to develop and use their strengths are more engaged and loyal. They perform better, produce more, learn their roles quicker, and more positively affect their organization's profits."[40]

How do you encourage employees to cultivate their strengths? Determine what they do well and enjoy doing and find opportunities for them to engage in those activities. For example, when I was a secretary, my boss, who was a county supervisor, allowed me to represent her at various events. I enjoyed going to the events and was good at making little speeches on her behalf, and I really appreciated her for allowing me to do that.

Being a training and development specialist is absolutely the right job for me because it allows me to utilize my strengths and receive positive recognition for doing so. Also, I don't have to file anything.

Uncover Skills

Whether you are trying to determine the strengths of a longtime employee being considered for a promotion or an applicant hoping to

---

[40]O'Keefe, "How Successful Organizations Maximize Employee Strengths."

get hired into an entry-level position, try to determine whether their strengths match your position. Use questions like these to help you uncover talents, interests, and strengths.

Knowledge, skills, experience

- What do you know about _____?
- What is your experience with _____?
- Explain how you would _____.
- Tell me about a time when you _____.
- What are your qualifications for this position?
- Tell me about a problem you had and how you solved it.
- Tell me about a conflict you had and how you resolved it.
- Tell me about the worst on-the-job experience you had and what you learned from it.
- What specifically have you done over the last year to improve your performance?

Preferred work environment

- Tell me what you liked best and least about your previous job.
- Describe the work environment that best suits you.
- Describe the management style that works best for you.
- What do you know about our company?
- Why do you want to work here?

Strengths

- What do you do well and like doing?
- What do you not do well or like doing?
- How would your previous employer describe you?
- If you could do anything you wanted to for a living, what would you do?

CHAPTER 6

AVOID A
CULTURE CLASH

I n addition to making sure employees are a good match for their positions, you want to hire people who will fit in at your workplace. Gen Z can be very sensitive to the "vibe" of an office or organization, so be sure that you are honest and open about your company's culture when you are interviewing candidates. Of course, before you can explain your organization's culture to a candidate, you have to recognize and define that culture.

"When people say they have a 'culture,' it's an amorphous thing," says Keith Swenson, a principal at William Mercer, Inc. "If you can define the culture in some ways, then you can hire for it."[41]

Unfortunately, many organizations can't adequately identify their cultures, which may be generally defined as some blend of a company's values, goals, rules, regulations, and preferences. Company culture includes highly visible components, such as dress codes and office arrangements, and deeply intrinsic elements, such as executive pay scales and ethical standards.

---

[41]David M. Sobocinski, Price Harding, Jennifer P. Sobocinski, and Bill Peterson, *Cultural Considerations in Hiring*, *CarterBaldwin Executive Search*, accessed May 30, 2020, https://carterbaldwin.com/wp-content/uploads/2016/11/CBWP-CulturalConsid-2014.pdf.

Swenson admits that it can be challenging to find the correct balance between shared values and diversity of viewpoints, and the process must start with a clear understanding of and agreement on the organization's values. Those values should be exemplified and used as benchmarks at every stage of the employment process—from recruitment and hiring to training to promotion and termination decisions. It's not an easy task.[42]

Morris R. Shechtman, an employee retention and development strategist and author of *Working Without a Net: How to Survive & Thrive in Today's High Risk Business World,* says hiring based on shared values is a great idea—as long as the values are apparent to the company. Unfortunately, "99 out of 100 companies we deal with confuse their goals with their values," he says.[43]

According to Shechtman, "Goals are where you're going; values are how you're going to get there. Values are absolutely critical, but most companies don't know what those values are. They're intent on where they're going, not on how they're going to get there." Organizations that fail to identify their core values tend to repeat the same hiring mistakes, he says. "If you don't know what your culture is, you'll keep replicating the same problems in every hire. We see that epidemically throughout corporate America."[44]

Risky Legal Business

As organizations get a clear sense of their own corporate culture and values, they must be sure not to emphasize them to the exclusion of other important factors—such as legal concerns. According to labor and employment attorney Elaine Fox, who is quoted in *Leadership: Research Findings, Practice, and Skills* by Andrew DuBrin, employers must be aware of certain risks when hiring based on a cultural fit.

"One of the biggest problems that can occur when hiring based on culture is if the culture you're comfortable with doesn't open the way for women and minorities." When conducting job interviews, hiring managers should factor in perceptions of how someone might fit into

---

[42]Ibid.

[43]Morris R. Shechtman, *Working Without a Net—How to Survive & Thrive in Today's High Risk Business World* (New York: Pocket Books, 1994).

[44]Ibid.

a workplace culture. "You can't get away from that, but you have to be very careful that these choices aren't based upon ethnic, racial, or gender issues," says Fox.[45]

Anna Segboia Masters, an attorney who specializes in labor law, employee litigation, and business litigation, believes training is one way for companies to minimize the potential for risk in hiring. In *Human Resources* by Fred Maidment, Masters says, "I think that's one reason companies spend so much time and energy training those people that do the interviews—to make sure they understand the difference between trying to get someone that meets professional and cultural needs but, on the other hand, not relying on stereotypes and first impressions."[46]

Cultural considerations extend beyond the hiring process. "You have to be very careful, not only when you hire, but in integrating employees once you have them and being sensitive to different cultural issues," says Fox. "Hiring is only the first step. Those same types of decisions also come into play when selecting employees for special assignments, when offering promotions, when taking disciplinary action or when making termination decisions."[47]

"If you're hiring for fit, does it mean that you're ignoring diversity issues?" asks Sally Haver, career management consultant and vice president of the Ayers Group, a human resources consulting firm. "The answer is absolutely, totally not."[48]

Haver and many others think diversity and cultural fit are not mutually exclusive but can, in fact, be complementary goals. This is possible if the company finds acceptable methods—both legally and practically—to avoid inadvertently underutilizing various types of employees and to ensure that any employee "profile" does not hinder the influx of new ideas and perspectives.

"The way I look at it, hiring for value systems that match doesn't mean necessarily that you might not be somewhat diverse," says Swenson, the William Mercer principal. "In terms of our own firm, we're

---

[45]Andrew DuBrin, *Leadership: Research Findings, Practice, and Skills* (Mason, OH: South-Western Cengage Learning, 2012).

[46]Fred Maidment, *Human Resources 2000–2001* (Guilford, CT: Dushkin/McGraw-Hill, 1999).

[47]DuBrin, *Leadership.*

[48]Ibid.

somewhat diverse and bring different perceptions, but I think we share some very similar core values as an organization. I don't think they have to be naturally conflicting."[49]

Culture versus Skills

Although a cultural fit is important, applicants still must possess the right skills to do the job. Unfortunately, not all employers do a very good job of identifying the skills that successful employees will need to bring to the workplace day in and day out.

Paul Storfer, founder of HR Technologies—a consulting firm that helps clients develop competency-based approaches to staffing—says that "one of the traps people fall into is not identifying what the job-relevant competencies are and behaviors that are appropriate; then they pick someone they like or someone who fits with them."

Without a detailed and unambiguous identification of the competencies necessary to succeed in a position, Storfer says that "the hiring evaluation could be done only on the basis of chemistry—'Do I like him or her, or not?' That's not a very good predictor of future success in the position."[50]

Identifying the competencies that predict success in a position can be difficult and time consuming, but it is critical. When Storfer first began working with Arthur D. Little, a management consulting firm, the company had identified only eleven competencies. "We narrowed these competencies to identify what they really mean and ended up with 47 competencies in the 11 clusters," Storfer says.

Too often, competencies are vaguely defined. At Arthur D. Little, one of the original competencies was "communication skills." This category was later expanded with several individual competencies.

Shechtman suggests a way of testing applicants that can simultaneously reveal competencies and cultural fit. "The recruiting process has to be uncomfortable and has to have the kind of difficulties in it that the candidate will encounter when she or he takes the position. If it doesn't, it's a waste of time," he says.

For example, if you're hiring someone to deal with rejection, the

---

[49]Sobocinski et al., *Cultural Considerations in Hiring.*
[50]DuBrin, *Leadership.*

recruiting process should have some potential rejection built in and some confrontation to see how the candidates respond. If you're hiring someone to give feedback, then you should demand that the candidate give feedback during the hiring process—about the interview process, about the company, anything to get an actual indication of the candidate's style and response.

Kat's Take

Be wary of trying to build in too many "uncomfortable difficulties" when you are interviewing Generation Z, especially for entry-level positions. Do you remember when you first started working? Do you remember how much you didn't know?

I moved to Los Angeles a week after graduating from college. Although I had work experience on campus and from my high school years, I had never worked in a true corporate environment. I was applying for positions in Hollywood (anything I could find) and was excited when I was asked to interview as an agent's assistant at one of the most prestigious agencies in the nation. I had experience with phones, data entry, and an office environment, so I thought I would be a good fit.

But that interview shook me to my core.

I was shown into the office of a premier agent, who appeared flustered. I introduced myself, but a phone in the back of her office began to ring before she responded to me. Not on her desk, but in the back corner. It rang a few times and then she looked at me and asked me if I was going to answer it.

Flummoxed, I walked over and nervously answered. I didn't know the agent's name, so I simply answered "Hello?" Mistake #1.

An angry person on the other end of the phone demanded to talk to the agent. I asked for his name; he said Jason. Turning to the agent, I told her Jason was on the phone. Mistake #2.

Glaring at me, the agent asked, "Jason who?"

Hating myself for not asking, I turned back to the phone and asked the caller to give me his last name. Rudely, he answered: "It's casting. I need to talk to her immediately." Putting my hand over the receiver, I told her it was Jason from casting.

"Why didn't you say that to begin with?"

She took the call. When she hung up, my interview officially began.

I didn't get the job.

However, I did land a job as a talent agent's assistant at another firm—one with a more traditional interview process.

With years of hindsight and work experience, I can understand why an agency would put potential candidates through that kind of test. But I also know that those types of trial severely limit an agency's pool of potential candidates. If I had come from a background where I expected some kind of test, I would have walked in confidently and handled the situation much differently.

I counted myself privileged because I had been taught how to dress, how to act, and how to conduct myself in an interview. But I was completely unprepared for such an unorthodox test, and I imagine a number of young adults would have reacted the same as I did. And that was over fifteen years ago.

Today's recent college graduates are likely to be even less prepared. Generation Z grew up in a school environment that focused on testing and metrics, and few received the kind of practical experience that previous generations recorded. It's highly likely that your Gen Z applicant has no interview experience of any kind.

So, if you are going to add "real-world" tests into your interview process, think them through carefully and determine exactly what you will be measuring. Also consider which candidates you might be excluding unfairly and unwisely.

CHAPTER 7

PREVENT GROUPTHINK

As discussed in chapter 6, hiring employees who fit well into your company's culture can make the process easier on both your organization and the new hire. But paying too much attention to "culture fit" can wind up hurting your business in the long run.

That's because building a workgroup that is too similar may lead to what social psychologist Irving Janis identified in the 1970s as "groupthink." According to Janis, some groups have such high levels of conformity that their ability to critically evaluate ideas was hampered.[51] Despite Janis's warnings about groupthink decades ago, the same tendency exists today and may become worse when organizations try too hard to hire individuals who closely match corporate culture.

"Our experience is that companies hire to their pathology and not to their health," says Shechtman.[52] If the company is run by people who can't stand stability, they'll keep hiring people who will stir things up. If the company is run by people who avoid conflict, they will keep hiring people who are passive.

John Challenger, CEO of Challenger, Gray & Christmas, an outplacement firm, advises employers, "What you're really trying to do is

---

[51]Irving Janis, *Victims of Groupthink: A Psychological Study of Policy Decisions and Fiascos* (Boston: Wadsworth, 1972).

[52]Morris Shechtman, *Working Without a Net: How to Survive & Thrive in Today's High Risk Business World* (New York: Pocket Books, 1994).

sort out the bad apples, not trying to get too highly defined a 'type.'"Too many employees who perfectly fit one mold can minimize effectiveness because the workforce will lack "people who think about things differently or come at issues from different perspectives."[53]

Barbara Moses, a consultant who helps organizations implement career management programs, also has serious concerns about hiring based on culture:

> I often worry that what you end up having is a homogeneous group of people who are pretty good in carrying out a number of behaviors, but not excellent in any. When a group is too much alike, they can have a tendency to too readily agree with each other—to be too quick to support proposals, causes, and suggestions because those suggestions mirror their own thoughts and ideals. A lack of diversity of opinion, background, and perspectives can hamper a group. We have an innate tendency to avoid conflict, but conflict can result in new ideas or alternative solutions to problems—and diversity can provide an environment where healthy conflict can exist.[54]

Adding age diversity to your workplace is another reason that you should be looking to hire Generation Z workers. They can help your company avoid getting too tightly bound to its culture and sinking into groupthink. Because Gen Zers are just starting to enter the workplace in large numbers, it's a pretty good bet that your workplace is not overloaded with these youngsters.

If your company can't seem to attract or keep younger workers, take a long hard look at your company culture. Many business owners complain about not being able to attract younger employees, but they fail to realize how their company culture shuts out the younger generations.

Does your organization have a "my-way-or-the-highway" mentality? Does your company culture cater only to the needs and beliefs of one generation? Maybe the problem is not with the "flaky" or "overdemanding" Gen Z and Millennial workers. Maybe the problem is that your organization's views and culture fail to take their needs and viewpoints into account.

---

[53]Fred H. Maidment, *Human Resources 2000–2001* (Guilford: CT: Dushkin/McGraw-Hill, 1999).

[54]Ibid.

Kat's Take

I ran head on into a culture barrier when I was training to become the incoming president of the local branch of a volunteer organization. Our branch was known for being flexible and diverse in terms of ages, gender, and cultural background. Unfortunately, we were a bit of an anomaly in the bigger district.

I had earlier attended a regional camp with a number of young professionals who were asked to come up with ways to attract more people like us to the organization. We explored a lot of barriers to membership and brainstormed ideas to break down those barriers. I left the camp quite proud of what we had identified and discussed and the ideas we would try to implement in our regions.

A few months later, at the main training for my presidential year, I was eager and optimistic and proud to describe the flexibility and diversity of my organization. Another future president approached me in the hall to ask how our local group had created our success. This future president, who was from a different generation, described his own organization as very structured.

I discussed the efforts of our organization to encourage new ideas and create a warm and welcoming environment, described joint projects with other organizations, and explained that our organization's willingness to put young professionals in high positions of leadership kept ideas and viewpoints fresh. Our trust in young professionals not only got my generation involved, I told him, but also allowed us to learn from one another, to mentor and be mentored. We could then feel good about encouraging other young professionals to join our organization.

He was quiet for a moment and then said (and I quote), "Oh, our club wouldn't be comfortable putting young professionals in positions of leadership or on our board. Particularly women."

I was taken aback, wondering if my watch had suddenly teleported me to the 1950s. Too shocked to reply, I muttered something to excuse myself. I have since wished that I had worked up the gumption to tell him that his club's culture was repelling young professionals. If his group did not listen to young professionals' ideas, assigned them only the grunt work, and gave them no opportunities to grow and lead the organization, it would not get any young professional members. Period.

I'm happy to report that the culture of the larger organization is slowly shifting as more local chapters implement changes to attract more young professionals. Although the organization as a whole has a long way to go, incremental change is ongoing, and more young professionals are taking the lead, making changes, and being visible while doing so.

Beware of Name Bias

According to the Social Security Administration, most of Gen Z's parents gave their children names like Emily and Jacob. However, some members of Gen Z were also named Kal-El (son of Nicolas Cage), Shiloh-Nouvel (daughter of Angelina Jolie and Brad Pitt), and Zuma Nesta Rock (son of Gwen Stefani). Those kids will probably have no problem finding a job; however, people who don't have famous parents but do have names that are hard to pronounce may have more trouble.

In their study "The Name-Pronunciation Effect: Why People Like Mr. Smith More Than Mr. Colquhoun," university researchers Simon Laham and Adam Alter found that "easy-to-pronounce names [and their bearers] are judged more positively than difficult-to-pronounce names." According to the study, which was published in the *Journal of Experimental Social Psychology*, problems don't come from the length of a name, how foreign it sounds, or how unusual it is. Judgment is based solely on how easy it is to pronounce the name. In this study, people with easy-to-pronounce names wind up with more positive performance evaluations and higher status in the hierarchy.

Really? The fact that someone's name might be difficult for others to pronounce could actually hinder his ability to succeed at work? Yes, if you believe the results of the study. According to Alter, "People simply aren't aware of the subtle impact that names can have on their judgments."[55]

Here are some steps you can take to prevent name bias in the hiring process, according to Rebecca R. Hastings, an online editor/manager for the Society for Human Resource Management:

- Remove the names of applicants from resumes and applications before they are circulated among the hiring committee.
- Use multiple interviewers with diverse backgrounds.
- Ensure that all job candidates are treated equally, including being asked the same questions for the same position.
- Address the issue in antidiscrimination policies.
- Train those who are involved in hiring decisions about unintentional bias.[56]

Know the Law!

If you think you can solve the name bias problem by handing out nicknames to people with difficult-to-pronounce names, think again. Your employee may see such behavior as insulting rather than helpful. For example, the CEO of BJY, Inc., called employee

---

[55]Simon M. Laham, Peter Koval, and Adam L. Alter, "The Name-Pronunciation Effect: Why People Like Mr. Smith More Than Mr. Colquhoun," *Journal of Experimental Social Psychology* 48 (2012): 752–56, https://ppw.kuleuven.be/okp/_pdf/Laham2012TNPEW.pdf.

[56]Rebecca R. Hastings, "How to Prevent Name-Related Bias," Society for Human Resource Management, February 21, 2012, https://www.shrm.org/resourcesandtools/hr-topics/behavioral-competencies/global-and-cultural-effectiveness/pages/howtopreventnamerelatedbias.aspx.

Mamdouh El-Hakem "Manny" because he thought the nickname "would increase El-Hakem's chances for success and would be more acceptable to BJY's clientele." Instead, it led to a racial discrimination lawsuit, which the employer lost. According to court documents, the jury awarded El-Hakem $15,000 in compensatory damages, $15,000 in punitive damages, and $11,000 in wages.[57]

According to Shakespeare, "That which we call a rose, by any other name would smell as sweet." Keep that in mind during the hiring process. Names should not be important, or even considered, when determining a person's value. Make judgments and employment decisions based only on the person's qualifications and performance.

Kat's Take

As mentioned in chapter 2, internships can be a great way of attracting ambitious Gen Zers to your company. They can also be a great way of determining whether a person fits in well with your culture and has the skills needed in a particular position. But recognize that unpaid internships will also disproportionately favor wealthy students.

Many low- and middle-class students are not able to take unpaid work, particularly over the summers as they need to work to help pay for their education. Offering only unpaid internships will immediately eliminate a number of candidates who work really hard and often have great practical work experience because they have had to work their way to get where they are.

If your organization can afford to offer a selection of paid internships, you could open up a wider base of candidates from all backgrounds and income levels.

[57]Mamdouh El-Hakem v. BJY Inc., 2005, https://law.justia.com/cases/federal/appellate-courts/F3/415/1068/524916/.

CHAPTER 8

CHECK THEM OUT

S o you've found a Gen Z worker who you are pretty sure has the skills you need and will fit into your company culture while also bringing a breath of young air. How can you determine whether the prospect will actually perform as well as the interview indicates?

This is not an easy question to answer, but one thing I do know: contacting references is often a waste of time.

Do you ask applicants to provide you with a list of references? If so, you should realize that (1) they will only list people who will say good things about them and (2) the references might have no direct knowledge about their work experience or performance. (For example, I was asked by an acquaintance to be a job reference, but I had no idea what she did for a living.)

Instead of contacting references, I suggest you contact previous employers whenever possible.

Although many people think previous employers are legally prevented from saying anything about former employees, no federal laws prevent employers from discussing a former employee's job performance, qualifications, and eligibility for rehire with a prospective employer as long as their remarks are truthful and offered without malice. However, state laws differ on what former employers may say; therefore, explore your state laws before you ask and answer questions. (See appendix A for information about what to do if you are asked to provide a reference.)

Failure to contact previous employers could result in a negligent hiring lawsuit if you hire someone who causes harm that might have been prevented if you had talked to a former boss. That said, there are some things you need to know before you pick up the phone or send an email.

First, you need to get the applicants' permission by having them initial an authorization statement on an employment application or sign a release that allows you to investigate their work record and releases you and previous employers from liability related to such investigation. Then create a list of questions that you will ask former employers or their agents (such as supervisors or HR personnel) of all applicants applying for the same job. (You probably won't get the applicants' permission to contact a current employer, which is fine. Organizations sometimes retaliate if they discover an employee is looking for another job.) It's important to follow the same process for all applicants applying for the same job in order to avoid discrimination claims.

What to Ask

I prefer calling previous employers instead of emailing because they usually provide more information while talking than they do in writing. Let them know the applicant has applied for a position with your company and authorized you to contact them (you'll probably need to email or fax the authorization form before they'll talk). Then ask them the questions from your list, such as:

- What were the applicant's job title, duties, and dates of employment?
- How well do you know the applicant?
- How would you describe the applicant's work performance?
- What was it like working with the applicant?
- What are the applicant's strengths and weaknesses?
- Was the applicant dependable?
- Why did the applicant leave your company?
- Would you rehire the applicant?
- Is there anything else I should know about the applicant?

Any questions and follow-up questions that are job related are permissible as long as they don't pertain to any of the protected classes, such as "What is the applicant's religion?" or "How old is the applicant?"

Of course, just because the law allows previous employers and their agents to answer these questions doesn't mean they will. Most will only provide information about position held, dates of employment, and whether they would rehire the applicant or not. But even getting this little bit of information can be valuable because it allows you to verify whether your prospect has been truthful in your job application. According to a PrideStaff report, 44 percent of applicants provide false or misleading information about their work history—such as position held and dates of employment.[58]

As discussed in previous chapters, Gen Z workers rarely have a long list of previous employers. In fact, they might not have any! So ask them to provide contact information for a few teachers or coaches or pastors or leaders of volunteer organizations.

Kat's Take

Professors and former teachers can be great references for Gen Z candidates. As professors and teachers are always busy, here a few tips to maximize your time and get the most relevant information from these references:

- In my experience, professors rarely answer their office phones. They are typically overloaded teaching multiple classes, grading, lecturing, helping students, and keeping up with many other expectations, so answering phone messages will be lower on their priority list. You will have a greater chance of getting an answer by email or using email to schedule a quick phone call.
- Professors and teachers can answer questions about your

---

[58]PrideStaff, "Flushing Out Resume Lies: Getting to the Truth About Candidates," accessed May 30, 2020, http://pridestaff38.haleymail.com/i/14611227312.

candidate's integrity, involvement, curiosity, quickness to learn, attention to detail, and initiative.

- Professors and teachers can answer questions about whether a potential employee shows up to class, arrives on time, or exceeds work expectations.
- If a professor or teacher instructs in your industry (such as engineering or accounting), she can answer questions about particular skill sets.
- She might also be able to tell you more about the candidate's involvement in the field, whether he took advantage of opportunities on campus, and other information that might highlight his strengths.

WELCOME THEM

Section 3 Takeaways

- First days are important.
- Onboarding is better than orientation.
- Detailed plans and procedures are a must.
- Handbooks make life easier.
- Set SMART goals.
- Provide valuable feedback.

CHAPTER 9

FIRST DAYS FIRST

Y ou've spent time and money in the hiring process. Now, how do you retain your talented Gen Z employees once you've got them on board?

Leigh Branham analyzed twenty years of data collected from surveys of more than four thousand employees to determine why they left their employers. The top ten reasons in order were as follows:

1. Poor management
2. Lack of career growth and advancement opportunity
3. Poor communications
4. Pay
5. Lack of recognition
6. Poor senior leadership
7. Lack of training
8. Excessive workload
9. Lack of tools and resources
10. Lack of teamwork

Branham concluded that "most of the reasons employees disengage and leave are consistent, predictable, and avoidable."[59] In the following

---

[59]Leigh Branham, *The 7 Hidden Reasons Employees Leave* (New York: AMACOM Books, 2012).

chapters, we're going to give you lots of tips for how to address many of these issues, especially with Gen Z employees, so that you have a better chance of retaining the employees who bring the most benefits to your company.

First, take a look at your first-day routines. Making a new employee feel welcome and valuable on the first day of a job can go a long way to inspire the kind of loyalty that leads to a happy, productive employee.

What is the first day on the job like for new employees at your workplace? Are they put in a room for hours to complete piles of paperwork and watch decades-old videos? Are they handed off to the first available employee to be "trained"? Are they forced to work in the break room because their workspace isn't ready? If any of these apply, your new employees are likely to feel disconnected and disrespected and may begin looking for their first chance to bounce right out of your company.

Kat's Take

First impressions are everything. Although onboarding a new employee isn't always on an organization's priority list, what happens in a new employee's first few days can truly set the tone for how they will fit into the organization.

I've been onboarded myself into several entry-level positions. I was grateful in those jobs where someone took me around and introduced me to other people around the office, but I never really enjoyed being left in a room by myself to watch outdated videos. But one experience stands out more than the others—especially because I've heard versions of my story countless times from other Millennials and Gen Zers.

After spending two hours signing reams of paperwork that were not well explained (health forms, privacy policies, retirement contributions, etc.), I was placed in my new cubicle with a computer, a phone, and a notepad. Although I could log in to my computer, I had no access to any of the software I needed to start my job. I asked when I could get training, and someone told me they would get me access "soon."

I sat for another ten minutes with nothing to do, then walked back to the supervisor who had placed me in my cubicle. I asked her if I could start reading any training manuals or any work projects I could take on. My supervisor was busy with her own job. "No, not at the moment," she smiled at me. "Just sit tight. We'll get you going soon."

I sat tight for an hour. Terrified of getting on the internet (I remembered signing that document), I literally just sat. Watched coworkers walk by. Caught snippets of information.

After an hour with nothing to do, I found the cubicle for the lead in the department, introduced myself, and asked if she had any work I could do. Thankfully, she gave me a filing project. The next morning, she kindly took me around to introduce me to everyone.

However, I had to constantly search for things to do for the entire week. Accounts had not been set up for me; I had no key to the building; and training wasn't possible because the new cohort would not start for two more weeks.

Because I had worked in a few other corporate entry-level positions, I knew that I had to take the initiative to find something to do that first week for my own peace of mind. I would eventually become the queen of the filing system in that job because I completely reorganized how everything was put into folders, filed, and cataloged, due to that first week of having nothing else to do.

What a missed opportunity! I could have shadowed multiple people in my department to start learning the vocabulary, processes, and policies with real hands-on mentoring. The company could have started me two weeks later, with the rest of my training cohort, so I could work on the technical aspects of the position. They could have prepared software log-ins so I could have at least done some online training.

I would learn later that my first-week experience was rather normal for the organization. Not only did that week make me feel less than welcome at that organization, but it gave me plenty of opportunities to abuse the system. Did no one realize that I was sitting in my cubicle staring at the wall? Would they notice if I was not there at all? What would have happened if I had not returned from lunch one day?

Setting the tone those first few days is paramount, especially as you're introducing your new hire to your company culture. Don't make it an afterthought.

All on Board

Many organizations have created "orientation" processes for new employees. I recommend that you upgrade your orientation process into an onboarding experience.

Whereas orientation gives new employees a superficial overview of your organization, onboarding aims to help them feel connected to your workplace. Successful onboarding experiences can be critical to new employees' success and longevity and can be especially vital when bringing in Gen Z. Consider these onboarding strategies:

- Begin the process before a new hire's first day of work by sending a welcome letter that outlines where to go, what time, and whom to see on the first day. Encourage her to call with any questions.
- Prepare her workspace before she arrives. Have computers, phones, and any other equipment she will need ready to operate. Have keys or access cards available.
- On the new employee's first day, show her around when she arrives and introduce her to her new coworkers. Take her to lunch or arrange for other employees to take her to lunch.
- Provide a "welcome" packet that includes the required pamphlets for new hires, a company directory, and a checklist of all the information she will need to learn in the first few days.
- To kick it up a notch, have business cards, a company T-shirt, a welcome card signed by all employees, balloons, a bouquet of flowers, or a new plant waiting for the new arrival.
- Try to avoid paperwork overload by having the new employee complete only the required new employee forms (I-9, W-4, etc.) on her first day.

- Have her meet with her supervisor, trainer, or mentor.
- Show her how to use her computer, phone, and other applicable equipment.
- Go over the new hire's job description and set some short-term goals she can achieve within her first week so that she can experience a sense of accomplishment early.
- Check in at the end of the day to see how things went. Let the new hire know once again that you're glad she has joined your organization.

" Employers React to Gen Z

This population wants a road map and instant access to move their career. "

Extra Effort, Extra Payoff

It takes time and effort to help new employees feel connected; however, numerous studies have demonstrated that employers who make this kind of investment are rewarded with increased employee productivity, morale, and retention.

Tammy Rutledge, director of experience at Planned Parenthood California Central Coast, says her organization's new-hire packet includes a "Favorites and Appreciation" questionnaire, which lets her know how new employees prefer to receive feedback and some of their favorite drinks, candy, sports, or other ways they like to be recognized. "I have one staff person who really likes Goldfish crackers and one who loves Red Vines. This is helpful when I want to get them a treat to say thank you or just let them know I appreciate them," she says.

"New employees are assigned a mentor (we call it a 'champion') who spends time with them each week for their first few weeks to help them settle in," says Rutledge. "During their time together, they talk about items on their 'champion agreement' such as lunchroom etiquette, parking, and good lunch locations."

Kat's Take

Did you know what a 401(k) plan was when you were nineteen or twenty-three? Did you understand all the nuances of your health plan when you started your first job?

Then don't be surprised when Gen Zers don't understand your benefit forms, especially it's likely they will have never encountered them before. Remember that in contrast to prior generations, Gen Zers are less likely to have had a prior job, and they may have never learned anything about these forms from their parents or in their schools.

When you take a little time to explain the basics, you may save yourself a lot of trouble down the way. Even better, go a step further and create a packet with basic questions, definitions, and explanations about the benefits. Try to stay away from formal, legal definitions and put everything in simple terms.

CHAPTER 10

SOLID GROUNDING

Focusing on your onboarding process can help ensure that your new employees feel comfortable and productive in their first days on the job. Now what?

In her article "Employee Orientation: Keeping New Employees on Board!," Judith Brown says, "People become productive sooner if they are firmly grounded in the basic knowledge they need to understand their job. Focus on the why, when, where, and how of the position before expecting them to handle assignments or big projects."[60]

Especially important, according to Nancy Sutherland, human resources director at Lightspeed Systems, is the "why":

The most important thing for new Lightspeed employees to understand is WHY. Why the company exists, why the new employee is there, and why their work is important to the overall mission. Lightspeed helps schools transform education and inspire students by being online, collaborative, and connected. That's an important mission that anyone can get behind. And internally we live by the principles we want

---

[60]Judith Brown, "Employee Orientation: Keeping New Employees on Board!," International Public Management Association for Human Resources, accessed June 1, 2020, https://www.ipma-hr.org/docs/default-source/public-docs/importdocuments/pdf/hrcenter/employee-orientation/cpr-eo-overview.

to see in education: our core values are to always be learning, always be teaching. If new employees understand that, they see their new role as less of an isolated job and more of a connected mission.[61]

This may be especially true of Gen Z workers, who want to believe they are working toward a worthy cause.

Closely monitor a new employees' progress during their first ninety days and provide helpful feedback on their performance. And encourage them to give you feedback on their onboarding experience so you can continually improve the process.

Remember that Generation Z's formative years have been marked by economic uncertainty and a breakdown of past systems. Kat Clowes says these experiences make it easy for Gen Zers to be cynical and hard for them to believe that a corporation or company will operate ethically. They were young when they watched millions of people lose their jobs, homes, and investments during the Great Recession of 2008 and teenagers or young adults when they witnessed the economic upheaval caused by COVID-19. They have seen parents and family members who had been loyal to their employers for many years (sometimes to the detriment of their family) laid off or pushed out overnight.

Generation Zers have witnessed a breakdown in government institutions and chaos and seen various parts of the country institute different policies in response to COVID. They know governments throughout the world have chosen different tactics to battle the pandemic, and they are watching how those choices affect individuals.

Because of this breakdown of trust in formalized institutions, Gen Z is less likely to believe that a corporation might do the right thing and especially skeptical that an organization will be loyal to its workforce. Employers should realize Gen Z workers will be on high alert for policies or programs that seem to benefit the workplace over its workers. So, if you are looking for loyalty from Gen Zers, you will first have to prove your loyalty to them and frequently let them know where they stand.

---

[61]Nancy Sutherland, interview by Robin Paggi, March 25, 2018.

Employers React to Gen Z

I sometimes want to shout, "Did you go to school for this profession?" I find myself doing a lot of the teaching that I'd expect would have already happened. **"**

Be Precise

When you are bringing in Gen Z employees, the most helpful step you can take is to tell them exactly what you expect them to do and precisely how to do it. You may not be used to spelling out your directions in explicit detail, but the more specific you are with a Gen Zer, the better results you are likely to get.

These young workers are entering the workforce with less job experience than previous generations. As previously mentioned, only 19 percent of Gen Z reported working as teenagers compared with 48 percent of Baby Boomers.[62] In addition, they are "digital natives," meaning most of them didn't learn how to do things the "old-school" way. So, if you expect tasks to be done in specific order or according to specific guidelines, it's your job to tell your employees exactly what you expect.

For example, I asked my granddaughter to meet me at a fundraiser and gave her the address. She texted me and asked if the fundraiser was at a church because that's where Google Maps told her to go. The fundraiser was next door to the church. When she arrived, I showed her how to look at the numbers on the building to determine whether you're in the right place and, if you're not, how to get there.

A friend told me she asked her young assistant to light some candles. The assistant asked for a candle lighter, but my friend handed her a book of matches instead. "What do I do with these?" the assistant asked.

I don't offer these examples to make fun of young people or to imply that they're not intelligent. But I do want you to understand that you can't assume Gen Zers know how to do the things you know how to

---

[62]Knowledge@Wharton, "Make Way for Generation Z in the Workplace," Wharton School, University of Pennsylvania, January 22, 2019, https://knowledge.wharton.upenn.edu/article/make-room-generation-z-workplace/.

do. As the French writer Voltaire said, "Common sense is not so common." What is common sense to you is not necessarily common sense to everyone else. And you might be surprised at some of the things Gen Z can do that you have never even attempted.

Kat's Take

Unlike the Millennials who grew up on the old desktop computers with green screens, Space Invaders, and text-only internet, Gen Zers have always lived in a world with iPad and digital tablets, smartphones, and Siri. Social media has always existed in their world. So has touchscreen technology.

I came to realize this myself when I hired one of my first assistants. For mobility purposes (and because I had been my company's only employee for a time), the company phone number was connected to a cell phone that happened to be a flip phone that opened to reveal a small keyboard. Toward the end of the day, I asked my assistant to call a client and schedule an appointment. I had given her a script on how to answer the phone, shown her how to schedule appointments on the laptop computer she'd been provided, and given her other pertinent information about the phone. Fifteen minutes after asking her to make the call, I walked back into her office and noticed the phone was ringing. "Oh, go ahead and get that," I said, pausing.

She picked up the phone, blushed, and sheepishly admitted that she didn't know how to answer it. Naturally, I was shocked. She went on to explain that she knew how to answer her phone—a touchscreen device—but wasn't sure what to do with this flip phone as she'd never seen one like that in her life. She also admitted she had been afraid to ask earlier.

I showed her how to answer it and then learned she didn't know how to check voicemail, so I explained that as well. Then I told her that she should never be afraid to ask any question, even if it seemed like a simple question, like how to operate the phone.

In the years since this experience, I've discovered that many of my clients have no idea how to operate devices that seem commonplace to me. Although they can operate their phones and tablets expertly, they are often unfamiliar with anything that is *not* a touchscreen. Many of them even struggle with a desktop computer because they mostly use Chromebooks or tablets in school.

Standard Operating Procedures

In my performance management workshops, I frequently ask the supervisors who attend to write down the instructions for making a peanut butter sandwich. If there are twelve people in the workshop, they will invariably submit twelve variations for how to make the sandwich. That's why it's important for organizations to create standard operating procedures for tasks that need to be done consistently. Without step-by-step procedures, employees will complete tasks the way they want to instead of the way you want them to.

Spell out exactly how to do something according to your company standards. Don't expect employees—especially Gen Z employees—to know precisely what you want if you don't tell them. Left to figure it out on their own, employees will approach a task in a way that feels most comfortable or familiar. Or they may let Google or YouTube tell them how to perform a task.

" Employers React to Gen Z

They truly believe that Google can teach them whatever they don't know that they need to know. Since they don't know what they don't know, they typically come back with, or take action on, partially correct information, without context or out of context, no discussion or confirmation they are on the right track, and don't quite hit the target. Then they are crushed when sent back for rework. **"**

My first training assignment was at an ice cream plant that did not define standard operating procedures. As a result, the product differed according to who was running the assembly line. Inconsistent products often lead to unhappy customers.

If consistent results are very important to your business, consider creating visual reminders of the standard operating procedures. Such visual aids should be concise and easy to read. Here's an example of one in the time of COVID-19:

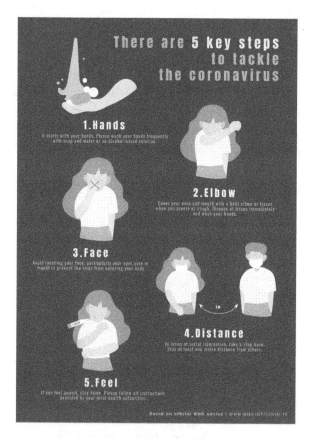

Employee Handbooks

Carefully crafted company handbooks are one of the most important communication tools you can use to make sure your employees are firmly grounded in the knowledge they need to understand your company and their job responsibilities. Effective handbooks spell out what the company expects from employees and what employees can expect from the company.

Handbooks should contain information on policies such as working hours, absenteeism, use of company property, dress codes, and other expectations. Describing the behavior you want from employees helps to ensure that you get it.

Handbooks should also contain information on benefits provided by the employer, such as holidays, sick leave, vacation, and insurance. They should also explain employees' statutory rights, including leaves of absence, and workers' compensation.

Providing this information in an easily accessible source helps promote a common understanding that can enhance employee productivity and help resolve issues when conflicts arise. On the other hand, the absence of a formal handbook, or the presence of a poorly drafted one, can put employers at a disadvantage if they face lawsuits based on policies, procedures, or accusations of discrimination or sexual harassment. (See appendix B for precautions about creating probationary periods and at-will worker clauses.)

Here are some things to keep in mind when creating a handbook:

- **Do it right.** Using another company's handbook or printing a generic one from the internet is dangerous because you don't know who drafted it or whether it was done correctly. Additionally, because some laws apply to businesses based on their size, a small company's handbook would not include all of the laws that apply to a large company, and a large company's handbook would include laws that don't apply to small companies. The safest course of action is to have an employment attorney draft your handbook, or at least review it.
- **Follow the handbook.** Employers who deviate from stated policies are at risk of being liable for breach of contract or claims of discrimination. Ensure that your supervisors are well versed in the handbook's content and apply the policies consistently. You can always end or modify policies after giving reasonable notice to employees.

- **Communicate policies to employees.** Simply distributing handbooks and having employees sign an acknowledgment form that they have read them isn't enough. Monthly staff meetings are a great time to carefully explain policies and answer questions about them. This communication helps prevent the "I-didn't-know-that-was-company-policy" excuse.
- **Hold employees accountable.** Make it clear that employees are expected to follow the policies in the handbook. However, don't detail disciplinary actions for policy violations so that you can have more flexibility in handling situations. Before taking disciplinary action, first determine whether the policy was clearly communicated, whether there is sufficient evidence of a violation, and whether extenuating circumstances led to the policy violation.

CHAPTER 11

GOOD GOALS

As part of onboarding a new hire, you need to set out some goals related to the job description. This helps a new employee, especially an inexperienced Gen Z worker, know how to get started in your organization.

Once you have communicated the ground rules and established a firm footing for new employees, review the job description to remind them of their overall responsibilities. Each essential job duty listed on the job description should be accompanied by at least one SMART goal that shows the employee how to successfully perform the duty. A SMART goal is

- Specific
- Measurable
- Attainable
- Relevant
- Timebound

For example, if a job duty is to provide excellent customer service, a SMART goal would be to "answer all incoming calls within three rings." Another part of the job description will be to explain what you expect your employee to say when answering a call.

Want to know why "attainable" is part of a SMART goal? It's because unattainable goals can lead to mischief and mayhem.

Many years ago, I was a waitress at a restaurant that was promoting a certain brand of wine. Our manager instructed the wait staff to sell at least three glasses of wine each shift or face disciplinary action. The wine was unsellable, so most of my coworkers and I ended up buying enough ourselves to meet our quota and avoid being written up or terminated. Then we drank the wine at the bar when our shifts were over.

Was our behavior unethical? As someone who facilitates ethics workshops, I can argue that it was because we weren't selling the wine to customers, which was clearly our manager's intent. We were essentially cheating to meet our sales goal.

I can also argue that our behavior was typical because decades of research have demonstrated that "incentive programs" like our manager's can cause ethical people to do what they need to do to survive.

Sales and other performance goals can be good because they tend to motivate employees to perform. However, if goals are not achievable, they can do more harm than good. Help your employees ethically meet their goals by ensuring that those goals are attainable as well as specific, measurable, relevant, and timebound. That way, your employees and your company can both profit.

Unwise Incentive Structures

A more complex version of our wine scheme unfolded in recent years at Wells Fargo, explains Gary Drevitch in his 2017 article "The Mystery of Motivation," published in *Psychology Today*. According to Drevitch, bank employees opened millions of phony bank and credit card accounts because of company "incentive structures that tied a substantial piece of their compensation, not to mention their continuing employment, to steep sales targets."[63]

Much like my former coworkers and me, Wells Fargo employees had to make sales goals to avoid discipline and remain employed. Unlike

---

[63]Gary Drevitch, "The Mystery of Motivation," *Psychology Today*, January 3, 2017, https://www.psychologytoday.com/us/articles/201701/the-mystery-motivation.

us, they were also rewarded for their sales. According to banking and economics reporter Victoria Finkle, "Wells Fargo's high-pressure sales quotas sent low-paid customer reps scrambling to meet unachievable growth goals."[64] And their increased income for meeting those goals created the perfect storm.

After more than five thousand customer reps were fired because of bogus accounts, Drevitch says, "The company's new head of community banking said that her first act would be to remove incentives that could promote bad behavior."[65]

That's probably because Consumer Financial Protection Bureau director Richard Cordray told her to. "Tying bonuses and job security to business goals that are unrealistic or not properly monitored can lead to illegal practices like unauthorized account openings and deceptive sales tactics," Cordray said in a statement. "The CFPB is warning companies to make sure that their incentives operate to reward quality customer service, not fraud and abuse."[66]

We can shake our heads disapprovingly at Wells Fargo and its former employees, or we can understand a fundamental fact about human behavior. Drevitch quotes George Loewenstein, professor of economics and psychology at Carnegie Mellon University: "If goals are unrealistic, but you can achieve them by cheating, then people will cheat. They will commit fraud to obtain the incentive."[67] Or to keep their job.

Loewenstein is considered to be one of the founders of behavioral economics, the study of psychology that attempts to explain why people make certain decisions, especially financial ones. Although there are no easy explanations about our decision-making in general, one thing is evident: people decide to do some stupid stuff when it comes to making money.

---

[64]Victoria Finkle, "The Wells Fargo Fake Account Scandal Proves 'There's No Such Thing as a Good Bank,'" Quartz, September 29, 2016, https://qz.com/795435/the-wells-fargo-fake-account-scandal-proves-theres-no-such-thing-as-a-good-big-bank/.

[65]Drevitch, "Mystery of Motivation."

[66]Consumer Financial Protection Bureau, "CFPB Warns Financial Companies About Sales and Production Incentives That May Lead to Fraud or Consumer Abuse," November 28, 2016, https://www.consumerfinance.gov/about-us/newsroom/cfpb-warns-financial-companies-about-sales-and-production-incentives-may-lead-fraud-or-consumer-abuse/.

[67]Drevitch, "Mystery of Motivation."

The Experiential Learning Cycle

You've spent time making your new employee feel welcome, spelled out your company's policies, provided an employee handbook, reviewed the job description, and established several SMART goals. Now you should be able to step back and expect the new employee to start smoothly and expertly handle all his responsibilities—right? Well, maybe, if you have an exceptional new hire.

But most of the time, you are going to experience some bumps in the road and watch your new hire make some mistakes—no matter how clear your directions have been. There are multiple reasons this might happen, but it may be that your new Gen Z employees are simply learning on the job and will have to make some mistakes before they can internalize the process you want them to master.

A couple of decades ago, I taught public speaking classes at a junior college. I would tell and show my students how to write and deliver a speech, and then I'd expect them to do it the way I taught them. Frequently, they did not, and I could not understand why. Then I learned about Kolb's experiential learning cycle.

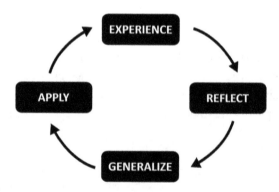

According to this model, we learn by having an experience, reflecting on what went well and what didn't go well, generalizing what we learned from the experience, and then determining how to apply what we learned the next time. We usually need to go through this cycle three or four times before we really learn how to do something well.[68]

Once I learned about this model, I began using it to coach students. After they had given a speech, I would ask:

·   What do you think went well? What didn't go well?
·   What did you learn from the experience?
·   How will you apply what you learned in your next speech?

You can use this tool with your employees, especially after they make mistakes.

Kat's Take

Although they have grown up with metrics, Gen Zers have had less experience with accountability when they fail to follow procedures or make mistakes. All too often their parents have pushed more responsibilities to the school system—or taken matters into their own hands when their child did make a mistake.

On top of that, Gen Zers have seen celebrities and world leaders escape accountability for their words or actions and watched society blur the lines between opinions and facts. Is it any wonder that Gen Zers are less likely to take full accountability for their own actions?

In my opinion, this reluctance is not because Gen Zers are malicious in any way but because they lack experience in being confronted or criticized. I often hear a parent or student blame a teacher when a student does poorly in a class, rather than admit that the student truly struggled but did not seek help. Or that the student had not turned in homework or kept up with the reading. I fully expect that Gen Z employees will transfer these attitudes into the workplace and try to blame others when things go wrong, rather than admit their own shortcomings.

---

[68]Saul A. McLeod, "Kolb's Learning Styles and Experiential Learning Cycle," Simply Psychology, October 24, 2017, accessed on May 5, 2020, https://www.simplypsychology.org/learning-kolb.html.

So, it will be important to use the experiential learning cycle and performance evaluations (see chapter 12) when dealing with Gen Z employees. Explain that learning is a process and that it's important to reflect on what went right *and* what went wrong. This type of feedback can make them feel less threatened and more likely to admit that they can make improvements.

Also let Gen Z employees know that their performance will be evaluated. Set the expectation up front that they will receive a "grade" for their work. Be clear on which metrics will be used in the evaluation so they can see where the bar is and how to exceed it.

Explain early on that during the evaluation process, all employees get feedback on how they can improve their performance so they can continue to grow and develop more skills to do better in their position. Framing it this way will help prepare them for potential criticism.

Check for Understanding

One of my favorite quotes is attributed to Ralph Waldo Emerson, who said, "The biggest problem with communication is the illusion we have achieved it." All too often, we think others understand what we're saying only to discover later that they didn't.

When a boss asks, "Do you understand?," most employees will be inclined to say yes. If you ask, "Do you have any questions?," the usual answer will be no. Then off we go thinking we're on the same page when we're not.

When you're dealing with a new employee, it's better to initiate a two-way conversation instead of just giving directives and asking closed questions that elicit one-word answers.

For example, you're trying to liven up a PowerPoint presentation for your next sales meeting. You go to the new communications guy and say, "I need you to add some graphics to this PowerPoint to make it more interesting." Then, instead of asking, "Do you understand?," ask, "What do you think would look good?"

You may be shocked to find out that your Gen Z illustrator is thinking about adding an embedded video or an animated GIF when all you want is a stock photo of a sunset. By engaging in an extra two minutes of conversation, you just saved yourself and your new employee a lot of time and frustration!

" Employers React to Gen Z

Coaching, coaching, coaching. It takes patience and that gets hard. But I find that when I give coaching, these folks tend to listen. "

CHAPTER 12

PERFORMANCE EVALUA-TIONS AND FEEDBACK

As Kat pointed out in chapter 11, Generation Zers in general do not react well to criticism or to being held accountable for their actions. And because most of them have little work experience, they have likely never experienced a performance review. So, it's going to be important that you create a highly effective performance review process to get the best results from your Gen Z workers.

Employers often ask me to provide them with a generic performance evaluation form they can use to evaluate their employees. I explain that an employee performance evaluation should reflect the job description because that's what the employee is being evaluated on.

For example, suppose an employee's job description includes the following essential job duties:

- responsible for recruiting, interviewing, and evaluating job candidates; and
- responsible for working with community resources to develop creative staffing solutions

Then the performance review should evaluate how well the employee performs those tasks, ranking the performance according to a numerical scale or using labels such as "Below Expectations," "Exceeds Expectations," and so on. Figure 1 provides a sample performance review form.

Essential Job Duties	1 Far exceeds expecta- tions	2 Exceeds expecta- tions	3 Meets expecta- tions	4 Falls short of expecta- tions	5 Falls far short of expecta- tions
Recruiting, in- terviewing, and evaluating job candidates					
Working with community resources to develop creative staffing solutions					

Figure 1. Performance review grid

I recommend showing all new employees the performance evaluation during the onboarding process so they understand how they will be evaluated. This helps to clarify your expectations, reduce misunderstandings, and prevent unhappy surprises during the performance evaluation meeting.

Supervisors should record noteworthy conversations, such as commendations or disciplinary action, on the performance evaluation forms throughout the year (which makes it less onerous to complete when it's due). Then these forms are used periodically for formal discussions and to evaluate an employee for raises, bonuses, or promotions. The formal discussion also presents a great opportunity for both employee and supervisor to discuss future goals and training prospects.

Never wait until an annual performance review to discuss a performance success or issue. There should be no surprises on the evaluation form.

Performance evaluations should memorialize an employee's performance for a specific period, and employers should use the documentation to explain their decisions.

"In addition to annual performance reviews, we schedule quarterly feedback interventions that encourage communication, not just work performance," says Tammy Rutledge of Planned Parenthood California Central Coast. "Some examples of our quarterly check-in opportunities have been 'stay interviews' (what makes employees stay with their employer); 'how I work best' conversations and team and personal SWOT [strengths, weaknesses, opportunities, and threats] assessments."

🙶 Employers React to Gen Z

They need a lot of continuous positive feedback and take critique very personally.

🙷

Bad Rap

If you're not a fan of performance evaluations, you're not alone. Samuel Culbert, author of *Get Rid of the Performance Review!*, appears to hate them. "It's the most ridiculous practice in the world," he told NPR's Neal Conan. "It's bogus, fraudulent, dishonest at its core, and reflects stupid, bad, cowardly management."[69] That seems a bit dramatic to me.

Culbert does have a point, though. When asked what words came to mind when giving or receiving a performance review, respondents of a ReviewSNAP survey said: time consuming, frustrating, dread, burden, headache, and pain.[70]

---

[69]Samuel Culbert, interview by Neal Conan, "Putting Performance Reviews on Probation," *National Public Radio,* November 9, 2010, https://www.npr.org/templates/story/story.php?storyId=131191535.

[70]Alexandra Bradley, "Taking the Formality out of Performance Reviews: Managers Need to Step Up Their Communications with Employees on Performance Issue," *Questia,* accessed June 1, 2020, https://www.questia.com/magazine/1G1–228331257/taking-the-formality-out-of-performance-reviews-managers.

Perhaps that's why a survey conducted by Kelton Research discovered that

- 68 percent of respondents had not received useful feedback from their supervisors;
- 82 percent had not established their career goals with their supervisors; and
- 53 percent did not have a clear understanding of how their role contributes to company objectives.[71]

Some people think performance evaluations are outdated. In his article "Performance Reviews Are Dead. Here's What You Should Do Instead," Thomas Koulopoulos says,

as with most industrial era models (annual performance reviews) were built primarily for scale in large organizations that were rapidly growing. Their rigor, checklists, metrics, and one or twice yearly application was never particularly good, especially for smaller organizations, but we accepted them as just part of the corporate tedium.[72]

Others just think performance reviews are ineffective. In their article "More Harm Than Good: The Truth About Performance Reviews," Robert Sutton and Ben Wigert say, "Performance evaluations are an imperfect tool that only captures snippets of information. They communicate what is and is not important for employees to do—for better or worse."[73]

---

[71]Jude Carter, , "Investing in Employee Loyalty," Marlin, accessed June 1, 2020, https://www.themarlincompany.com/blog-articles/investing-employee-loyalty/.

[72]Thomas Koulopoulos, "Performance Reviews Are Dead. Here's What You Should Do Instead," *Inc.*, accessed June 1, 2020, https://www.inc.com/thomas-koulopoulos/performance-reviews-are-dead-heres-what-you-should-do-instead.html.

73Robert Sutton and Ben Wigert, "More Harm Than Good: The Truth About Performance Reviews," Gallup, May 6, 2019, https://www.gallup.com/workplace/249332/harm-good-truth-performance-reviews.aspx.

Frequent Feedback

Despite these observations, the performance evaluation itself isn't the problem. But it *is* a problem if you're only talking to employees about their performance once a year.

"Using feedback on performance to course correct once a year, or even twice a year, is akin to trying to navigate a minefield by reviewing your performance after you've crossed it," Koulopoulos says. "Only on this minefield the landmines are shifting underground as you walk through them!"[74]

Not being honest with employees is another problem. As a human resources manager, I have sometimes seen supervisors rate employees higher than they deserved because they didn't want to cause any hurt feelings. This practice is a disservice to the employee and can end up causing lawsuits for employers.

Know the Law!

In the case of *Vaughn v. Edel*, favorable evaluations of an employee who did not deserve them led to a lawsuit. According to court documents, employee Emma Vaughn received favorable performance evaluations, merit increases, and no criticism of her work performance before being terminated by Texaco, her employer.

Texaco management stated that Vaughn was terminated for poor performance, even though its documentation demonstrated otherwise. In its defense, Texaco management stated that it refrained from confronting Vaughn about her poor performance because she was black.

---

[74]Koulopoulos, "Performance Reviews Are Dead."

Ironically, the judge said, "This direct evidence clearly shows that [her supervisor] acted as he did solely because Vaughn is black. . . . Vaughn has, consequently, established that Texaco discriminated against her."[75]

Two key components of performance discussions are frequency and honesty. When these are included, "performance evaluations can also paint a well-rounded picture of contributions, opportunities for improvement and plans for what's next," say Sutton and Wigert.[76]

To clarify, a formal performance evaluation doesn't need to be given frequently. What needs to be given more frequently is feedback, which is simply your reaction to your employees' actions. When employees are new, and especially when they're young, they need guidance to ensure that they're on the right path. Feedback provides them with this guidance.

According to a Gallup poll cited by Sutton and Wigert, employees who receive weekly feedback are

- 5.2 times more likely to strongly agree that *they receive meaningful feedback;*
- 3.2 times more likely to strongly agree that *they are motivated to do outstanding work; and*
- 2.7 times more likely to be *engaged at work.*[77]

In addition, the Center for Generational Kinetics says that 66 percent of Gen Z employees said they want feedback from their managers every few weeks if not more.[78]

---

[75]Vaughn v. Edel, US Court of Appeals for the Fifth Circuit, December 6, 1990, https://law.justia.com/cases/federal/appellate-courts/F2/918/517/24304/.

[76]Sutton, and Wigert, "More Harm Than Good."

[77]Ibid.

[78]Center for Generational Kinetics, *The State of Gen Z 2018*, Fall 2018, https://genhq.com/wp-content/uploads/2018/10/State-of-Gen-Z-2018.pdf.

❝   **Employers React to Gen Z**

I tell them repeatedly that just because you don't hear back on a particular assignment doesn't mean it wasn't good. If anything, it means the exact opposite. . . . While it's good to hear positive feedback every now and then, your worth and quality of your work shouldn't be dependent on it. Be confident in yourself and the work that you do.   **❞**

Gauging the Need

Figuring out how much feedback your employees need and prefer can be tricky, and generational differences can play a part in misunderstandings and miscommunication.

One Millennial supervisor told me she likes continual feedback and thought her employees would like it too, so she tried to meet with them individually once a week to provide feedback. She was puzzled when one of her older employees told her, "Honey, no news is good news." The supervisor didn't know what that meant. I explained that older employees were often used to hearing from managers only when they had done something wrong. So, "no news is good news" probably meant the employee didn't want weekly feedback. Moreover, the employee might have felt degraded by her younger supervisor constantly talking to her about her performance.

On the other hand, one Baby Boomer supervisor told me she was fed up with a young employee always asking whether he had done a good job on the tasks she assigned him. Although the employee was performing his job well, the supervisor refused to tell him so because of "his neediness." I explained that younger generations are generally used to getting more feedback and praise from their parents and teachers, and that if he was doing a good job, she should tell him. She finally did and was pleasantly surprised when he stopped "bugging her" after that.

I had a similar experience. I was setting up for a workshop and asked a young employee to put numerous handouts at each place on the tables. When she completed the task, she asked, "Did I do a good job or what?" The voice in my head said, "Yes, you did a great job putting papers on tables—good for you!" Fortunately, what I said aloud was "Yes, thanks for being so conscientious—the tables look very neat."

So, do you have to give older employees less feedback and younger employees more feedback? Why can't you just give the amount of feedback you want to give and have employees to adapt to your style? Because of a basic life principle: if you give people what they need, they will probably give you what you need in return.

It's not that hard to take a minute or two to tell employees (especially if they ask) when they meet or exceed your expectations, and your effort will often inspire them to meet or exceed your expectations in the future. Be sure to be specific when giving positive feedback, so employees know exactly what they did to deserve your praise.

Kat's Take

I went to work for a small shop after finishing college, and my employer didn't give much in terms of feedback. The lack of feedback made me paranoid. Was I doing an okay job? Was there more I could be doing? My coworker also wondered about her performance but decided to take a "no-news-is-good-news" viewpoint, assuming she was doing a good job if the business owner didn't tell her otherwise.

I, on the other hand, thought that if I wasn't hearing feedback, it must be because my boss was angry with me for not doing enough. Because of this, I took on extra projects, creating work for myself when the shop was slow by organizing and cleaning. I liked the job and wanted to keep it. My coworker continued to step back, spending her time goofing off, playing on her phone, or talking to her boyfriend when there were no customers.

After a few months, the business owner seemed to be unusually quiet over the span of a few days. Internalizing that, I finally built up the courage to ask her directly if she was angry with me or if I was doing something wrong. Was there more I could be doing to do better at my job?

She looked at me as if I had sprouted two heads. "No, of course not. You're doing a great job. For the first time, I feel like I can leave the shop in an employee's hands and not worry about what you're doing while I'm gone," she confessed. "Thank you for asking. I've never had anyone ask me that."

I told her that since I hadn't heard anything from her, I assumed I was doing poorly. She told me she rarely gave feedback, not on purpose, but usually because her mind was on the business. It had nothing to do with me. Clearing those channels of communication really helped, and we agreed that if I was doing something she didn't approve of, she would tell me so. Her faith in me to run the shop made me work even harder.

Unfortunately, my coworker was let go a month later. She, too, had begun the job with the potential to be a good employee. But the lack of guidance had prompted her to do less work, and she ended up without a job.

Honest—and Tactful

In his article "The Best Gift Leaders Can Give: Honest Feedback," Joseph Folkman says, "Strong employee engagement is closely aligned with the ability to give honest feedback in a helpful way." He cites a study he conducted that showed leaders who ranked in the top 10 percent in their ability to give honest feedback received engagement scores of 77 percent from their direct reports. Folkman believes that "giving honest feedback is a fantastic gift, but apparently people only experience it as a gift when it is delivered well."[79]

Well, yes.

We've already discussed how hard it is for Gen Zers to take criticism, but are they the only ones who take critique very personally? I don't think so. Google something like "do people take feedback personally"

---

[79]Joseph Folkman, "The Best Gift Leaders Can Give: Honest Feedback, *Forbes*, December 19, 2013, https://www.forbes.com/sites/joefolkman/2013/12/19/the-best-gift-leaders-can-give-honest-feedback/#22788c2f4c2b.

and you'll find pages and pages of advice on "how to not take feedback so personally." I have to work on not becoming defensive when someone gives me feedback that I don't like, and you probably do too. So, I don't think it's fair to say it's just a Gen Z thing.

I spend a lot of time teaching people how to critique in a constructive (rather than destructive) manner. This format works for almost every situation, including failure to meet expectations, policy violations, and discussing personal issues (such as body odor or bad breath). Emphasize how to help the employee be successful, and the employee will usually be more receptive to the feedback. For example:

- **Door opener statement:** "Robin, I'd like to talk to you about yesterday's workshop."
- **Statement of the issue:** "The workshop ended twenty minutes late, which cut into the participants' schedule."
- **Ask for the employee's input:** "Did something prevent you from ending on time?"
- **Tell the employee how to be successful** (what you say here depends on the employee's response): "Let me show you how to organize the workshop so you end on time in the future."

Many people think they always have to say something positive if they're going to say something negative. For example, "Robin, the participants thought your workshop was great, but I received a complaint that it ran overtime."

Adding a positive comment is a good idea; however, you will get a better reception if you avoid the word "but" or one of its synonyms. That's because any positive statement is negated by whatever statement follows the "but."

Use the word "and" instead: "That was a good presentation *and* enlarging the graphics will make it even better."

There are situations where replacing "but" with "and" won't work ("You're a great employee and you're fired"). However, it can help prevent a positive statement from being negated and make a negative statement sound constructive.

SECTION 4

TRAIN THEM

Section 4 Takeaways

- Teach, train, coach.
- Manage their expectations.
- Professionalism and civility don't come naturally.
- Regulate cell phone use.
- Create social media policies.
- Prevent cyberloafing and tardiness.
- Consider what they wear.
- Teach how to communicate verbally, nonverbally, and on the phone.
- Provide training on emails and emojis.
- Don't let bad habits fester.
- Give second chances.

CHAPTER 13

WHAT DO THEY KNOW?

In 2018, personal finance reporter Andrew Keshner said Gen Z is poised to be the most highly educated of the generations so far.[80] But that statistic may be misleading for employers for several reasons.

One reason is that the working world changes at a remarkable speed these days, making it hard for high schools and colleges to keep up. "The skills critical to success in any job are changing rapidly," write the authors of "3 Critical Skills College Doesn't Teach You."[81] "If you learned a programming language in school, chances are it already changed by the time you graduated."

Larry Summers, the former president of Harvard University, echoes that sentiment when he says, "For something that's all about ideas and for something that's all about *young* people, the pace of innovation in higher education is stunningly slow."[82]

[80]Andrew Keshner, "Meet the Post-Millennials—The Most Educated, Ethnically Diverse Americans, *MarketWatch*, November 19, 2018, https://www.marketwatch.com/story/meet-the-post-millennials-youve-never-seen-such-a-group-2018-11-16).

[81]StudySoup, "3 Critical Skills College Doesn't Teach You," WayUp—Community, April 21, 2017, https://www.wayup.com/guide/community/3-critical-skills-college-doesnt-teach/.

[82]Tyler Cowen, "Larry Summers on Macroeconomics, Mentorship, and Avoiding Complacency," *Conversations with Tyler*, September 20, 2017, https://medium.com/conversations-with-tyler/tyler-cowen-larry-summers-blog-secular-stagnation-twitter-421a69ed84c8.

Kat's Take

There's been a shift in what college is designed to do. Previously, a student went to college to learn how to learn and think through complex problems. They were taught in certain fields of expertise, yes, but for the most part, colleges emphasized a broad range of subjects and helping students gain critical thinking skills that they could apply to any job.

Vocational training was provided for apprenticeships and hands-on training either at the high school level or in specialized programs—not in colleges or universities. Vocational training allowed students to learn solid skills in a particular field so they could enter the workforce immediately.

But parents, high schools, and our entire society, in fact, began pushing kids to go to college, hoping they would find better opportunities through a college degree. Even as the price of college skyrocketed, more and more people began to see a college degree as a necessity for gaining employment. In addition, high schools cut vocational training, leading to the rise of for-profit schools and private vocational schools charging tens of thousands of dollars for that same training.

As college became a more popular path for more kids, many people began to believe that a college degree should teach you all you need to know to go into a specific field. Employers began to expect that college graduates should be fully prepared for their jobs. The purpose and mission of college, however, has not changed. A college education is not designed to be job training; it is designed to prepare students to think through big problems.

Colleges have scrambled to provide more robust career services, internships, and specialized training to students in particular majors, but employers should not expect recent college graduates to arrive knowing all there is to know about the field. And employers who require a college degree and years of experience for entry-level positions are just making it harder on young workers. Students lament on online forums that they're in this odd catch-22 where they have an expensive college degree, tried for as much experience as they could, but don't have the threshold requirements for what should be entry-level positions.

Employers, loosening requirements on your positions and being prepared to teach Gen Z will pay dividends for your organization in the end. You will be able to attract (and hopefully retain) the best candidates for various positions.

Another Side of Gen Z

So, Gen Z college graduates may not know as much as you expect them to know when they enter your workplace. But what about the ones who never make it to college at all? Many books and articles about Gen Zers tend to talk about them as college students or recent graduates, but this is only one segment of this age group.

Although the statistics showing Gen Z may end up being the most educated generation are true, these statistics are also true:

- The likelihood that a child lives in a high-poverty area in the United States has risen 44 percent since 2000.
- In 2018, 13 percent of all kids—nearly 9.5 million—lived in areas of concentrated poverty.
- 27 percent of kids lived in families that receive public assistance.[83]

Before the COVID-19 pandemic, Katie Davis noted in her article "How Disparities in Wealth Affect Gen Z's Experiences With Technology" that "income has an enormous impact on young people's educational experiences with technology, just as it does on other aspects of school life: teacher quality, class size, curriculum offerings, and so on."[84]

During the pandemic, as many schools switched to online

---

[83] Annie E. Casey Foundation, "Generation Z in the Statistical Spotlight," June 18, 2018, https://www.aecf.org/blog/generation-z-in-the-statistical-spotlight/.

[84] Katie Davis, "How Disparities in Wealth Affect Gen Z's Experiences with Technology," Pacific Standard, April 2, 2019, https://psmag.com/ideas/how-disparities-in-wealth-affect-gen-zs-experiences-with-technology.

instruction, the differences between the haves and the have-nots became even more visible. Some children were home with parents continuing their education on their personal laptops or tablets, but other children had no parents or technology at home.

In my California county, the superintendent of schools estimated in spring 2020 that 40 percent of students lacked the electronic devices or internet connectivity to continue their education online.[85] Although most students were provided with those things, they often still did not have the essential resource they needed to be successful: parents adept at using technology.

In an April 2020 article in the *Bakersfield Californian*, Ema Sasic writes, "As teachers navigate distance learning, relationships with students remain a priority." Sasic describes Bethany Gonzales, a third-grade teacher at McKinley Elementary School: "Out of 22 students in her classroom, she connects regularly with five. Even through various messaging apps, such as ClassDojo, where she has 90 percent of parents connected, only three reply. It's disheartening to not be able to connect with all her students, especially since many live in violent neighborhoods and she worries about their safety, but she's constantly thinking of new ways to engage with them."[86]

In a segment for NPR, Anya Kamenetz said, "Research done in past disasters suggests that it is teenagers who are the most at risk when school is interrupted. Many are forced to work to earn money or have to stay home and take care of younger siblings. They are more likely to drop out and less likely to go on to college."[87] These teenagers are also members of Gen Z—and you may be hiring one or more of them in the next few years.

---

[85]Ema Sasic, "KCSOS Turns Attention to Strengthening Distance Learning amid School Closures," *Bakersfield Californian*, April 2, 2020, https://www.bakersfield.com/news/kcsos-turns-attention-to-strengthening-distance-learning-amid-school-closures/article_96ad5fe6–751e-11ea-a7fa-77c34394f9e7.html.

[86]Ema Sasic, "As Teachers Navigate Distance Learning, Relationships with Students Remain a Priority," *Bakersfield Californian*, April 23, 2020, https://www.bakersfield.com/news/as-teachers-navigate-distance-learning-relationships-with-students-remain-a-priority/article_2ccf66e4–85a1–11ea-8bd6–7379fb84af61.html.

[87]Anya Kamenetz, "4 in 10 U.S. Teens Say They Haven't Done Online Learning Since Schools Closed," National Public Radio, April 8, 2020, https://www.npr.org/sections/coronavirus-live-updates/2020/04/08/829618124/4-in-10-u-s-teens-say-they-havent-done-online-learning-since-schools-closed.

The Secret Sauce

So, what happens to the young workers who will be arriving in your office in the next few years? How can you make sure they get a shot at being successful in your organization—and thus bring value and results to your company?

Train them.

People all over the world are familiar with the green mermaid on the Starbucks logo (seriously, the company has stores in over sixty countries). Despite its tremendous success at branding, Starbucks CEO Howard Schultz has said, "Starbucks is not an advertiser; people think we are a great marketing company, but in fact we spend very little money on marketing and more money on training our people than advertising."[88]

Employers wanting to attain even a smidgen of Starbucks' success should follow suit.

Training employees to perform their jobs well seems like a no-brainer; however, data indicates that few employers provide any kind of formal training program. Indeed, most employees receive some kind of on-the-job training similar to this experience described on Alison Green's blog, *Ask a Manager:* "Training (at a busy downtown hotel) consisted of my showing up and immediately being thrown behind the front desk with another employee who was expected to do his job while I observed him and did what he did."[89]

In a 2014 article, Pascal-Emmanuel Gobry says employers and managers know that training employees is good for business but don't do it because "by the time you're done with the day-to-day blocking and tackling, it's time to go to sleep to be ready to do it all over again the next day. You're not thinking about next week, next month, next year."[90]

In addition to time, training takes money, which is usually in short supply for most small- and medium-size businesses. However,

---

[88]BrainyQuote, "Howard Schultz Quotes," accessed June 1, 2020, https://www.brainyquote.com/quotes/howard_schultz_579235.

[89]Alison Green, "Why Are Employers So Bad at Training People," *Ask a Manager,* May 19, 2012, https://www.askamanager.org/2012/05/why-are-employers-so-bad-at-training-people.html.

[90]Pascal-Emanuel Gobry, "All Companies Should Train Employees. Few Do. Here's How to Fix That," *The Week*, February 11, 2014, https://theweek.com/articles/451619/all-companies-should-train-employees-few-heres-how-fix-that.

not providing training could cost even more. For example, let's say that turnover of new hires cost an employer $10,000 annually. Training supervisors on how to conduct effective interviews might cost the employer $1,000. If turnover is reduced even 20 percent as a result of the training, the employer saves $2,000. So, the training paid for itself and then some.

Employers often say they don't want to invest in training because they fear employees will leave after being trained. In response, I offer this quote by author Zig Ziglar, "The only thing worse than training employees and losing them is to not train them and keep them."[91]

Kat's Take

Gen Zers are adept at doing research on the internet, gaining instant answers to almost any question. On the other hand, not knowing what they don't know, the answer they get may not be complete, well researched, or the best answer to their problem. They go for the quick answer as opposed to the possible correct answer.

There's another incomprehensible trend that I have witnessed firsthand with my Gen Z clients: they don't even use Google to answer questions. The fact is, Google has become such a staple that teens are shunning it—although they don't seem to have a better option. I have no answer for this, and I hope it has to do more with maturity and being a teenager in general than a generational characteristic.

The students who do use Google typically look only at the first two or three results and take those at face value. As the US education system pushes for more metrics and testing, students are not getting lessons in critical thinking and some of the original skills that were taught to facilitate that thinking. Prior generations did have the card catalog, which taught you the difference between primary and secondary research, how to gauge the accuracy of

---

[91] Zig Ziglar, Ziglar, Inc., accessed October 3, 2020, https://www.ziglar.com/quotes/employees/.

the information you were researching, and the basic process to research.

Now with tools like Google, that research training has all but disappeared. They are no longer being taught how to use the library, how to research, how to judge the quality of information, or how to apply that information to a hypothesis, problem, or original question.

So I highly encourage employers to give your Gen Z employees specific instructions and training. Encourage them to look up questions to gain further information and have a conversation about what your industry considers credible sources: handbooks, policy manuals, industry code books, primary research, guidelines, and so on.

The more specific you can be, the less miscommunication will result in the long run.

Successful Training Ingredients

To ensure that a training program is successful, employers should do the following:

- **Identify who needs what training.** A one-size-fits-all approach rarely works.
- **Determine the outcome.** Decide before training begins what you want your employees to learn. For example, "trainees should be able to effectively handle customer complaints independently."
- **Develop the training material.** This could be as simple as a checklist.
- **Identify a competent trainer.** Be careful with this. Just because an employee is good at his job doesn't mean he is a good trainer.
- **Deliver the training.** Morning hours are usually best. Food makes the process better.
- **Evaluate the training.** Because training should be an ongoing process, it's important to evaluate the program to determine how it can be more effective in the future.

Employees who are well trained perform their jobs better. Customers return to a business because of the service they receive—not because of the company's brand.

" Employers React to Gen Z

The biggest challenge I've faced with this group is managing their expectations. When they feel they master something, it seems they expect a reward or deserve a promotion over someone who has much more training or experience. **"**

Manage Their Expectations

One of your first steps in successfully training your new Gen Z hires will be to help them manage their expectations. Young workers who show up expecting to find an unrealistically easy path to riches and a quick trip up the corporate ladder may become disgruntled very quickly. Help them envision a more realistic future.

According to the "2018 Yello Recruiting Study—Inside the Minds of Millennial Job Seekers," 41 percent of current college students expect to make at least $60,000 a year after graduation.[92] If that seems far-fetched to you, I'll confess that upon my graduation from college, I expected to make at least $50,000—and that was in 1987!

High school students are repeatedly told that college graduates make more money, so young college graduates tend to say, "Show me the money!" Additionally, Gen Z has spent about two decades advancing from one grade to the next, one achievement to the next—as long as work is satisfactory, you move on to the next level. So, it should come as no surprise that people fresh out of school think that's the way the world works.

To prevent unpleasant surprises for your Gen Z hires, be clear about pay and advancement opportunities during the hiring process. When new employees are on board and settled, help them create a career

---

[92]Yello, "2018 Yello Recruiting Study—Inside the Minds of Millennial Job Seekers," accessed June 25, 2020, https://yello.co/blog/inside-the-minds-of-millennial-job-seekers/.

development plan that identifies their career goals, what they need to do to achieve them, and how your organization might be able to help.

" Employers React to Gen Z

We've added an extra step between job positions—sort of a midway point between the entry-level positions and the supervisory. This gives them the perception of advancement more quickly and also adds new tasks for learning, which seems to satisfy that "itch" for advancement. "

For example, let's say you've hired a human resources assistant to help with payroll. When you discuss his career goals, he tells you he'd like to be a human resources manager someday. So let him know that HR managers in your organization must be HR certified and proficient in all aspects of payroll, benefits, workers' compensation, compliance, and training.

Without making any promises about his future employment or pay, help your new hire create a plan to get the education, training, and resources he will need to meet his goal. Continue to meet with him on a consistent basis to gauge his progress, provide input, and determine whether you're able to help in any other way, such as providing cross-training or tuition reimbursement.

Giving employees a realistic perspective of their career opportunities can help keep them motivated. And even if employees leave your organization to meet their career goals, your company will still benefit from their increased knowledge and abilities while they're still with you.

Kat's Take

Growing up as a Millennial, I was told my job was to achieve the best grades possible and work really hard to get into the best college possible, which would guarantee me a great, solid, successful career. At the time, it was what every adult told me and my entire generation. Why would there be reason to believe tough times were ahead? I graduated from high school at the height of the dot. com boom; people were making millions from technology start-ups and software companies, and the housing market was exploding. But after getting into the best college possible ("Don't worry about the cost. It's an investment in your future! You'll pay those loans off when you get that great job after college," every adult told me) and working hard, I realized a few events had shattered that promise.

The dot.com bubble burst. Then 9/11 happened my junior year of college. A recession followed and work was hard to come by. Student debt exploded and loan payments were due. My generation worked hard in college to gain degrees that were now required for jobs that a decade before had required no college degree. We were priced out of the housing market. Then came the Great Recession. The job market was cutthroat and salaries fell. Millennials still haven't recovered.

Even in the face of that recent history and the COVID-19 pandemic, we keep telling Gen Z to work hard and go to college, so they can get a great job. And we wonder why they're graduating with huge expectations for their careers?

Like Robin, I expected to be at the top of management about a year out of college, but I had no idea how to truly get there. There was no planning. No mention of personal or professional development, no pathway that I could follow, as I had my entire life.

Showing that pathway to Gen Z employees can help calm unrealistic expectations immediately and also show them how to achieve that next step. Explaining what skills they need to learn or sharpen will inspire many of them to take on additional project responsibilities and seek more training and professional development opportunities. It could eliminate a lot of their frustration about lack of advancement and a lot of your frustration about Gen Z's "sense of entitlement." Creating transparency and opening opportunities for skill advancement could also help you keep them around longer.

CHAPTER 14

CULTIVATE PROFESSIONALISM AND CIVILITY

W hat does it mean to be a professional in your field? How do you define professionalism in your workplace? If you are expecting Gen Z employees to behave "professionally" on the job, you are going to have to let them know how your organization defines the concept.

Misunderstandings can arise between people because we sometimes have different definitions of the same words. These misunderstandings can multiply in a workplace with people from a variety of age groups and backgrounds.

A few years ago, I was asked to be a judge at a fashion show involving business majors at a local college. For the show, students modeled three versions of business attire: inappropriate, business casual, and dressy. The students and I agreed on what constituted inappropriate attire; however, it soon became clear that we had different ideas about business casual and dressy!

A recent survey from York College of Pennsylvania's Center for Professional Excellence demonstrated that HR managers and front-line supervisors define professionalism differently than do many of their new hires, especially younger ones.[93] According to the survey, HR managers and supervisors typically say interpersonal skills, work ethic, appearance, and communication skills are important parts of professionalism, and they complained that younger employees were the ones most likely to lack professionalism. However, most respondents also admitted that their companies did not have any kind of formal program describing what professionalism looks like or sounds like. They undoubtedly assumed the employees would know and then dinged them when they didn't.

I'm willing to bet that those younger employees, like the business majors at my fashion show, believed they were behaving in a professional manner. They just define it differently than their older bosses or coworkers do.

If you want employees to look, sound, and behave professionally, tell them how you want them to look, sound, and behave. Assuming they have the same ideas about "professional" behavior leads to needless misunderstandings and problems.

" Employers React to Gen Z

Parents and teachers need to start teaching children at a young age how they should act in the workplace; otherwise, when they get to the workplace, the managers, supervisors, and experienced workers have to do it. "

Define Your Terms

Respondents to the York College survey named four areas as being important components of professionalism.[94] Take a look at those areas and how the managers and supervisors described them. Would you

[93]Center for Professional Excellence, *2013 National Professionalism Survey: Workplace Report*, York College of Pennsylvania, accessed May 29, 2020, https://www.ycp.edu/media/york-website/cpe/York-College-Professionalism-in-the-Workplace-Study-2013.pdf.
[94]Ibid.

define these behaviors in the same way? Start with this list to create your own picture of professionalism.

Interpersonal skills. Survey respondents said that being courteous, showing others respect, exhibiting behavior that is appropriate to the situation, and using proper etiquette demonstrate one's interpersonal skills.

Work ethic. According to survey respondents, having a good work ethic means working instead of abusing tech. Excessive tweeting and Facebooking, inappropriate use of the internet, text messaging at inappropriate times, and excessive cell phone usage for personal calls were considered signs of a poor work ethic. On the other hand, showing up for work every day on time demonstrates a strong work ethic. According to the York survey, employees are most likely to be fired because they too often miss work, arrive late, or leave early.[95]

Having a strong work ethic also is defined as demonstrating a commitment to the employer ("What can I do for the company?") rather than displaying a sense of entitlement ("What can the company do for me?").

But before you start accusing your younger workers of feeling "entitled," think about what previous generations said about you when you were new to the workforce. "It's worth noting that every generation has been accused of being 'entitled' by the previous generation," says Jamie Belinne in her book, *The Care and Feeding of Your Young Employee.* "It's safe to say entitlement is more a symptom of youth than a generational definition."[96]

Appearance. YORK survey respondents noted that a person's appearance demonstrates professionalism and impacts hiring, promotions, and perceptions of competence. Attire, facial piercings other than earrings, visible tattoos, unnatural hair color, and personal hygiene can affect hiring or promotions decisions.[97]

Communication skills. The York survey results don't provide much information on what "communication skills" means other than "competent verbal and written communication." Therefore, I'll take the liberty of providing my own definition. We communicate to get a desired response from our audience. For example, if we give a directive, we want it followed;

---

[95]Ibid.

[96]Jamie Belinne, *The Care and Feeding of Your Young Employee: A Manager's Guide to Millennials and Gen Z* (self-published, 2017).

[97]Center for Professional Excellence, *2013 National Professionalism Survey.*

if we ask a question, we want an answer; if we tell a joke, we want a laugh. Every time we communicate, we want a specific response.

Having good verbal communication skills means being able to express yourself in a way that inspires people to respond how you want them to respond. Good written communication means knowing and following spelling, grammar, and punctuation rules, even in emails and texts.

Kat's Take

Remember that your Gen Z workers may have never been directly taught what is expected in a professional workplace. Office etiquette is rarely taught in schools or most college programs. Some Gen Z parents instill the concepts in their kids, and some Gen Zers might get a taste of professionalism through an internship or during a workshop at school, but most don't.

So mentoring your young workers about your expectations for professional behavior, teaching them what they don't know, and setting clear guidelines will eliminate frustration on both sides.

Remember too that professionalism in a Silicon Valley start-up will be different from professionalism at a bank. If you don't clearly communicate what you expect at your organization, how will your new employee know what you want?

Promoting Civility

If you think civil behavior has gone the way of rotary phones and eight-track tapes, you're not alone. According to the survey *Civility in America VII: The State of Civility*, 75 percent of Americans think incivility has reached "crisis levels."[98]

You don't need to watch TV, listen to the radio, or get on social media to be subjected to incivility—just go to work. "Rudeness at work

---

[98]Weber Shandwick and Powell, in partnership with KRC Research, *Civility in America VII: The State of Civility*, accessed June 20, 2020, https://www.webershandwick.com/uploads/news/files/Civility_in_America_the_State_of_Civility.pdf.

is rampant, and it's on the rise," according to Christine Porath, an associate professor at the McDonough School of Business at Georgetown University and author of *Mastering Civility*. A survey she conducted in 1998 revealed that nearly half of the respondents said they were treated rudely at least once a month. That number rose to 55 percent in 2011 and 62 percent in 2016.[99] I can't wait to see the 2020 numbers.

What does incivility at work look like? Here's a personal example.

While I was conducting a workshop for a client, two employees came in late, sat in the back of the room, and spent the rest of the workshop talking and laughing with each other while texting. Their supervisor—who also came in late—sat by them but did nothing about their behavior.

Were they being rude? Most people seem to think so. Showing up late, having side conversations, and texting during meetings appear on just about every "examples-of-rude-behavior" list on Google.

Is rude behavior so bad? According to University of Florida professor Amir Erez, it is. A series of studies he conducted demonstrated that being subjected to rude behavior impacts our brain's ability to function, specifically the ability to be creative, help others, and solve problems.[100] I can attest to that. I felt so disrespected by the talking/laughing/texting training participants that I could hardly persevere through the workshop. My brain was shutting down and I just wanted to shut down with it.

Kat's Take

Being civil—or not being rude—is another area that is rarely covered in school these days. Depending on your family, avoiding rudeness could be a cornerstone of your family expectations, or something that is never discussed at all.

With a rise in social media videos of people harassing one another, yelling at one another, and throwing punches at retail

---

[99]Christine Porath and Christine Pearson, "The Price of Incivility," *Harvard Business Review*, January-February 2013, https://hbr.org/2013/01/the-price-of-incivility.

[100]Christine Poratch, and Amir Erez, , *Does Rudeness Really Matter?: The Effects of Rudeness on Task Performance and Helpfulness*, Social Science Research Network, May 16, 2007, https://papers.ssrn.com/s013/papers.cfm?abstract_id=986441.

employees or at restaurant staff, is it any mystery that the younger generation lacks a healthy respect for civility? Generation Z grew up with reality television and social media where everything is filmed for drama, harassment, or humor. The days of *Leave It to Beaver* or *Family Ties* are long gone.

Teach Gen Zers the basics of etiquette so they have more in their tool kit to draw from. Show them that civility includes manners and displaying care and respect for the people around them. They might not have been taught not to gossip or laugh at a coworker's mistake. They might not know that you think it's rude to pull out their phone during a meeting.

With a little instruction, you can make your company a more pleasant place to work—and increase the civility quotient in our world!

Manners Lessons

If you want your employees to mind their manners, take these steps:

- **Set clear expectations about behavior.** Don't assume people will naturally behave the way you want them to. Tell employees what's expected of them, such as "No side conversations or texting during meetings."
- **Provide training and coaching.** You need to train people how to behave appropriately? Yes. Coaching is for those folks who need specific one-on-one attention.
- **Model appropriate behavior.** If you're going to tell people to mind their manners, you have to mind yours too.
- **Hold people accountable.** Don't let employees get away with behaving inappropriately. You get what you tolerate.

Getting professionals to behave professionally requires that you tell them, teach them, show them how, and then ensure that they follow suit. People don't behave professionally just because they have a job.

The Problems with Multitasking

I present lots of trainings in workplaces, and I'm sure the people who stare at their laptops or cell phones during my presentations undoubtedly think they can effectively listen to me and use technology at the same time. After all, they've probably been told that multitasking is not only possible—it's necessary. But multitasking has many downsides—and it often seems flat-out rude.

In her article "Top 10 Reasons Employers Want to Hire You" on CareerBuilder.com, Rachel Zupek says employers value multitaskers. She provides this quote from Susan Stern, founder and president of a public relations and marketing communications agency, as evidence: "Business today moves at supersonic speed, and effectively managing a variety of different projects simultaneously is essential."[101]

Unfortunately, the definition of multitasking is "the performance of multiple tasks at one time," not "*effectively* managing a variety of different projects simultaneously." Thus, we're led to believe by Zupek and others that we need to be able to (or can) perform several tasks concurrently when we really can't. This false belief has led to a number of serious problems, which Amanda MacMillan lists in her article "12 Reasons to Stop Multitasking Now!"[102] MacMillan cites numerous studies about multitasking and its negative effects on us:

Multitasking dampens our creativity. It "causes the brain to burn through fuel so quickly that we feel exhausted and disoriented after even a short time," said cognitive psychologist and neuroscientist Daniel J. Levitin. A University of London study demonstrated that multitasking dumbs us down (the IQ of multitasking participants dropped to the average range of an eight-year-old child).

Multitasking slows us down. A University of Utah study demonstrated that participants took longer to reach their destinations when they talked on their phones while driving.

---

[101]Rachel Zupek, "Top 10 Reasons Employers Want to Hire You," *CareerBuilder*, 2009, https://edition.cnn.com/2009/LIVING/worklife/11/02/cb.hire.reasons.job/.

[102]Amanda MacMillan, "12 Reasons to Stop Multitasking Now!," *Health*, July 14, 2016, https://www.health.com/condition/adhd/12-reasons-to-stop-multitasking-now?.

Multitasking causes us to make mistakes. In the article "Multi-tasking—a Medical and Mental Hazard," Patrick J. Skerrett described a medical mishap in which a resident was using her cell phone to send an order to stop a medication from being administered to a patient. Midway through, she received a text from a friend about a party. She responded to the text and then forgot to finish the order. As a result, the patient received too much medicine and had to have open-heart surgery to save his life.

Multitasking is stressful. Employees with constant access to email had higher heart rates, according to one University of California, Irvine, study.

Multitasking makes us miss out on life. In a Western Washington University study, 75 percent of college students walking across campus while talking on their cell phones didn't see a clown riding a unicycle.

Multitasking negatively affects our memory. Interrupting one task to focus on another can disrupt short-term memory, according to a University of California, San Francisco, study.

Multitasking hurts our relationships. A University of Essex study demonstrated that just having a cell phone nearby during personal conversations causes friction and a lack of trust.

Multitasking makes us overeat. A review of twenty-four studies revealed that being distracted while eating prevents us from feeling full.

Multitasking can be dangerous. According to the US Department of Transportation, 3,477 people died and 391,000 people were injured in motor vehicle crashes caused by drivers who used their cell phones in just one year.[103]

If multitasking is so problematic, why do we do it? Levitin said it's because dopamine is released each time we switch tasks (like switching from listening to someone to looking at a text), which feels good for a while because of the dopamine hit and because of the perception that we're getting a lot accomplished while doing it.[104]

But we're not getting a lot accomplished. In fact, a 2013 University of Utah study demonstrated that participants who said they had above-average multitasking skills actually scored worse on multitasking tests. In other

[103]Ibid.
[104]Ibid.

words, if you think you're really good at multitasking, you're probably really not.[105]

Moreover, trying to multitask while people talk to us causes problems for the speakers. Even techie guru Anthony De Rosa, former editor in chief of *Circa*, the first media organization focused on producing news for mobile consumption, said our frequent attention to our phones while interacting with others has eroded fundamental human courtesies.

De Rosa told *New York Times* writer David Carr, "I'm fine with people stepping aside to check something, but when I'm standing in front of someone and in the middle of my conversation they whip out their phone, I'll just stop talking to them and walk away. If they're going to be rude, I'll be rude right back."[106]

Why is it considered rude to look at your computer or phone when someone is talking to you? Mostly because as Americans we're taught that making eye contact is a sign of respect: no eye contact = no respect.

You will almost certainly need to teach your Gen Z employees the downsides of multitasking and the importance of putting away technology during trainings, meetings, or even conversations. And truth be told, your older employees may need these lessons too.

Kat's Take

When you try to talk about multitasking to your youngest employees, keep this in mind: Gen Z grew up with technology.

Being connected and having a phone in your hand or at arm's distance is not only normal, it's a part of their routine. So when you ask Gen Zers to put their phones down or away in their bags, you may be creating a sense of anxiety that results from being "disconnected" or missing something important.

During meetings, conferences, and other events, it's not uncommon to see people on their phones. You should not assume, however, that they're being rude or ignoring you. In fact, they

[105]Ibid.

[106]David Carr, "Keep Your Thumbs Still When I'm Talking to You," *New York Times*, April 15, 2011, https://www.nytimes.com/2011/04/17/fashion/17TEXT.html.

might be using their phones to take notes. More robust than ever, smartphones can be used to take notes, pictures, and other useful actions during training. I'm often guilty of snapping pictures of presentations or PowerPoint slides for future reference.

Am I guilty of trying to multitask? Yes. Am I successful at it? No. However, when I'm using technology for documentation of presentations or training, I tend to be using technology to my advantage as an asset, not to distract.

CHAPTER 15

REGULATE CELL PHONES

The one item that most defines Generation Z is the smartphone. It's also the one item most likely to create discord and harden generational divides in the workplace. To avoid conflict and promote professionalism in your office, you must create well-defined cell phone policies and ensure that all employees know and follow those policies. This is especially important when Gen Z starts arriving in your organizations.

According to the Center for Generational Kinetics, "95% of Gen Z between the ages of 13 and 22 already has a smartphone."[107]

According to Kat Clowes, if today's teenagers were asked, "What necessity do you think you couldn't live without?," every one of them would answer, "My phone."

Gen Zers view the phone as the lifeline to the world. Actually, Gen Zers view the phone as their world. The phone informs them, entertains them, wakes them in the morning, reminds them of important events, tracks their exercise and calorie intake, and keeps them in instant

---

[107]Center for Generational Kinetics, *The State of Gen Z 2018*, Fall 2018, accessed October 3, 2020, https://genhq.com/wp-content/uploads/2018/10/State-of-Gen-Z-2018.pdf.

contact with friends and family all over the world. You need to realize that if you ask new Gen Z employees to turn off their phone or keep it put away while at work, you're asking them to disconnect from their entire world.

" Employers React to Gen Z

They always have to be on their phone playing games, texting, or posting on social media. "

Love and Hate

So, if cell phones are likely to cause trouble at work but banning cell phones at work is also likely to cause trouble, what's a wise office manager supposed to do? Create a wise cell phone policy. To do that, let's consider some of the reasons to love *and* hate cell phones at work. When you have realistically considered the pluses and minuses, you will be in a better position to create a policy that takes advantage of the positives and reduces the negatives.

Productivity

Love. Cell phones can increase productivity because of their many capabilities, including apps that can help entry-level employees be better at what they do. Otter can help employees transcribe or take notes during meetings; Evernote can keep them organized, and reminders can be set through various organizational apps. If you keep an open mind, you might discover that your new Gen Z intern or employee is already using a new app that might make your whole office more productive.

Hate. A Cornell University study concluded that having to listen to a coworker's cell phone conversations significantly detracts from cognitive performance. According to an article in the *Cornell Chronicle*, "overhearing half a conversation—a 'halfalogue'—is more distracting than other kinds of conversations because we're missing the other side of the story and so can't predict the flow of the conversation."[108]

Furthermore, in this age of multitasking, numerous studies have demonstrated that trying to juggle phone calls and emails while working can negatively impact productivity. René Marois, neuroscientist and director of the Human Information Processing Laboratory at Vanderbilt University, states in an *Orlando Sentinel* article that "we are under the impression that we have this brain that can do more than it often can . . . a core limitation is an inability to concentrate on two things at once."[109] So, employees who check email on their phones while in meetings or training seminars are most likely missing much of the information they are being paid to receive. In fact, a 2017 study demonstrated that the mere presence of your smartphone in a meeting can affect your attention skills.[110]

Confidentiality

Love. Cell phone users can move to more isolated spaces to make or take phone calls so that coworkers won't be forced to listen in on conversations. In addition, texting instead of talking allows employees to attend to personal or office affairs quietly and privately.

Hate. A Nokia survey revealed that respondents said phone users who speak too loudly were the second most irritating thing about people using cell phones in public (playing noisy movies, games, or music was the first).[111] So, cell phone users are much more likely to breach confidentiality if they speak too loudly in places where they can be easily

---

[108]Susan S. Lang, "Overhearing Cell Phone Chats Reduces Cognitive Performance, Study Finds," *Cornell Chronicle*, May 24, 2010, https://news.cornell.edu/stories/2010/05/half-heard-phone-conversations-reduce-performance.

[109]Steve Lohr, "Multitaskers Might Need Speed Bumps," *Orlando Sentinel*, March 25, 2007, https://www.orlandosentinel.com/news/os-xpm-2007-03-25-a2story25-story.html.

[110]Adrian Ward, Kristen Duke, Ayelet Gneezy, and Maarten Bos, "Brain Drain: The Mere Presence of One's Own Smartphone Reduces Available Cognitive Capacity," *Journal of the Association for Consumer Research*, April 3, 2017, https://www.journals.uchicago.edu/doi/abs/10.1086/691462.

[111]*Yahoo! News*, "Nokia Users Share Their List of Most Annoying Mobile Habits," July 29, 2011, https://sg.news.yahoo.com/nokia-users-share-list-most-annoying-mobile-habits-090115415.html .

overheard. In addition, cell phone calls and texts can be more easily intercepted. In her article "Who Did You Say Is Listening to My Cell Phone Calls?," Anat Hazanchuk says, "Anyone with your cell phone number has the ability to hear your calls, read your texts and track your location (even if GPS is turned off)."[112]

Also, gossip can run rampant through text or messaging apps. Although Gen Z workers might be quicker to fire off a snarky text, this behavior is not limited to younger workers, so address this issue in your cell phone policy.

Safety

Love. Cell phones increase personal safety by providing users an easy means of contacting others during an emergency.

Hate. The National Highway Traffic Safety Administration (NHTSA), which defines distracted driving as any activity that diverts attention from driving, has said that texting is the most alarming distraction of all. In 2018, 1,730 drivers, 605 passengers, 400 pedestrians, and 77 bicyclists were killed because of distracted driving. According to the NHTSA, even hands-free devices do not reduce distraction or make cell phones any safer to use while driving.[113] A University of Utah study concluded that people who drive while talking on their cell phones are as impaired as drunk drivers with a blood alcohol level of .08 percent.[114] Therefore, employees who talk on the phone while driving are putting themselves and their employers at risk.

---

[112]Anat Hazanchuk, "Who Did You Say Is Listening to My Cell Phone Call?," *Ooma*, April 4, 2017, https://www.ooma.com/blog/who-can-listen-to-cell-phone-calls/.

[113]National Highway Traffic Safety Administration, "Distracted Driving," accessed June 23, 2020, https://www.nhtsa.gov/risky-driving/distracted-driving.

[114]University of Utah News Center, "Drivers on Cell Phones as Bad as Drunks," June 29, 2006, https://archive.unews.utah.edu/news_releases/drivers-on-cell-phones-are-as-bad-as-drunks/.

Civility

Love. People are usually quick to use their phones to help others when necessary, such as calling for help when they witness an accident or if someone falls ill.

Hate. Christine Pearson, professor at the Thunderbird School of Global Management, says in a *New York Times* article that "electronic devices lead to more incivility because of their powerful ability to claim our attention—no matter where we are or what we're doing."[115] Indeed, French president Nicolas Sarkozy was advised to behave in a more statesmanlike manner after being caught texting during an audience with the pope and a meeting with the Chinese prime minister.[116] Pearson considers taking calls, texting, and checking emails while talking with coworkers to be uncivil and damaging to our workplace relationships. Ultimately, it sends the message that the cell phone is more important than the coworker.

Kat's Take

Gen Z is far more likely to pull out a cell phone and start taking pictures or filming something—with or without permission. This could range from a video of an irate customer or client or a seemingly innocuous snapshot of another employee that could possibly turn into a harassment issue.

For a reason that isn't clear to me or anyone I've asked, Gen Z often takes selfies in the bathroom. This could open the door to some embarrassing moments in the company bathroom.

---

[115]Christine Pearson, "Texting in Meetings: It Means 'I Don't Care,'" *New York Times,* May 16, 2010, https://www.nytimes.com/2010/05/16/jobs/16pre.html.

[116]Sherry Turkle, *Alone Together: Why We Expect More from Technology and Less from Each Other* (New York: Basic Books, 2017).

Setting Boundaries

After you have considered the advantages and disadvantages of cell phones and the realities of your workplace, then you can set up some specific cell phone guidelines for your workplace. Consider your setup and what your workers do each day and get some input from employees about what restrictions they consider reasonable and helpful.

Obviously, the cell phone rules for an employee who spends most of the day alone in an enclosed office reading book manuscripts can be different from the rules for employees who share tight quarters while making calls to clients. Cell phone rules for employees who drive or operate dangerous machinery should be the most stringent. Explain to your employees—especially the Gen Z workers who may not understand the reason for any rules—that your rules are not arbitrary restrictions but protocols intended to increase productivity and reduce coworker friction.

Here are some suggested points for an office cell phone policy:

- Keep your distance from coworkers when talking on the phone.
- Let calls on personal phones go to voicemail and return calls once an hour.
- Do not allow phones at meetings.
- Refrain from talking about business in public places.
- While in the office, do not send texts about coworkers, supervisors, clients, or customers.
- Do not talk on the phone while driving, even on a hands-free device.
- Avoid taking calls or texting when you're already engaged in a face-to-face conversation.

Cell phones can be an asset and a liability at work. Setting guidelines for your employees' use of them can help your entire organization benefit from this amazing tool while avoiding all the ways it can cause harm.

The Danger of Cell Phones

Evidently, some employees think using their cell phone is more important than doing their job.

In 2011, Iraq War veteran Omar Gonzalez scaled the fence, bolted across the lawn, and burst through a door at the White House before being apprehended by two Secret Service agents. According to news reports, a US Department of Homeland Security review revealed that the Secret Service officer who was supposed to be stationed at the North Lawn with an attack dog could have stopped Gonzalez long before he reached the building. However, the officer wasn't at his post; instead, he was sitting in his van making a personal call on his cell phone.[117]

In 2009, a San Antonio bus driver caused a wreck because of texting while driving. A trolley operator caused a 2009 crash in Boston while texting, and about fifty people were injured.

The danger of employees injuring themselves and others because of the distractions caused by cell phones has led some employers, such as FedEx, to prohibit them at work. Of the ban, one FedEx employee told a WTHR news reporter, "I think it is infringing on everyone's right."[118]

Obviously, this employee does not know that it is a privilege—not a right—to have a personal cell phone at work. And employers have the right to take that privilege away.

---

[117] *NBC News*, "'Harsh' Report Finds Guard on Cell Phone During White House Breach," November 13, 2014, https://www.nbcnews.com/news/us-news/harsh-report-finds-guard-cell-phone-during-white-house-breach-n248196.

[118] Alex Daniel, "15 Things Dictator Bosses Banned at Their Companies," *Best Life*, July 18, 2017, https://bestlifeonline.com/horrible-bosses-banning-stuff/.

CHAPTER 16

TAME SOCIAL MEDIA

Generation Zers not only grew up with social media, they also were more likely than older generations to broadcast their life on social media and to tie their self-worth to the reactions they receive. As has been proven by the rise of Instagram influencers and TikTok dance videos, everything is broadcast and anyone can be a star. Gen Zers have few expectations of privacy, and they have always lived in a world where people are publicly praised and shamed online for the way they dress or eat or dance or behave.

Gen Zers are less likely to set their social media profiles to private and also more likely to blend their personal and work lives online. It's not uncommon for them to post about being drunk at a huge party one day and share a quick snap about life at work the next.

Rest assured that the news isn't all bad! Social media can be great for your business, and Gen Z employees can be great brand ambassadors online. They can help your company reach a new audience and generate awareness about products, events, or your organization's inspirational community outreach. Kat Clowes says, "The savvy that my Gen Z employees have on social media has been an asset to my company, as they're already familiar with the platform, the audience, and how best to communicate a message to our target clients."

But Gen Z employees can also bring negative publicity to your company with their social media posts or photos. Even though they are highly sophisticated at using the various social media platforms, many Gen Zers seem surprisingly naïve about how a quick post can lead to long-term consequences. Kat says she regularly has entire conversations about how social media posts can affect college admissions. In fact, in recent years, many colleges have rescinded admissions offers to students after seeing their tweets, online harassment, or inappropriate videos.

So, if your organization does not already have a well-defined social media policy, you better get one ready before the Gen Z wave hits your workplace. It is imperative that you have a clear social media policy and that you update it regularly as new social media platforms emerge. Address the gray areas as much as you can by giving concrete examples and detailed instructions.

Can employees post photos of work events without permission? What about photos of coworkers? If they're at a work party and there's alcohol, are pictures appropriate? Are there limits to political or social opinions on their own social media accounts? Can they discuss office drama on public or private forums?

Kat's Take

I also recommend that you address "vaguebooking" in your office social media policies. Vaguebooking, a term that became popular first on Facebook but can now apply to many platforms, happens when someone hints at a huge event but is just vague enough to attract attention. Users ask questions and offer guesses, often revealing the user's "secret." Office drama can easily be "vaguebooked," creating conflict and hurt feelings at work.

Legal Considerations

Creating a social media policy for your organization is a good idea because it can prevent conflict in the office and help your organization avoid unwanted attention. It can also keep you out of legal trouble.

In 2019, 343 Philadelphia police officers were investigated for racist and offensive Facebook posts. The investigation concluded that 193 of the officers violated the police department's social media directive. As a result, some were terminated, some were suspended, some faced other disciplinary action, and some were ordered to undergo training and counseling.

But doesn't the First Amendment give the police officers the right to say whatever they want to? Some believe it does. *Philadelphia Inquirer* reporter Chris Palmer writes, "The police officers' union has said it believes any firings over the Facebook posts would be 'completely out of bounds.'"[119]

But there are always exceptions to the freedom of speech. For example, it is illegal to make false statements that damage a person's reputation, to threaten others, or to incite violence. In addition, the First Amendment prevents the government from making any law that prohibits our freedom of speech. Therefore, the protection the First Amendment provides is from our government, not from our employers.

The First Amendment does not prevent employers from restricting the speech of their employees—at work or away from it—and numerous employers have legally fired employees for comments they posted on Facebook and other social media.

For example, Juli Briskman lost her job as a marketing analyst at Akima LLC days after she was photographed flipping off President Trump's motorcade as it passed by while she rode her bike. The photo went viral but didn't identify Briskman as the bike rider. However, she posted the photo on her Twitter and Facebook pages and was subsequently fired for violating the company's social media policy.

Briskman sued for unlawful termination, but the company's attorney argued that private employers don't have to abide by free speech provisions of the Constitution and that "the company found out about a rude and profane act and . . . decided it wasn't interested in continuing with that particular person." The judge agreed and dismissed the wrongful termination count, according to an article in the American Bar Association's *ABA Journal*.[120]

---

[119]Chris Palmer, "Philadelphia Police Department to Fire 13 Officers over Offensive Facebook Posts," *Philadelphia Inquirer*, July 18, 2019, https://www.inquirer.com/news/philadelphia-police-facebook-scandal-15-cops-fired-christine-coulter-20190911.html.

[120]Debra Weiss, "Judge Tosses Wrongful Termination Claim by Woman Forced to Resign after Flipping Off Trump Motorcade," *ABA Journal*, July 2, 2018, https://www.abajournal.com/news/article/wrongful_termination_claim_trump_motorcade.

NLRB Guidelines

The National Labor Relations Board (NLRB) often rules on terminations based on social media postings. This independent federal agency enforces the National Labor Relations Act (NLRA), which protects the rights of employees to discuss the terms and conditions of their workplace. It has ruled in favor of both employers and employees in social media cases, walking a fine line between the rights of both parties.

For example, the board ruled in favor of an employer who fired a BMW salesman for photos and comments he posted of an embarrassing accident at a nearby Land Rover dealership, also owned by the employer. Because his photos and comments were not about his own working conditions, the employee's speech was not protected.

However, the board has consistently ruled against employers who fired employees for posting discussions about work and for having overly broad social media policies. (See appendix C for more discussion about such policies.)

In general, employees are protected from being fired or punished when they engage in lawful conduct when away from work and off duty—except when their behavior creates a conflict of interest for their employer. This normally occurs when an individual's personal interests are at odds with the professional interests they owe to those who employ them.

For example, if I posted that most employers are stupid and deserve to be sued, it could financially hurt the organization that employs me—a human resources outsourcing company whose customers are employers. My personal interest in expressing my opinion would conflict with the professional interest I owe my employer to generate revenue.

That's essentially the line crossed by the police officers when they posted racist and offensive material. If your job is to be fair and impartial, you have to appear to be fair and impartial, even on your Facebook page.

According to an article on Constitutioncenter.org, the speech of government employees can be restricted when it is incompatible with their status as a public official, that is, when it creates a conflict of interest.[121]

---

[121]Geoffrey R. Stone and Eugene Volokh, "A Common Interpretation: Freedom of Speech and the Press," National Constitution Center, December 1, 2016, https://constitutioncenter.org/blog/a-common-interpretation-freedom-of-speech-and-the-press.

The First Amendment does not give us the right to say whatever we want to without consequences. A lot of people have learned that the hard way. See appendix C for more discussion on the legal intricacies of creating a social media policy.

Draft Carefully

I encourage employers to incorporate such policies into their workplace because they help to clarify employers' expectations of their employees. However, the NLRB's rulings demonstrate that social media policies need to be very carefully drafted. So, what does the NLRB allow? Among other things, the board has ruled in favor of policies that

- prohibited the use of social media to "post or display comments about coworkers or supervisors or the Employer that are vulgar, obscene, threatening, intimidating, harassing, or a violation of the Employer's workplace policies against discrimination, harassment, or hostility on account of age, race, religion, sex, ethnicity, nationality, disability, or other protected class, status, or characteristic";
- forbade employees from making "slanderous" comments that appeared on a list of prohibited activity including "sexual or racial harassment" and "sabotage";
- prohibited employees "from using or disclosing confidential and/or proprietary information, including personal health information about customers or patients, and . . . from discussing . . . 'embargoed information,' such as launch and release dates and pending reorganizations"; and
- prevented employees "from publishing any promotional content."[122]

A carefully drafted policy is critical to avoiding the wrath of the NLRB. But the board has also decided that employers will not be liable

---

[122]National Labor Relations Board, "The NLRB and Social Media," accessed June 20, 2020, https://www.nlrb.gov/about-nlrb/rights-we-protect/your-rights/the-nlrb-and-social-media.

for discipline resulting from an overly broad policy if the employer can show an employee's social media postings interfered with the employee's work, with other employees' work, or with the employer's operations and that the interference was the reason for the discipline.

Hundreds of millions of people use social media every day. Having a social media policy that meets the approval of the NLRB helps prevent employers and employees alike from being hurt by it.

Because this is such a complex topic, I suggest that you have an employment attorney review your social media policy and that you consult with an attorney before taking disciplinary action related to an employee's social media postings.

Monitor Your Own Social Media Posts

When you are creating a social media policy for your company, also give some thought to your own social media usage and how it might be used against you. At the very least, if you're being sued by some of your employees, don't post derogatory comments about them on your company website or Facebook page unless you want to get an additional lawsuit. That's what happened to Coyote Ugly founder and franchise president Liliana Lovell who, in addition to being sued for violating the Fair Labor Standards Act (FLSA), was sued for retaliation because of posts she and one of her managers made about the employees after they filed the suit.

Former bartender Misty Blu Stewart filed a lawsuit against Coyote Ugly alleging an illegal tip-pooling practice and failure to compensate employees for all time worked (which are violations of the FLSA). Shortly thereafter, Lovell posted the following on the Coyote Ugly website: "This particular case will end up pissing me off cause it is coming from someone we terminated for theft. I have to believe in my heart that somewhere down the road, bad people end up facing bad circumstances!" She then went on to call Stewart a derogatory name using some colorful language.

Meanwhile, bartender Sarah Stone, who had joined Stewart in the FLSA lawsuit, was working an anniversary party at the saloon attended by Coyote Ugly director of operations Daniel Huckaby, who knew that Stone was in on the suit. Stone said that while he was sitting across the bar from her, Huckaby made the following post to his Facebook page: "Dear God, please don't let me kill the girl that is suing me . . . that is all . . ." Huckaby was intoxicated at the time and doesn't recall making or later removing the post; however, Stone, who at the time was Facebook friends with Huckaby, saw the post an hour after it was posted while looking for Facebook updates on her cell phone while at work.

The following night, after hearing that a customer had fallen down some stairs and was threatening to sue, Huckaby yelled out in front of Stone, "Why does everyone sue? I'm tired of all these [sexist slur] taking their issues out on our company. They're [expletive] idiots." Stone quit the following day and, as in the case with the Facebook posting, Huckaby had no recollection of the incident.

Both former employees then filed retaliation lawsuits. Stewart said she was retaliated against when Lovell posted her message on the Coyote Ugly website saying she was fired for stealing (although she was not mentioned by name). Stone said she was retaliated against when Huckaby posted his Facebook message (she also was not mentioned by name) and yelled disparaging remarks in front of her.[123]

The former waitresses lost in court; however, paying attorneys to defend you is not cheap. Employers wishing to avoid a similar fate should refrain from

- making disparaging remarks about employees or former employees who file complaints with the government against you on social media sites;
- revealing confidential information, such as why you fired someone, to anyone who doesn't have a need to know;
- implying that you'd like to kill an employee;
- being Facebook friends with your employees;
- posting on Facebook while intoxicated;
- being intoxicated while at work; and
- allowing employees to check social media while on the clock.

---

[123]Jon Hyman, "When Coyote Posts Get Ugly," *Workforce.com*, October 13, 2013, https://www.workforce.com/news/when-coyote-posts-get-ugly.

According to social media coach Tasha Turner, "Social networking is about building people up in your network NOT tearing them down."[124] As this case demonstrates, employers who use social media to air their grievances about their employees after they have filed a complaint against them are perhaps the ones who are the idiots.

[124]Tasha Turner, Goodreads, accessed October 3, 2020, https://www.goodreads.com/quotes/621825-social-networking-is-about-building-people-up-in-your-network.

CHAPTER 17

CLAIM YOUR TIME

Gen Z often seems to have a different sense of time than older generations. You might be surprised to watch your bright young hires stroll in late day after day. Or marvel that they never seem to think twice about updating their Instagram accounts or doing a little online shopping during work hours.

As we've been saying throughout this section, Gen Z workers rarely behave this way because they want to challenge your authority or prove themselves to be irresponsible. They just have not learned how much employers frown on such behaviors. So, it's up to you to teach them better.

Prevent Cyberloafing

Did you hear about the US software developer who got caught outsourcing his job? According to an *ABC News* article, the developer's company security team discovered someone was logging in from Shenyang, China, using the developer's credentials. The team discovered that the developer had been paying someone in China to take care of his work. What was the developer doing while someone else did his job? His web-browsing history revealed that he spent most of his day surfing the internet.[125] Although most employees don't go to those lengths, far too many of them spend far too much time aimlessly browsing online sites.

"Of all workplace distractions, the Internet is the greatest productivity drain," says Cheryl Conner in her article "Who Wastes the Most Time at Work?"[126]

" Employers React to Gen Z

Challenges that I have with them are reliability, consistency, and attendance.

"

According to a Salary.com survey, 39 percent of respondents spent less than one hour, 29 percent spent one to two hours, 21 percent spent two to five hours, 8 percent spent six to ten hours, and 3 percent spent more than ten hours each week using their work computer to update their Facebook status, watch videos of piano-playing cats, shop on Amazon, or follow endless news-related links. In other words, they were cyberloafing.[127]

It's no surprise that employees spend time on the internet when they should be working. So what? Well, let's say a full-time employee (who works 2,080 hours, or 260 days a year) spends ten hours each week cyberloafing. That's 520 hours (or sixty-five workdays) each year that employee is being paid for not doing his job. There is not enough research yet to show whether Gen Z employees are bigger cyberloafers than other employees, but anecdotal evidence points in that direction.

---

[125]Susanna Kim, "US Software Developer Caught Outsourcing His Job to China," *ABC News*, January 17, 2013, https://abcnews.go.com/Business/us-software-developer-busted-employer-outsourcing-job-china/story?id=18230346.

[126]Cheryl Conner, "Who Wastes the Most Time at Work?," *Forbes*, September 7, 2013, https://www.forbes.com/sites/cherylsnappconner/2013/09/07/who-wastes-the-most-time-at-work/#3d661fef6c39.

[127]Salary.com, "Why & How Your Employees Are Wasting Time at Work," accessed June 24, 2020, https://www.salary.com/articles/why-how-your-employees-are-wasting-time-at-work/.

Security Risks

In addition to being a drain on productivity and money, some employee cyberloafing could lead to liability issues for employers. For example, in a Barna Group survey of one thousand adults nationwide, 63 percent of male respondents and 36 percent of female respondents admitted to watching porn on a computer at work (and that's just the ones who fessed up).[128] If an employee is involuntarily subjected to a coworker's porn, the employee could make a harassment claim against the company.

Internet surfing could also lead to office security issues if employees accidentally download viruses and other malicious programs. Here's a fun fact: employees are three times more likely to download a virus from a church website than from a porn site. According to Dan Seitz, author of the article "Church Websites Are Three Times More Likely to Give You a Virus Than Porn Sites," that's because the adult industry has the money to ensure that their sites are secure, but nonprofit religious organizations often do not.[129]

Before You Ban

Obviously, with so many risks, employers should just deny access to the internet, right? Wrong for many reasons. First, most employees need the internet to do their jobs. And if you restrict it from company computers, many employees will just use their phones to get online. Also, making a no-internet policy is oppressive and unnecessary.

Instead of an outright ban, create internet usage policies that are reasonable and workable. Consider what your employees need to do their jobs and consider what poses the biggest risks for you and your organization. Then craft a well-defined policy and make sure all your employees understand it and understand your rationale. Your workplace

---

[128]Cision PR Newswire, "2014 Survey: Find Out How Many Employees Are Watching Porn on Company Time," August 19, 2014, https://www.prnewswire.com/news-releases/2014-survey-find-out-how-many-employees-are-watching-porn-on-company-time-271854721.html.

[129]Dan Seitz, "Church Websites Are Three Times More Likely to Give You a Virus Than Porn Sites," Uproxx, July 11, 2013, https://uproxx.com/technology/church-websites-are-three-times-more-likely-to-give-you-a-virus-than-porn-sites/.

needs will dictate the specifics of your policy, but you may want to take all or some of these steps:

- Deny access to certain websites, such as porn sites. Numerous software programs are available that allow employers to restrict access to websites based on various criteria. Make sure your employees know that those sites are off limits and why.
- Monitor employees' online activity. Those software programs can also track which websites employees are visiting and for how long.
- Restrict internet usage for business purposes, except when employees are on breaks or during their meal periods. Findings from a University of Melbourne study found that employees who were allowed to access social networks were actually more productive than those who weren't because a quick visit to their social media pages reinvigorated them.[130]
- Tell employees they have limited access and are being monitored. Put this in writing in a handbook or stand-alone policy and have them sign it.
- Enforce consequences for employees who violate the policy. Not surprisingly, a Kansas State University study revealed that just having a policy did not prevent cyberloafing. Says researcher Joseph Ugrin, "Even when they [employees] knew they were being monitored, they still did not care."[131]

One more thing. If you know your employees are spending too much time cyberloafing, you may want to find out why. In a Salary.com survey, employees said they were likely to spend work time online when they were not being challenged or were bored. Want to make sure your employees work when they are at work? Then make sure they have lots

---

[130]Reuters, "Facebook, YouTube at Work Make Better Employees: Study," April 2, 2009, https://www.reuters.com/article/us-work-internet-tech-life-idUSTRE5313G220090402.

[131]Kansas State University, "Policy, Enforcement May Stop Employees from Wasting Time Online at Work," January 31, 2013, https://www.newswise.com/articles/policy-enforcement-may-stop-employees-from-wasting-time-online-at-work-researcher-finds.

of challenging work to do.[132]

Tackling Tardiness

Many employers report that chronic tardiness is a huge pet peeve.[133] This frustration is not surprising since 55 percent of employees in a CareerBuilder survey reported being late to work once a month or more and 34 percent said they are late to work at least once a week or more.[134]

Why are they late? Traffic is the number one excuse, followed by lack of sleep, kids, and bad weather. I would add another reason to the list—not being held accountable for being late by their employer or supervisor.

In her article "How Do Employers Contribute to Tardiness?," Amanda McMullen says, "Employees are more likely to be late when employers don't notice tardiness, don't take action against it, or fail to follow through with threats of disciplinary action."[135] This may be especially true for Gen Z employees, who have rarely been held accountable for being on time.

Kat's Take

I confess that I am mystified by Gen Z's chronic lateness—especially when they don't even bother to notify anyone that they are running late.

Cell phones and a plethora of message apps make it far easier than it used to be to tell someone when you're running a few

---

[132]Salary.com "2013 Wasting Time at Work Survey," July 29, 2013, https://www.salary.com/chronicles/2013-wasting-time-at-work-survey/.

[133]Intelligence for Your Life, "Biggest Pet Peeves of Employers," accessed June 24, 2020, https://www.tesh.com/articles/biggest-pet-peeves-of-employers/.

[134]CareerBuilder, "More Than Half of Workers Late to Work at Least Once a Month, According to CareerBuilder.ca Survey," February 19, 2015, http://press.careerbuilder.com/2015-02-19-More-Than-Half-of-Workers-Late-to-Work-at-Least-Once-a-Month-According-to-CareerBuilder-ca-Survey.

[135]Amanda McMullen, "How Do Employers Contribute to Tardiness?" *Chron*, accessed June 24, 2020, https://smallbusiness.chron.com/employers-contribute-tardiness-38323.html.

minutes late. It's also easier to schedule your time with the countless amounts of apps and alarms we can set on our phones to make sure we are on time. And then there's Google Maps that even lets us know about traffic conditions and estimates our time of arrival down to the minute.

Still, the teenagers I work with are often late and rarely give me a head's-up.

In school, being late doesn't have the consequences it once did. In my local school district, for example, late work is given full credit as long as it's turned in by the end of the quarter. Unfortunately for teachers, they often have an avalanche of late work turned in at the last minute—all of which, by school policy, receives full credit.

However, I don't think this tendency toward tardiness is simply generational. As the pace of life increases and people work more hours, they are just trying to make the most of the hours they have. I attribute the increased pace of life to the increase of lateness in younger generations. Millennials and Gen Z don't view lateness in the same way that Baby Boomers and Generation X do. Work-life balance carries greater importance than showing up at the office as the clock strikes eight.

Turning a blind eye to tardiness can actually be used against employers if they suddenly decide to terminate or discipline employees for being late. In one New York City case, an employee who took medication for schizophrenia that made him feel drowsy was often late for work. His supervisors in the city's Human Resources Administration (HRA) explicitly or tacitly approved his late arrivals for ten years and then decided to begin disciplinary action against him for being late to work. The employee sued, alleging violations of the ADA among other things, and eventually won his case. The Court of Appeals said the HRA's approval of late arrivals for ten years indicated that arriving to work at a specific time was not really an essential function of the employee's job.[136]

This case demonstrates that employers who consistently allow employees to be late are communicating that being on time is not an essential part of the job. If being on time *is* a requirement because tardiness interferes with getting the job done or prevents others from getting their job done, hold employees accountable when they are not.

Start by telling new hires what time they are expected to be at work, ready to perform their job. If they're late, remind them of the start time. If they're late again, begin disciplinary action in the form of a documented verbal warning. Another tardy gets a written warning, and another might merit a final written warning, suspension, or even termination.

At-will employers are not required to follow this sort of progressive discipline; however, it's always a good idea to give employees several chances to correct their behavior, especially Gen Z employees who might be working for the first time. It's more cost effective than firing for the first offense, and employers who give people several chances to succeed are looked upon more kindly by judges and juries—and employees.

---

[136]McMillan v. City of New York, United States Court of Appeals for the Second Circuit, accessed June 24, 2020, https://cases.justia.com/federal/appellate-courts/ca2/11-3932/11-3932-2013-03-04.pdf?ts=1410918648.

CHAPTER 18

FASHION A DRESS CODE

Fashion experts have proclaimed, "It's a new era in fashion—there are no rules." Want to wear white before Memorial Day? Go for it. Want to wear gold and silver jewelry at the same time? You can do that too. Style today is not about rules—it's all about the individual and his or her personal style.

Although that's a relief on some fronts—I do like to wear my white jeans all year long—it can present problems for employers. What if you have employees whose personal fashion statement seems to be: "I just rolled out of bed"?

Many changes in the norms of society, education, industry, and even manufacturing have led to increasing confusion about appropriate attire for the office. As it has become cheaper to produce clothes from "comfortable" fabrics and stretchy knits, we've seen more and more people wearing yoga pants and running shorts far beyond the gym or trails.

And more lines were blurred as CEOs and executives from tech start-ups began wearing jeans, hoodies, and raggedy T-shirts to work. Clothes that had been staples on college campuses began showing up in the professional world. Facebook founder Mark Zuckerberg, for example, rocked the professional world when he began showing up for meetings, presentations, and speeches in his signature hoodie, jeans, and tennis shoes. As far as Gen Z knows, such clothes are perfectly normal in a professional environment.

If your organization does *not* consider jeans, T-shirts, and tennis shoes as "professional attire," you need to say so, especially for your Gen Z employees, who will need to know exactly what you expect. Create a policy that clearly communicates what clothing is allowed and not allowed.

Kat's Take

As a former costume designer who studied fashion, I think Gen Z's confusion about a proper workplace wardrobe can't be blamed entirely on the "you-do-you" mentality. In my opinion, it's as much about lack of instruction as it is about society's "whatever-goes" mentality.

For decades, home economics classes in public schools taught students life skills like budgeting, manners, cooking, sewing, and other important "adulting" skills. The curriculum included books (in fact, I have a small collection of them) that taught young men and women the rules of dress and grooming. You might recall watching some of those old videos that introduced you to two students, one who dressed well and took care of personal grooming and the other who did not.

The curriculum described which clothes were best for your shape, gave advice about haircuts, explained how to mend your clothing, and covered other standards of society. Most of these practical classes were phased out of the curriculum during the 1980s and 1990s, leaving a huge hole in students' practical knowledge. Many students were no longer learning a lot of the life skills covered in those classes, including how to dress appropriately for various occasions.

We have an entire generation whose only knowledge about how to dress professionally comes from what they learn from fashion magazines, at the mall, or through friends and family members. Actually, I think this lack of knowledge extends beyond Generation Z; I'll include my generation—Millennials—in this as well.

Are Dress Codes Legal?

Some organizations may be reluctant to establish formal dress codes because they worry about whether they are legal. If those standards are reasonable, the answer generally is yes.

State and federal laws say it's reasonable for employers to request that employees dress professionally (e.g., no miniskirts or low-cut blouses), present a neat appearance (no ripped or wrinkled clothing), and have good hygiene (washed hair and no body odor). It's also reasonable for employers to require most employees to have natural-looking hair color and hairstyles, to cover tattoos, and to remove jewelry from places such as noses, lips, and eyebrows.[137]

Additionally, employers may generally set a different standard for women and men; for example, women can be allowed to have long hair while men are required to have a short haircut. But you need to proceed very cautiously here. You will run into trouble if the standard is not based on social norms, differs greatly between the sexes, or imposes a greater burden on one sex than the other.

Be sure that your dress and grooming standards allow your employees to

- comply with religious beliefs or practices, such as wearing skullcaps or beards;
- dress in their traditional national attire;
- dress consistently with their gender identity; and
- dress comfortably because of a disability.

In these cases, you're required to provide employees with an accommodation unless it presents an undue hardship for the employer. Failure to do so could result in a discrimination claim.

And the NLRB has determined that employers cannot restrict employees from wearing clothing and accessories that express their feelings about their employment. (See appendix D for more information.)

---

[137]In California, the CROWN Act protects against discrimination based on ethnic hairstyles and hair texture.

" Employers React to Gen Z

My Gen Z female employees accused me of "body shaming" them because I asked them to dress more professionally. **"**

Code with Care

If you'd like to implement a dress and grooming policy, you should ensure that your policy is carefully considered and articulated. Here are some tips to help in that effort:

- Have good business reasons for your policy, such as safety or maintaining the company image. Explain the reasons in your policy.
- Provide clear expectations by specifically identifying what is *not* considered to be professional attire: T-shirts, jeans, flip-flops, and so on.
- Explain what will happen if employees do not comply with the policy.
- Have employees sign an acknowledgment form that they understand and will comply with the policy. The form then goes in their personnel file in case they later claim they didn't know what was expected of them.
- Apply the policy consistently, except for those cases where accommodations must be made.

A carefully drafted dress and grooming policy can help all your employees understand what is expected of them. And it can be especially important for Gen Z workers, who may have a different idea about "professional" attire than older workers in your organization. They need to understand that even if society no longer has fashion rules, your workplace does.

CHAPTER 19

COACH COMMUNICATION

Few people are eloquent when they are young. And people who grow up using text messaging apps as their primary method of communicating tend not to develop outstanding verbal communication skills. That's why your Gen Z employees will probably need some coaching to improve their communication abilities.

Of course, the rest of your employees could probably benefit from some communication coaching as well. My clients frequently request communication workshops for all their employees, and when I'm asked to provide one-on-one coaching, it tends to be with a middle-aged male.

My communication training and coaching always include the following points:

- Our communication style is influenced by our personality, gender, age, culture, and everything else that makes us who we are.
- Our natural style communicates easily with some people (meaning we get the responses we want) but not others.
- We usually get along better with people who communicate as we do and struggle with people who don't.
- When we become aware of our style and the style used by others, we can adjust our natural tendencies—and encourage them to adjust their own—in order to communicate more effectively.

For example, some people need a lot of details when they receive information while others don't. When you provide more details to the person who needs them and fewer details to the person who doesn't, your interactions will be more effective.

How can you tell who needs what? By their response to your usual communication. If you're not providing enough information, the "more-details" person will ask a lot of questions. If you're providing too much information, the eyes of the "fewer-details" person will glaze over as you continue to talk. If you're providing the right amount of details, the interaction goes more smoothly.

When we give people what they need, they tend to give us the response we need or want—such as changing their behavior or completing a task we assigned. If that sounds manipulative to you, consider this: when you travel to a foreign country, do you learn a few important words (such as "bathroom") in that country's language? Learning to speak the language of your environment can prevent accidents from happening. Making small adjustments in how you communicate is just another way of learning to speak someone's language.

Kat's Take

Communication is one of Gen Zers' strongest and weakest qualities. They are in constant contact with their friends and can convey a huge amount of information with nothing but emojis. They juggle multiple lines of communication and information and may receive more than a hundred messages and notifications a day.

But proper communication is a challenge for many of them because they rarely learn how to write a letter or a formal email or even leave a proper voicemail in school or at home.

I've begun instructing my clients on how to write a formal email and how to leave a proper voicemail. I've also taught a number of them how to set their voicemail message and showed them how to check their voicemail.

" Employers React to Gen Z

They would prefer to text you than pick up the phone or verbally communicate or talk face-to-face in person.

"

Phone Coaching

You may be surprised to discover that Generation Zers—the ones who can't live without their phones—rarely use that device for voice conversations and may know little about the professional etiquette of answering phone calls, taking messages, or dealing with voicemail.

You might remember having to hide in the closet with your family phone, the cord stretched all the way across the hall and into your bedroom for some privacy. Because your family shared one phone line, you learned very young how to answer the phone, how to take a message if the caller was looking for a family member who was unavailable, and how to leave that message on the refrigerator so it could be found easily. You also learned how to leave messages when the person you were calling was not home.

When families began to hook up answering machines to their phones, you began checking your answering machine the second you walked in the door to see if someone had called. And you learned how to leave a message on a machine: say your name, say why you're calling, and then say your phone number clearly and slowly to ensure a return call.

Few members of Generation Z ever got those lessons because most family members have cell phones and answer their own calls and retrieve their own messages. So Gen Zers never had to jot down a message on a piece of paper and put it in the designated place for their parents to see it. They didn't learn how to answer the family phone or check the family answering machine.

You'll need to keep this in mind as you're training new employees, particularly Gen Zers, in entry-level positions. Skills that you take for granted might not have been developed as the world shifted. If you expect them to answer the phone, give them a script for what they should say: "Hello, this is ABC Consulting. How can I help you today?"

And give them a script for taking messages: "He's not in his office at the moment. May I take a message?"

Tell them what information you expect in a message: name of caller, summary of business, contact information for return call, date and time of call. Explain how this message should be passed on: written on a memo and left in a particular place or sent by email or inner-office message app.

" Employers React to Gen Z

They don't know how to leave a voicemail.

"

Also show them how to check your office voicemail and what to do with messages left there. Kat Clowes says one of her biggest surprises about Gen Zers is that they don't check their voicemail—and how many of them don't have it set up at all.

Sophie Cullinane addresses this quirk of Gen Z in her article "Why Are We All So Terrified of Leaving Voicemails?" According to Cullinane, many in Generation Z would prefer to send a text rather than leave a voicemail because people can tell if you're nervous on a voicemail. Also, Gen Z members rarely listen to voicemails when they receive them, so they assume no one else does either![138]

Nonverbal Communication

Nonverbal communication in your workplace is an important part of communication that is often overlooked or undervalued.

The first scientific study of nonverbal communication was published in 1872 by Charles Darwin in his book *The Expression of the Emotions in Man and Animals*. Even though people have studied and talked about nonverbal communication for well over a century, many of us are

---

[138]Sophie Cullinane, "Why Are We All So Terrified of Leaving Voicemails?," *Grazia*, June 18, 2014, https://graziadaily.co.uk/life/real-life/terrified-leaving-voicemails/.

unaware of the messages we are sending nonverbally, and that could be to our detriment.

In a famous study on nonverbal communication, psychologist Albert Mehrabian determined that when we communicate,

- 55 percent of the message is conveyed through body language;
- 38 percent is expressed through tone of voice; and
- only 7 percent is communicated through words.[139]

In other words, our messages are conveyed more through body language and tone of voice more than the words we actually speak. Thus, the old adage "Action speaks louder than words."

And even when people don't speak, they are communicating. The good news is that being aware of and managing our nonverbal communication can help us convey positive messages about ourselves and make stronger connections with others.

When you understand more about nonverbal communication, you can teach your employees, especially your youngest ones, how to convey competence. People appear most competent when they

- exhibit few speech errors ("ums," "uhs");
- speak with slight rapidity (about 125 to 150 words per minute);
- face the listener directly;
- sustain eye contact about half of the time (do not look away while making a point); and
- assume an open and relaxed posture.

Another impression many people want to convey is likability and dynamism. Persuasive communicators are often extremely likable because they are good at expressing their liking of others. Those who are dynamic are interesting to listen to and observe when they're talking. The elements of likability and dynamism are

- standing relatively close to the listener (between two and six

---

[139]Wikipedia, s.v. "Albert Mehrabian," accessed June 24, 2020, https://en.wikipedia. org/wiki/Albert_Mehrabian.

feet);

- positive facial expressions;
- leaning toward others;
- standing or sitting parallel with the listener;
- moderate physical contact (as appropriate for the situation);
- eye contact about half the time;
- a moderate amount of gesturing (particularly to help the listener understand);
- a voice that is relaxed, not nasal or monotonic but vocally animated; and
- the absence of fidgeting.

Curtail Workplace Cursing

The summer I was fifteen and working at my dad's bait-and-tackle shop, he posted a sign by the cash register that said No Cussing. The sign was to remind customers that swearing was not allowed around my delicate ears. My ears are not so delicate any more, but I encourage you to curtail the use of cursing in the workplace—by you, your employees, and your customers.

Every time we send a message we are attempting to gain a desired response. Employers and supervisors communicate with their employees primarily to get results. Therefore, they should ask themselves whether their communication inspires greater engagement, commitment, and performance or whether it inspires a negative response.

Communication full of four-letter words inspires a negative response because that's what swearing does to our bodies. According to Richard Stephens, a senior psychology lecturer at Keele University who studied the effects of cursing, "Swearing increases the heart rate and sets off the body's flight-or-fight response."[140] That's great if you have to fight somebody or run away but not so great when you're just trying to do your job.

Excessive cursing helped get former Yahoo! CEO Carol Bartz fired, according to some insiders. In their article "The Management Mistakes

---

[140]Richard Stephens, John Atkins, and Andrew Kingston, "Swearing as a Response to Pain," *Neuroreport* 20, no. 12 (2009): 1056–60

of Carol Bartz," Karlee Weinmann and Aimee Groth say, "Her brazenness earned her some respect, but also a reputation that clashed with Yahoo!'s board and top management—not to mention employees."[141] Indeed, Bartz told the Women in Economy conference audience that the one thing she would have done differently during her tenure was to not use the f-word.[142]

So, if you want scared and angry employees, curse away. If that's not the response you're looking for, then learn to broaden your vocabulary.

Failing to curtail your employees' cursing could get you sued. Cursing is not illegal; however, it might infringe upon the religious rights of some employees, which is illegal.

In his article "When Employees' Cursing Gets You Sued," Dan Wisniewski describes such a situation. Kellymarie Griffin worked for the City of Portland and repeatedly let her coworkers know that she was opposed to their use of profanity, especially when they used the names of God and Jesus as curse words, because of her religious beliefs. One day Griffin sneezed loudly, startling a coworker who exclaimed, "Jesus Christ!" Griffin complained to her team lead, who responded by saying she was sick of Griffin's Christian attitude, her Christian [expletive] all over her desk, and her Christian [expletive] all over the place. Griffin sued, claiming a hostile work environment. The court found that "a rational jury could find that at least some of this profanity occurred because of Griffin's religion" and sent the case to trial.[143]

Finally, you might want to follow my dad's lead and ensure that your customers keep their language clean while in your establishment. That's what the owners of Mount Royal Tavern in Baltimore did after getting fed up with "the endless barrage of blue language that was on

[141]Karlee Weinmann, and Aimee Groth, "The Management Mistakes of Carol Bartz," *Business Insider*, September 9, 2011, https://www.businessinsider.com/carol-bartz-management-style-2011–9.

[142]James Poulos, "Fired Yahoo Chief Carol Bartz Wishes She Didn't Drop So Many F-Bombs," *Forbes*, May 25, 2012, https://www.forbes.com/sites/jamespoulos/2012/05/25/fired-yahoo-chief-carol-bartz-wishes-she-didnt-drop-so-many-f-bombs/#14b39c0e6372.

[143]Dan Wisniewski, "When Employees' Cursing Gets You Sued," *HRMorning*, January 3, 2014, https://www.hrmorning.com/articles/when-employees-cursing-gets-you-sued/.

the increase in the high-ceilinged barroom," according to Frederick N. Rasmussen's article in the *Baltimore Sun*.

Tavern owner Ron Carback said, "I thought we needed a little civility around here," and set up a large plastic pretzel jar with a sign taped to it that said "Mount Royal Tavern Cuss Bucket. 25 cents a cuss." Customers and employees are now watching what they say more closely, lest they be fined. And the money collected when someone slips is donated to charity.[144] Sure, customers who don't appreciate the endless barrage of blue language can always go elsewhere, but that's just the point—they take their business elsewhere.

Mark Twain said, "Under certain circumstances, urgent circumstances, desperate circumstances, profanity provides a relief denied even to prayer." I agree but suggest those circumstances should be rare at work.

[144]Frederick N. Rasmussen, "City Restaurant Installs 'Cuss Bucket,'" *Baltimore Sun*, May 16, 2011, https://www.baltimoresun.com/maryland/baltimore-city/bs-md-ci-mount-royal-tavern-20110516-story.html.

CHAPTER 20

EXPLAIN EMAIL AND EMOJIS

E mail has in many ways become the formal way of communicating business. Although there may still be the need for letters to be typed or printed and sent through the mail, most business correspondence is handled by email these days. And you may be thinking that Gen Zers will be great with email because they grew up with computers and technology. Unfortunately, that is rarely the case.

Gen Zers grew up using text messaging, SnapChat, and Instagram—not email. And as we have mentioned so many other times in this book, they received little in the way of education about how to write professional emails. So, if you're expecting your new Gen Z hires to handle any amount of email correspondence for your company, you should spend a little time teaching them about professional practices.

Because Kat Clowes coaches high school students about how to get into and succeed in college and beyond, she has developed specific, easy-to-follow instructions to teach her clients how to write an email, which are included here. Feel free to use this format in your own training or to modify or supplement to make it fit your business needs.

How to Write a Professional Email

by Kat Clowes

This might sound like the most basic thing in the world, but there is a format that you should follow when writing an email. Trust me in saying that a number of your colleagues and higher-ups will judge you by your emails if they are not done correctly (I hear this constantly). I must confess, bad grammar and punctuation cause me to judge, and I'm not very judgmental. The best way to avoid this is to learn the proper email format.

Let's go over the unspoken rules of professional emails first and then I'll show you a few examples of good emails and bad emails.

The Unspoken Rules of Professional Emails

The Basics

Never write in all caps. It will read as though you're screaming at the reader.

Always use proper grammar and spelling. I highly recommend installing Grammarly on your computer or opening up a Grammarly account (https://www.grammarly.com/). It will suggest edits in real time to your emails and will give you a monthly report of your most common mistakes, allowing you to improve. It's inexpensive, and I've found it to be the most helpful. You can also use Grammarly in other areas, such as posting in social media, Google Drive, and other word-processing programs.

Don't use abbreviations, unless it's in reference to something that's usually abbreviated at the company. For example, always write out "you" instead of saying "u." If a company software is referred to as "SAP," then it is acceptable to abbreviate.

Attachments

If you're including an attachment, say so in your email.

Don't send huge files as attachments. This especially pertains to pictures but could also include regular files. If you have to send a big attachment, send it as a zipped file attachment, which compresses the size.

Always try to send attachments in PDF form, especially for documents. PC and Mac computers use different software for files (though this is becoming less and less the case). To guarantee that someone can open your file no matter what computer they have, send it as a PDF. I also highly recommend this if you're sending out resumes and cover letters as well.

Never email highly confidential or sensitive information as an attachment, especially client information. Some industries have strict rules about client information and confidentiality.

Professionalism

Never write huge, novel-like emails. Keep everything short and simple. Huge, long paragraphs automatically make the brain glaze over. Break things up and keep as succinct as you possibly can.

Never Reply All unless it is absolutely necessary. No one in the company needs 230,839,089,032 emails that fill up their in-box with a simple "Sounds good" in reply to a full company email.

Always have a professional signature. Your signature usually contains your name and, underneath it, your title, contact information, and the company. Don't get fancy here, and make sure to use any company templates for your signature, if your company has one. (See the examples below for signature examples.)

If you're unsure of someone's gender, put the recipient's first and last name in the greeting: Dear Riley Clowes.

Never assume someone's marital status in her title. Ms. is always a safe prefix instead of Mrs. or Miss for a woman. If the contact has a doctorate (PhD), use Dr. regardless of gender.

Don't write anything in an email that you wouldn't want on the front page of the newspaper. You don't know who might eventually see your email, and you really don't want to be embarrassed if you mistakenly hit Reply All. This goes for complaints, talking about coworkers, or any other subjects that could get you in trouble.

When scheduling an appointment through email, offer at least two days and times that might work to eliminate excessive back-and-forth emailing.

Subject Line

Your subject line, which serves as the "title" of your email, should be succinct and quickly demonstrate to the recipient what your email is about.

If you're responding to a previous email, use the prefix RE: in front of your subject line to reference that previous email.

Samples

Subject Lines

First Email—Subject: March Consulting Consultation
Responding Email—Subject: RE: March Consulting Consultation

First Email—Subject: Inquiring after the TPP reports
Responding Email—Subject: RE: Inquiring after the TPP reports

Requesting Information

Dear Ms. Clowes,
We're updating our workbook that outlines the college admissions process for seniors in the area. We'd like for you to review your previous articles in the workbook and add any updates you think are relevant to this incoming class.

If you could make those changes and send them to us by June 5 at 5 p.m., we would appreciate it.

Best,

Kat Clowes
CEO March Consulting Publishing
Cell: 555–555–5555
Office: 555–555–5557

Scheduling an Appointment

Dear Ms. Clowes,
I would like to schedule an appointment with you to discuss the upcoming changes we're making to our annual admissions workbook.

Currently I have available June 4 at 3 p.m. or June 12 at 10 a.m. Would either work best for your schedule?

Best,

Kat Clowes
CEO March Consulting Publishing
Cell: 555–555–5555
Office: 555–555–5557

Privacy and Emails

Make sure you let employees know that their personal emails may not be private. Gen Z employees especially need to hear this.

In 2012, CIA director David Petraeus resigned his post because, like numerous well-known figures in politics, sports, and business before him, his emails shed light on an inappropriate relationship. According to numerous news reports, the emails were discovered during an investigation that was triggered by a complaint against Paula Broadwell, Petraeus's purported lover.

When Broadwell was accused of sending harassing emails to another woman, the FBI investigated, and the emails between Broadwell and Petraeus were found. National scandal aside, this case is interesting because it demonstrated once again that personal emails can destroy careers—and lives.

Anecdotal evidence suggests that many employees still believe that emails they deem to be private may not be viewed by their employers. This is simply not the case. Although the Fourth Amendment to the US Constitution gives people the right "to be secure against unreasonable searches and seizures in their persons, houses, papers, and effects," employers do not violate that right when the employee should have no reasonable expectation of privacy.

For example, if an employer states in writing (whether in a handbook or individual policy) that company equipment is to be used for business purposes only and that emails will be monitored, then there should be no expectation of privacy. However, if there is no policy, or if a policy exists but is rarely enforced, then employees may have a reasonable expectation of privacy and employers could get in trouble for perusing employees' emails without their consent. Even in that situation, however, private emails can be reviewed as part of an investigation into misconduct.

Explicit policy or not, employees should refrain from sending personal (especially inappropriate) emails or texts using company equipment, as can be seen in the court case of the *City of Ontario v. Quon*.[145] In this case, Sergeant Jeff Quon claimed his supervisor told him that text messages on his city-issued pager would not be audited as long as Quon paid for any overage charges. However, his text messages were later reviewed to determine why he was exceeding the message limit. The review revealed that the majority of Quon's messages were personal and often sexually explicit. Quon sued the city for violation of privacy, but the US Supreme Court found in favor of the City of Ontario.

Note that Petraeus used a personal account and not his CIA account when emailing Broadwell. This demonstrates that, in some cases, employees can get into trouble for their personal emails even when they are not sent on company equipment.

Of course, because of his former position as the director of the CIA, the Petraeus situation was much more than just an inappropriate email exchange. However, it was the inappropriate email exchange that led to his demise and to his total lack of privacy afterward. Employees don't need to be the head of the CIA for that to happen to them as well.

---

[145]City of Ontario v. Quon - 560 U.S. 746, 130 S. Ct. 2619 (2010), accessed October, 3.2020, https://www.lexisnexis.com/community/casebrief/p/casebrief-city-of -ontario-v-quon.

Kat's Take

As mentioned previously, privacy is a different concept to Gen Z. When I had to let go of a Gen Z employee, they were surprised to find they had lost access to their company email. You can imagine my surprise at their surprise!

Later, when transferring pertinent information to our company drive, I discovered the employee had been using company email for personal uses. Songs, movies, and other such files were stored in their drive. Not only was that not appropriate and against company policy, but this particular employee was frustrated to no longer be able to access their email or files.

Thoroughly review privacy and storage of client information (or any other sensitive information, for that matter) with your employees, particularly Gen Zers. It's one of the first things that we cover now when training our new employees. It's an effort to eliminate any embarrassing or possible liability concerns later.

Emojis

Most people are familiar with "emojis" by now—those colorful cartoon characters (faces, hearts, animals, etc.) that are used in electronic communications like emails, social media posts, or text messages, often to clarify, illustrate, or amplify messages.

In her article "Oxford's 2015 Word of the Year Is This Emoji," Katy Steinmetz says, "They act like punctuation, providing cues about how to understand the words that came before them, as an exclamation point might. Emoji typically add to ideas rather than replace words."[146] Thanks to numerous lawsuits, they also add one more thing you need to worry about your employees doing that could get you into trouble.

Why worry? Because along with emails, texts, and tweets, emojis are now admissible in court hearings. Numerous courts, including

---

[146]Katy Steinmetz, "Oxford's 2015 Word of the Year Is This Emoji," *Time*, November 16, 2015, https://time.com/4114886/oxford-word-of-the-year-2015-emoji/.

the US Supreme Court, have ruled on cases involving the use and intent of emojis. The Supreme Court reversed the conviction of a man whose violent electronic threats against his wife were followed by a face sticking its tongue out, which he said proved he was just joking about killing her.

One problem with emojis is that they might clarify messages too well. For example, let's say you have an employee who emails a coworker this message: "What do you think of the new intern?" The coworker responds with this message: "She's fine" and an emoji of a winking face with puckered lips and a heart. The words "She's fine" are ambiguous; however, with the emoji added, the message now has romantic overtones, which could present a problem when trying to fight a sexual harassment claim.

Would employees really use emojis like the one described above in their business communications? Yes.

According to the Oxford Dictionaries team that chose the "Face With Tears of Joy" emoji as the word of 2015, "Although emoji have been a staple of texting teens for some time, emoji culture exploded into the global mainstream over the past year." In a *Fortune* article about emojis, tech writer Robert Hackett says the "emoji has begun to reshape the language of business."[147] Indeed, in a survey commissioned by Cotap, a mobile messaging company, of one thousand American workers with smartphones, 76 percent said they had used emoji in business communication.[148]

Even when people know not to put a particular thought into words, they seem to thoughtlessly say the same thing with emojis. In his article "Emoji-gosh! How Emojis in Workplace Communications Can Spark a Lawsuit (or Make It Harder to Defend One)," attorney Peter T. Tschanz says most employees wouldn't dream of sending a message that the new intern is attractive but seem to believe communicating that same message with emojis is somehow acceptable. "Because many people view this sort of humor as

---

[147]Robert Hackett, "This Is Apple's Weird New Emoji," *Fortune*, September 21, 2015, https://fortune.com/2015/09/21/apple-new-emoji/.

[148]Kelly Creighton, "Do Emojis Belong in Business Writing?," *Grammar Phile Blog*, October 26, 2017, https://www.proofreadnow.com/blog/do-emojis-belong-in-business-writing.

creative and not really inappropriate. It's just a joke," according to Tschanz.[149]

In light of these legal headaches, should you ban the use of emojis at work? I wouldn't. Instead, simply remind employees that all their business correspondence, including emails, texts, tweets, and now emojis, can be used as evidence in court so they should not send anything they wouldn't want to be seen by a judge and jury. If you're sending this message via electronic communication, leave off the smiley face.

Teach your Gen Z employees that emojis are rarely appropriate in a professional environment, especially in formal communication with clients or prospects. Nor should they be used in social media unless your target audience responds or communicates in emojis, and even then, they should be used sparingly and be approved ahead of time.

Extend this emoji policy to text abbreviations as well, reminding employees that they should skip abbreviations such as BRB (be right back), TTYL (talk to you later), and other text speak in professional messages. You may even need to tell an employee not to use "r" in professional communication in place of the word "are."

Kat's Take

Unlike any generation before them, Gen Z has grown up in a world of emojis. I've seen them use entire emoji strings in place of sentences, a talent that I unfortunately do not have.

However, if you haven't forayed far into the world of emojis, be aware that there are vulgar emojis. And that perfectly benign emojis can be combined to create vulgarities.

---

[149]Peter T. Tschanz, "Emoji-gosh! How Emojis in Workplace Communications Can Spark a Lawsuit (or Make It Harder to Defend One)," *Barnes & Thornburg*, accessed June 25, 2020, https://www.lexology.com/library/detail. aspx?g=413f3f6f-b845–49f3–840d-69201810f6f8.

CHAPTER 21

ADDRESS BAD HABITS

M any years ago, I shared an office with a coworker who chewed her gum voraciously. She snapped and popped it loudly all day long while I sat nearby gritting my teeth. Finally, I asked her if she could chew more quietly. She laughed and said, "People tell me all the time how annoying my gum chewing is" and continued to snap and pop away.

If you have an office with people working in close quarters, your employees will almost certainly experience conflict at one point or another. This may be especially true if you have a wide mix of ages, where employees don't always agree on workplace etiquette. When should you address irritating behavior and what can you do about employees' bothersome habits?

First, determine whether the habit is "a" problem or "your" problem. For example, if you are irritated because an employee frequently says "like" or "you know," but it doesn't seem to bother anyone else, then that's "your" problem. However, if an employee has frequent temper tantrums that scare coworkers, then that's "a" problem.

"Be very clear on the real impact of the bad habit," says John Stark, associate dean of the School of Business and Public Administration at California State University, Bakersfield. Stark also teaches management classes and advises that correcting employees' benign bad habits could result in a loss of goodwill that is more harmful than what you consider annoying behavior.[150]

But don't ignore bad behavior that is causing problems for the organization or others. First determine whether the behavior violates company policy or procedure. Behavior that is against the rules, such as destroying company property, is usually easier to address because of its objective nature. Behavior that doesn't violate any specific policy—such as audible gum chewing—is more subjective and, thus, a reprimand can be taken more personally by the offender. So, you'll want to be extra tactful when addressing these issues.

Have a Conversation

"Once you have your basis for addressing the habit, then you have a conversation with the employee," says Stark. Here is a format that should help that conversation be successful.

Make a door-opener statement. "Robin, I need to talk to you about an issue that involves you."

State the problem directly and tactfully. If it's a policy violation, you can say: "You have a habit of losing your temper. Yesterday you became so angry that you threw your telephone through the window, which broke both things." If it's a personal issue, you can say: "You have a habit of chewing your gum so loudly that other people can hear it."

State how the problem affects the business. "Destroying company property is a policy violation, which will result in disciplinary action. Moreover, you have lost your temper so many times that some of your coworkers are now afraid of you." "Your audible gum chewing is distracting for some of your coworkers and is affecting their ability to work."

State how the problem affects the employee. "Not being able to control your temper could result in future disciplinary action or could prevent you from being promoted to a supervisory position." "I think you should know that chewing your gum so loudly is hurting your professional image."

Ask and explore. "Is there something that's causing you to lose your temper that I can help with? When you feel frustrated, is there

---

[150]John Stark, interview by Robin Paggi, March 4, 2019.

something you can do to avoid losing your temper?" "Is there a reason you need to chew gum? Is there something you could do instead?"

Once the conversation is over, periodically check in with employees to ensure that they stay on track. Be patient with their progress. Stark says, "Habits change only with thousands of repetitions, so we need to be patient and supportive of our employees, especially if they are putting in a good-faith effort to change!"

Kat's Take

If you show care, respect, and that you're genuinely trying to help (instead of blame or criticize), workers will be much more receptive to what you are likely to say. I think this is true for anyone, but it is especially true for younger workers, particularly for Gen Z.

Showing a path to improving behavior or breaking a bad habit or simply offering your support goes a long way toward alleviating any negative responses.

If I'm quick to criticize work done on an essay, for example, without showing how to improve it, Gen Z shuts down. It's far more effective if I discuss the problem, suggest different paths toward a different result, and follow up in a supportive manner.

Everyone needs a cheerleader once in a while. Or an accountability partner.

Give Them a Second Chance

Some business and consultants allow little room for employees to make errors or reform their bad habits. In his article "Hire Slow, Fire Fast," Patrick Hull tells readers that "if a person that you hire is not working out, don't hesitate to move on quickly. . . . I know many businesses that took time to try and change someone. I haven't seen it be successful. People don't change."[151]

---

[151]Patrick Hull, "Hire Slow, Fire Fast," *Forbes*, March 27, 2013, https://www.forbes.com/sites/patrickhull/2013/03/27/hire-slow-fire-fast/#4411ea9c5a6a.

I disagree with that approach, especially when you are dealing with young and inexperienced Gen Z workers.

I have coached a number of employees who needed to change their behavior in order to remain employed. Some were able to do it and some weren't, but offering an opportunity to improve is important for a couple of reasons.

Blind to the Problem

People usually are oblivious when their behavior is a problem. We don't see ourselves as other people see us. For example, we might think that we're confident and assertive while others think that we're an aggressive know-it-all. We might think that we're fun and charismatic while others think that we're inappropriate.

People are also oblivious that their behavior is a problem because other people are not honest and candid with them. Employees need to have honest feedback about how their behavior affects the workplace in order to improve. It's amazing what can happen when employees are told specifically what they are doing—or not doing— that is problematic.

Many years ago a manager told me he refused to promote an employee to a supervisory position because the employee "was weird." Although the employee had applied for a promotion numerous times, the manager never told him why he was being turned down. I encouraged the manager to discuss the problematic behavior, and with specific feedback and guidance, the employee was able to change. A couple of months later, the manager told me he wanted to promote the employee.

The employee benefited because he got the promotion he desired, and the manager benefited because the employee now behaved in an appropriate manner.

❝ Employers React to Gen Z

How long do you allow them to learn it and demonstrate proficiency? How do you determine this isn't going to work out? ❞

Protect Yourself

The second reason to give employees an opportunity and the tools to improve is, frankly, because it makes employers look better if they have to defend a termination in court. Firing employees too fast is one of the top ten things employers do to get sued, according to "Hostile Work Environment—10 Things Bully Bosses Do to Cause Lawsuits." The article author, a defense attorney, writes,

Employers who take a long time to try to improve a negative situation with an employee, and who can show gradually increasing discipline over that time period are the ones who will look better in court. Juries like it when it looks like the employer went well beyond the minimum legal requirements and tried everything possible to "save" the employer-employee relationship, but despite the boss's training and coaching the employee just refused to do the work.[152]

But Not Too Many Chances

Obviously, I'm in favor of giving employees a chance to learn new behaviors to improve their performance. However, I'm not in favor of giving employees too many chances. Doing so doesn't inspire employees to be accountable, and it can backfire on employers.

An excellent example of such backfiring is an unemployment hearing that was documented in the article "Should Employees Be Given Second Chances?" by the Troutman Pepper's Labor and Employment Group. Despite committing numerous infractions (stealing time, excessive tardiness, and being rude during a counseling session), an employee was offered a different work shift instead of being fired. The employee declined and was subsequently terminated. At the unemployment hearing, the employee said he was fired for not accepting the position. In the employer's defense, the manager presented the list of the numerous infractions the employee had committed, to which the hearing officer asked:

---

[152]"Hostile Work Environment—10 Things Bully Bosses Do to Cause Lawsuits," ToughNickel, June 18, 2020, https://toughnickel.com/business/Hostile-Work-Environment-How-Bully-Bosses-Cause-Lawsuits-Part2.

- If you have documented evidence that he was stealing time, why didn't you terminate him then?
- If arriving to work on time is an essential function of his position, why did you wait until he was tardy forty-two times before terminating him?
- If he was unprofessional during a counseling session, had already stolen time, and demonstrated a pattern of excessive tardiness, why didn't you terminate him at that point?
- And why after all of the aforementioned issues with his job performance did you offer him another position within the company?[153]

The employee did not get unemployment benefits; however, this example demonstrates that courts could suspect an employer's motive to terminate when the employer allows an employee to repeatedly behave inappropriately without consequences.

Something else that causes suspicion is a lack of documentation. If you are giving employees more chances, be very diligent about documenting the performance issues or the delay in termination will generally backfire too.

I suggest you give wayward employees the opportunity and tools to improve. If they can't turn their behavior around in a reasonable time period, then guide them toward the door.

---

[153]Troutman Pepper's Labor and Employment Group, "Should Employees Be Given Second Chances?," *HR Law Matters*, July 24, 2012, https://www.hrlawmatters. com/2012/07/should-employees-be-given-second-chances/.

WORK WITH THEM

Section 5 Takeaways

- Communicate commitment and cultivate love.
- Promote positivity and negate negativity.
- Employees respond to freedom and recognition.
- Great teams are not built in a day.
- Making work fun can make businesses more successful.
- Equip leaders to manage conflict and communicate well.

CHAPTER 22

COMMITMENT AND LOVE

I f you have ever been married, chances are you were madly in love when you decided to become engaged. And you probably thought this magical feeling would last a lifetime. Spoiler alert—it doesn't. In the article "Exactly What to Do When the Honeymoon Phase Ends in Your Relationship," marriage and family therapist Jane Greer explains that our bodies naturally shift out of the lovey-dovey mode after about a year because of self-preservation. In other words, we can't handle the hormonal overload that causes that lovely feeling for much longer than that.[154]

I propose (pun intended) that this phenomenon occurs in work relationships as well. When we hire someone or accept a job offer, we're often enamored with each other and think that feeling will last. Your Gen Z employees may be especially starry eyed if this is their first real job. But just as in relationships, the "too-good-to-be-true" feelings are exactly that: too good to be true. Workers can become disillusioned if the job or the organization does not live up to their expectations, and

---

[154]Alexis Jones, "Exactly What to Do When the Honeymoon Phase Ends in Your Relationship," *Women's Health*, October 7, 2019, https://www.womenshealthmag.com/relationships/a29338359/honeymoon-phase-over/.

employers can become exasperated when their new hire does not immediately handle all tasks smoothly and expertly.

Demonstrating Commitment

In her article "Gen Z in the Workplace—5 Ways to Be a Better Employer," Sina Kaye Lockley says, "More than any other generation before them, the driving force behind Generation Z in the workplace are financial rewards and career advancement."[155]

As the consequences of COVID-19 drag on, many employers may not have the ability to offer a lot of rewards or promotions anytime soon. However, even before the pandemic, we knew that our need for human connection and commitment is more important than money, and there are still actions available that will help you cultivate employee loyalty and inspire productivity from your employees.

❝   Employers React to Gen Z

We have instituted strong leadership that cares about our employees and understands the generation. While we may not completely agree with some of the values of this generation, we are open to new ideas and solutions to solving new/old problems.

❞

Lead by Example

This basic leadership principle applies to any relationship. If you want employees to devote themselves to your organization, you need to prove that you are devoted both to them and to the company. For example, I once coached a supervisor who complained that his employees didn't always follow safety rules, such as wearing their hard hats. This made

---

[155]Sina Kaye Lockley, "Gen Z in the Workplace: 5 Ways to Manage Every Generation," *Staffbase*, accessed June 25, 2020, https://staffbase.com/blog/generation-z-in-the-workplace-5-ways-to-be-a-better-employer

him angry because they weren't doing what he told them to do. I asked if he always wore his hard hat? Guess what his answer was. The "do-as-I-say-and-not-as-I-do" philosophy won't get you the results that you want in any relationship.

Communicate

I believe miscommunication and a lack of communication are the sources of many of our personal and professional problems. When we don't talk about things or provide information, our employees will make things up to fill the void. If you don't provide information to your employees about things that affect them, they will imagine the worst-case scenario. Communication is essential to our well-being; our relationships can't be well without it.

Give Praise and Recognition

In his article "Why People Can Be Kinder to Strangers Than to Loved Ones," Dr. Alex Lickerman says, "We have the least tolerance for the negative qualities of those with whom we spend the most time."[156] In other words, when we become very familiar with someone, we stop seeing the great things they do and start focusing on the tiny things that drive us crazy. But providing only negative feedback and never acknowledging employees' accomplishments makes them feel unappreciated. Psychologist Abraham Maslow theorized that we all have a need for praise and recognition, and I agree. When that need is unmet, it damages us and our relationships.

Be Available

Absence might make the heart grow fonder, but it can also destroy relationships. And just because someone is physically present doesn't mean

---

[156]Alex Lickerman, "Why People Can Be Kinder to Strangers Than to Loved Ones," *Psychology Today*, July 13, 2014, https://www.psychologytoday.com/us/blog/happiness-in-world/201407/why-people-can-be-kinder-strangers-loved-ones.

that they're mentally and emotionally available. If you are rarely around the office, are unavailable when you are there, and can't pay attention when your employees talk to you, they'll think you don't care about them. Being present, both physically and mentally, is essential to good relationships.

Clarify Expectations

We often think people have the same worldview we do, so we fail to communicate what we want and need from them. You expect your employees to complete some task and become frustrated when it doesn't happen. You didn't ask them to complete it, but you shouldn't have to, right? In your mind, their failure to anticipate your expectations demonstrates they're lazy and don't care about their jobs. News flash: no one knows what's in your head but you. Clarifying your expectations helps others to meet them and helps prevent you from being disappointed.

Demonstrate Interest and Concern

This really is a no-brainer at home and at work. If you don't show an interest in others, they won't be interested in you. How does one show interest? First, put your phone down and don't look at it during conversations. Next, really pay attention and acknowledge what's being said. Then, show you care about what was said by saying something like "I understand why that made you angry" or "You must have felt good about that." Demonstrating more interest in people than in your electronic gadgets is essential to connect with them.

Be Honest

Another no-brainer. Why would the people be honest with you if you're not honest with them?

Kat's Take

If you make your new Gen Z employee feel heard, you have taken a big step in creating a committed, productive working relationship.

One of the best practices we have instituted in my office is to more frequently ask employees what our next step should be. For example, if employees come to me with a problem, I ask what ideas they have to remedy it. Now, they are less likely to bring complaints; instead, they bring ideas for how to make situations or projects better.

They feel more heard now and that they have a bigger stake in what happens at work, the directions we take on projects, and the company as a whole. They have also become more comfortable in bringing up issues, because they know those issues won't be simply swept under the rug.

Show Some HR-Approved Love

While I frown upon romantic relationships between supervisors and their employees, I do encourage employers to take deliberate steps to create a "loving" workplace. By love I mean "any positive emotion that we share with another person in real time," which is the definition of love by emotion researcher Barbara Fredrickson, author of *Love 2.0: How Our Supreme Emotion Affects Everything We Feel, Think, Do, and Become.*[157] Fredrickson says this positive emotion "could be shared serenity, pride, or compassion, but the minute that it becomes shared, it is converted to an experience of love."

And what happens when we experience these moments of love at work? Says Fredrickson, "These micro-moments of connection are the key to unlocking more generative capacity."[158] In other words, they lead to greater creativity and productivity. If you're thinking this love-at-work

---

[157]Barbara Fredrickson, *Love 2.0: How Our Supreme Emotion Affects Everything We Feel, Think, Do, and Become* (Old Saybrook, CT: Gilden Media, 2013).
[158]Ibid.

stuff is a bunch of new-age hooey, I offer this scientific data.

In his paper "A Theory of Human Motivation," published in *Psychological Review* in 1943, psychologist Abraham Maslow proposed that humans are motivated to act because they have certain needs, including the need for love and belonging. Humans need to love and be loved—sexually and nonsexually—by others. Without this love, people suffer.[159]

Numerous scientific studies later, research has demonstrated that this need for love is caused by the hardwiring of our brains. Amy Banks, an instructor of psychiatry at Harvard Medical School, stated in a 2010 interview that "neuroscience is confirming that our nervous systems want us to connect with other human beings." And what happens when we don't connect with others? Banks said that "the distress of social pain is biologically identical to the distress of physical pain."[160]

Kat's Take

I have seen so much damage caused when established professionals do not connect well with their new Gen Z employees. Without frank communication, the Gen Z employee always ends up being terminated, and he rarely knows why.

Because the employee does not know that his boss is bothered by an action—or a lack of action—the employee continues with the same irritating behavior. The frustrated supervisor becomes increasingly irritated until she finds grounds to fire the person.

I've seen this happen multiple times with Gen Z employees, and employers frequently ask, "Why do these young people now _____?" Usually, I tell the employer that "those young people" just need to develop a specific skill and recommend that the employer help the young worker develop that skill. Nine times out of ten, when the employer follows my advice, the issue is resolved.

[159]Abraham H. Maslow, "A Theory of Human Motivation," *Psychological Review 50*, no. 4 (1943): 370–96, https://doi.org/10.1037/h0054346.

[160]Wellesley Centers for Women, "Humans Are Hardwired for Connection? Neurobiology 101 for Parents, Educators, Practitioners and the General Public," September 15, 2010, https://www.wcwonline.org/2010/humans-are-hardwired-for-connection-neurobiology-101-for-parents-educators-practitioners-and-the-general-public.

Most of the time, the employee had no idea what he was doing was wrong or inappropriate, and certainly didn't know he could be jeopardizing his job.

Gen Zers don't have years of life or professional experience yet to gauge what needs to be done or their employer's frustration levels. What seems obvious to you will not be obvious to them—that's why it's up to you to communicate.

Simply put, employees who feel connected to their employer, supervisor, and coworkers perform better than those who don't. Feelings of connection are created by moments of shared positive emotion—or love—in Fredrickson's definition.

I encourage you to take these deliberate steps to create a loving—and thus more productive—workplace:

- **Be present.** Interact with employees face-to-face and focus all your attention on them during these interactions. (Yes, this is pretty much the same advice as "be available," which I mentioned above, but it bears repeating.)
- **Be truthful.** People can't connect with others who aren't authentic. Tell employees when they have not met your expectations and what they should do to meet them.
- **Be tactful.** Say what needs to be said in a way that does not destroy people.
- **Be personable.** Let employees get to know you and get to know them. I'm not suggesting getting involved in each other's personal lives; I am suggesting a conversation now and then about something other than work.
- **Resolve conflicts.** Avoiding conflicts actually creates more barriers to connection.
- **Say "I'm sorry."** Apologize when you make mistakes. Sounds obvious, but people in positions of authority often have the misguided notion they always have to be right.

- **Keep people in the loop.** Provide monthly or at least quarterly updates on finances, new clients, operational changes, and so on.
- **Provide social opportunities.** You don't have to foot the bill for a lavish party; just bring in cookies or a pizza that employees can munch on while chatting.
- **Celebrate successes.** If you think people are supposed to do a good job and therefore don't need to be thanked when they succeed, you need to think again.

When you demonstrate commitment and love to your employees, you will realize that your actions don't benefit your employees alone. Moments of connection positively impact everyone who shares them.

Mother Teresa said, "Work without love is slavery." If you've ever had a job that you hated, then you know what she meant. Help your employees love their work by taking deliberate steps to connect with them and by showing your commitment to them. You'll love the effect it has on your employees, yourself, and your business.

CHAPTER 23

CULTIVATE A POSITIVE ATMOSPHERE

W hen an organization asks me to give a motivational speech to a group of employees who are marring the workplace with their negativity, I often suggest that I should speak to the managers and supervisors instead, because they are often the source of employee negativity.

Are your employees grumbling because no one asks for their input or values their opinion? Are they complaining about favoritism or unequal treatment in your company? Have they said they don't feel appreciated? Then maybe you should first examine the attitudes and actions of your organization's leaders.

Employers who offer their employees input, freedom, and recognition rarely struggle with negativity in the workplace.

In her article "9 Tips for Minimizing Workplace Negativity," human resources expert Susan M. Heathfield says that "the best way to combat workplace negativity is to keep it from occurring in the first place."[161] The following tips for preventing negativity and promoting positivity in

---

[161]Susan M. Heathfield, "9 Tips for Minimizing Workplace Negativity," The Balance Careers, August 9, 2019, https://www.thebalancecareers.com/tips-for-minimizing-workplace-negativity-1919384.

the workplace are all taken from Heathfield's article:

- **Allow employees to make decisions about their own job.** Says Heathfield, "The single most frequent cause of workplace negativity I encounter is traceable to a manager or the organization making a decision about a person's work without her input. Almost any decision that excludes the input of the person doing the work is perceived as negative."
- **Provide opportunities for employees to express opinions about workplace policies and procedures.** Not having a forum makes employees feel unheard and uncared for.
- **Be consistent in applying policies and procedures.** Remember that inconsistency breeds "contempt."
- **Don't overdo the policies.** If you overwhelm employees with rules and regulations and procedures, you make them feel like children. "Treat people as adults; they will usually live up to your expectations, and their own expectations," says Heathfield.
- **Help people feel included.** Keep everyone informed about what's going on and why.
- **Allow employees opportunities to grow and develop.** Not providing potential for growth makes employees feel stifled and confined.
- **Have a mission, vision, and goals for your workplace.** Help employees see they are part of something bigger than themselves.
- **Let employees know that their contribution is valued.** Says Heathfield, "The power of appropriate rewards and recognition for a positive workplace is remarkable. Suffice to say, reward and recognition is one of the most powerful tools an organization can use to buoy staff morale."[162]

If you want to prevent negativity in the workplace, look in the mirror and ask whether your actions or inactions are contributing to the poor attitudes. Then talk to employees to determine why they are feeling so negative.

Now address the issues you identify. Do policies need to be better

[162]Ibid.

clarified? Do decisions need to be better explained? Does appreciation need to be better expressed?

Whatever the cause, negative feelings need to be addressed because, as Heathfield says, "Like a seemingly dormant volcano, they will boil beneath the surface, and periodically bubble up and overflow to cause fresh damage."

Give Them Some Freedom

One of the ways you can create a positive atmosphere in your workplace is to make sure your employees have some freedom. This will be especially important for your Gen Z employees, who see little justification for restrictive rules about start and stop times or in-person meetings.

In his article "8 Things Your Employees Need Most," Jeff Haden, author of numerous books on business, says the number one thing employees need from their employers is freedom. "Whenever possible, give your employees the freedom to work the way they work best," he says.[163] Issie Lapowsky, a reporter at *Inc.* magazine, echoes this sentiment in her article "10 Things Employees Want Most": "In addition to deciding how they work, the experts say employees also appreciate having a say over when they work."[164]

People need to feel like they are given some freedom to perform their work when and how they work best. Employees also crave schedule flexibility so they can handle the countless other duties life brings with it.

According to a 2018 workplace flexibility study conducted by Annie Dean and Anna Auerbach, the flexibility employees desire most is the ability to adapt their location and schedule as needed, work remotely, travel minimally, and work part-time. A lack of flexibility negatively impacts their ability to care for others, health and wellness, productivity,

---

[163]Jeff Haden, "8 Things Your Employees Need Most," *Inc.*, accessed June 25, 2020, http://node.inc.com/jeff-haden/the-8-things-your-employees-need-most.html.

[164]Issie Lapowsky, "10 Things Employees Want Most," *Inc.*, accessed June 25, 2020, https://www.inc.com/guides/2010/08/10-things-employees-want.html.

and retention.[165]

Many employers have insisted for years that employees must commute to the workplace; however, the shelter-in-place orders issued because of COVID-19 demonstrated that many employees are capable of efficiently and effectively working remotely. In fact, Jack Dorsey, CEO of Twitter, announced in spring 2020 that all his employees could work from home forever if they want to, and other corporations have followed his lead.[166] As we are writing this book, it's hard to know what long-term effects the COVID shutdowns may have on workplace requirements, but it's going to be hard for employers to ignore the arrangements that have been made during the pandemic.

Although you are not expected to allow employees to dictate every detail of how and when they want to work, providing them with a say could lead to happier, healthier, more productive employees who stay with your organization longer.

If you still don't see the value in being flexible with your employees, consider these words by martial artist Bruce Lee: "Notice that the stiffest tree is most easily cracked, while the bamboo or willow survives by bending with the wind."

Update Your Employee Recognition Program

As we have explained in several places in this book, feedback and recognition are crucial components to building positive employee relationships, especially with Gen Z workers. I am a strong proponent of employee recognition, but I'm not a big fan of employee-of-the-month or tenure-based recognition programs.

What's wrong with employee-of-the-month programs? First, employees usually have no idea what they did to win the award—and neither do the people who are giving the award. Is the winner is chosen

---

[165]Annie Dean and Anna Auerbach, "96% of U.S. Professionals Say They Need Flexibility, but Only 47% Have It," *Harvard Business Review*, June 5, 2018, https://hbr.org/2018/06/96-of-u-s-professionals-say-they-need-flexibility-but-only-47-have-it.

[166]Jack Kelly, "Twitter CEO Jack Dorsey Tells Employees They Can Work from Home 'Forever'—Before You Celebrate, There's a Catch," *Forbes*, May 13, 2020, https://www.forbes.com/sites/jackkelly/2020/05/13/twitter-ceo-jack-dorsey-tells-employees-they-can-work-from-home-forever-before-you-celebrate-theres-a-catch/#3d9c8862e916.

based on who is most attractive, who walked in the door recently, or who most needs a pat on the back?

Furthermore, the reward is usually meaningless. Most employees of the month get their picture on a plaque that hangs in the lobby, which the employee rarely sees. Or maybe they get a hat with the company logo on it, which they can't even wear to work because of your dress code.

Another problem is there can be only one winner each month. What happens if two employees do something outstanding that is worthy of recognition? Do you recognize one this month and the other the next? By then, their outstanding accomplishment will be old news.

You might be thinking, "Ha! I don't have an employee-of-the-month program. I'm good because all my employees get recognized every five years on their work anniversaries." Now, that's a different problem.

Josh Bersin is the principal and founder of Bersin by Deloitte, an organization that provides research-based information for strategic HR management purposes. He says employers spend about $46 billion each year on plaques, statues, and other mementos (with the company's logo on them) celebrating the fact that employees are still around.[167]

Evidently, lots of companies reward people this way because 87 percent of recognition programs focus on those five-, ten-, fifteen-, and twenty-year awards. Unfortunately, this kind of recognition program doesn't work for two reasons:

- Most people really don't care about those mementos.
- Tenure awards have virtually no impact on organizational performance.

Effective Recognition Affects Performance

The business purpose of recognition programs is to positively impact the business. According to Bersin, organizations that effectively recognize their employees far outperform those that don't.[168] Employee engagement, productivity, and customer service are about 14 percent better

---

[167]Josh Bersin, "New Research Unlocks the Secret of Employee Recognition," *Forbes*, June 13, 2012, https://www.forbes.com/sites/joshbersin/2012/06/13/new-research-unlocks-the-secret-of-employee-recognition/#722b9a465276.

[168]Ibid.

than in organizations where recognition does not occur. So, if you want employees to be more engaged, more productive, and better with your customers, recognize them—wisely. Here are some specific recognition policies you should consider:

- Recognize employees based on specific results and behaviors that align with your company's values or goals. For example, if your company prides itself on delivering outstanding customer service, recognize employees when they deliver outstanding customer service.
- Recognize employees when they deserve recognition, not just once a month or every five years.
- Allow employees to recognize each other. The boss doesn't always know what goes on.
- Recognize employees the way they want to be recognized. For example, some employees like public recognition and others don't.
- Recognize employees with rewards that are meaningful to them. For example, give them a gift card to a store or restaurant that you know your employees enjoy instead of giving them a gift card to *your* favorite store or restaurant.

Of course, it's always a good idea to recognize employees when they've exceeded your expectations—even if you don't expect your business to get a direct reward. It's perfectly appropriate to recognize them because they are human beings and probably need a pat on the back.

Kat's Take

It may not come as a surprise, but Gen Zers prefer money or gift cards as tokens of recognition. But before you hand them that gift card to Applebee's, ask about their preferences.

At our office, we ask if employees would rather receive a Visa gift card, a Starbucks gift card, or a gift certificate to a local eatery. Most will opt for a Visa gift card during the holidays, while they might go for the Starbucks card during the summer. All appreciate being given options.

How did we come up with these choices? We asked everyone to submit their preferences in a quick email and then purchased the top three requests, allowing each employee input in our recognition awards.

We also made it easy for employees to recognize their coworkers. Because I don't see every detail of everyone's work, it's harder for me to recognize those who go above and beyond and/or solve a problem while working on a big project. Having a stock of gift cards available makes it easy for our management team to quickly reward any employee on the spot. Being "caught" doing something good boosts morale and makes everyone feel like they're recognized.

Learn Their Love Languages

In a Capital One commercial that ran years ago, comedian Jimmy Fallon stated, "According to research, everybody likes more cash . . . well, almost everybody." Fallon then turned to a toddler and asked if she would like more cash, to which the little girl replied no. Fallon then said, "But, it's more money," and got cereal thrown in his face.

Employers often think giving their employees an annual cash bonus is all that is really necessary to make them feel valued. However, does the cash really do the job of making all employees feel appreciated all year long? Probably not.

In his book *The Five Love Languages*, Dr. Gary Chapman identifies five ways that people generally show their love and feel loved.[169] Chapman and Dr. Paul White took that concept, applied it to the working world, and wrote *The Five Languages of Appreciation in the Workplace*.[170] When you recognize how various employees respond to various types of

---

[169]Gary Chapman, *The Five Love Languages: How to Express Heartfelt Commitment to Your Mate* (Chicago: Northfield Publishing, 1992).

[170]Gary Chapman and Paul White, *The 5 Languages of Appreciation in the Workplace* (Chicago: Moody Publishers, 2012).

recognition, you can more effectively make them feel appreciated using these five "languages":

- Words of affirmation. People who speak this love language often show their love and appreciation for others through their words. According to Chapman, "Verbal compliments, or words of appreciation, are powerful communicators of love" for these folks.[171] In addition to showing their love through words, they tend to hear whether they are loved through the words of others. At work, "words" people are quick to compliment others and usually like receiving compliments as well. Do people who thrive on words of affirmation appreciate a cash bonus? Probably. However, receiving cash once a year won't make up for a year without verbal affirmation.

- Quality time. Those who speak this love language show their love and appreciation for others by spending quality time with them, and they tend to determine how others feel about them by the amount of quality time they are given. Chapman says quality time "means that we are doing something together and that we are giving our full attention to the other person." At work, this would translate into keeping appointments and giving others your undivided attention when meeting with them. People who thrive on quality time undoubtedly enjoy receiving a cash bonus. However, receiving cash once a year doesn't make up for a year of missed meetings and interrupted conversations.

- Gifts. People who speak this love language usually show their appreciation for others by giving them carefully selected gifts. Unfortunately, recipients tend to feel loved only when a gift is carefully chosen just for them. Says Chapman, "You must be thinking of someone to give him a gift. The gift itself is a symbol of that thought. It doesn't matter whether it costs money. What is important is that you thought of him." People who speak this love language probably enjoy cash; however, receiving an annual bonus just like the bonus given to every other employee doesn't make up for a year without thoughtful, individual gestures.

---

[171]Chapman, *The Five Love Languages*. All the quotes in this list are from this source.

- Acts of service. People who speak this love language demonstrate their love and appreciation for others by doing things for them. According to Chapman, acts of service are expressions of love when "they require thought, planning, time, effort, and energy [and are] done with a positive spirit." At work, acts of service could include covering for an employee while she attends her child's school play or pitching in to help a coworker meet an important deadline. Those who determine whether others care for them through their acts of service undoubtedly enjoy receiving cash; however, receiving cash once a year doesn't make up for leaving them to struggle alone throughout the year.
- Physical touch. Those who speak this love language show their love and appreciation for others through physical touch, which HR professionals tend to frown upon at work, especially in the face of COVID-19. Although a handshake, fist bump, or high five could safely be used to show appreciation prior to the pandemic, in April 2020, Dr. Anthony Fauci, a key member of the White House coronavirus task force, said, "I don't think we should ever shake hands ever again, to be honest with you." Those who determine how others feel about them by physical contact undoubtedly like cash bonuses, but bonuses don't make up for a lack of human contact that, in the future, might just be an elbow bump.

Trying to always recognize employees by using your own love language is like trying to communicate in English to someone who speaks only Spanish. You can speak loudly and enunciate your words, but you still can't communicate. You need to learn the other person's language to get the message across.

You're probably thinking, "I don't have the time or the inclination to determine the love languages of my employees—if they don't want the cash, then I'll just keep it." Which is *not* the message we are trying to convey here. Give the cash, but consider putting the cash in a carefully selected card and writing a few nice words especially for that employee. Then give the employee the card during a private moment, accompanied by an elbow bump. You'll communicate your appreciation in every love language, and all your employees will feel it.

And remember to make use of the love languages throughout the entire year. Demonstrating appreciation for employees just once a year has the same effect as demonstrating love for your significant other just once a year. Not enough love and they're gone.

CHAPTER 24

BUILD A GREAT TEAM

"If you want to go fast, go alone. If you want to go far, go together."
This African proverb neatly explains why you should encourage your employees to work as a team: individuals can go fast, but a team can go far. There are many strategies and preferences to building a great team, and coaches have to follow their own instincts based on the personnel and task at hand. But all agree there are some common elements to a great team.

Dr. Gregory E. Huszczo identifies seven components for successful teams in his book *Tools for Team Excellence*.[172] A professor in Eastern Michigan University's master's degree program in human resources and organizational development, Huszczo has also served as a consultant for numerous big-name companies like Ford Motor Company. He says successful teams need a clear sense of direction, clear roles and responsibilities, constructive interpersonal relationships, reasonable and efficient operating procedures, constructive external relationships, effective reinforcement systems, and talented people. Let's examine those seven components:

A clear sense of direction. Employees need to know why their business exists, where it's headed, and what part they play in it. A few

---

[172]Gregory E. Huszczo, *Tools for Team Excellence: Getting Your Team into High Gear and Keeping It There* (Boston: Davies-Black, 2010).

tools commonly used to communicate those things are a mission statement, a vision statement, and goals.

A mission statement says what a business does and why it exists. Isn't the mission of a business to make as much money as possible? In "The Key to Better Business Culture: Establishing a Company Mission," psychotherapist Jasmin Terrany says, "Employees these days are not as motivated by simply a paycheck. If you want employees who are going to go to battle with and for you, they need to feel connected to a deeper purpose or mission."[173]

A vision statement indicates where the organization wants to be in the future. In the 1980s, Bill Gates's vision for Microsoft was to have a computer on every desk and in every home. His vision and talent helped make it happen.

Specific, measurable, attainable, relevant, and timebound (SMART) goals need to be set for every department and employee to make the vision a reality. See chapter 11 for more information on SMART goals.

" Employers React to Gen Z

We work hard on communicating company vision and team building. We believe in building trust, open communication, commitment to goals and objectives, and holding each other accountable as we strive to focus on positive company results. **"**

Clear roles and responsibilities. Employees need to understand what they are supposed to do and how they are supposed to do it. Job descriptions, employee handbooks, and standard operating procedures help with that. Organizational charts also help employees understand what everyone does and how it all fits together. See chapter 10 for more information on handbooks and standard operating procedures.

Constructive interpersonal relationships. Relationships are

---

[173]Matt D'Angelo, "The Key to Better Business Culture: Establishing a Company Mission," *Business News Daily*, April 12, 2018, https://www.businessnewsdaily.com/3783-mission-statement.html.

created through communication. Unfortunately, the way we communicate sometimes causes problems for others and prevents us from working effectively with them. Team building training can help with that.

"In team building training, we learned how our personality styles impact how we communicate, how we tend to annoy our coworkers, and what we can do to communicate more effectively with each other," Asta Fowler, operations manager of Empire Management Group, told me.

"Team building training was beneficial for our group because it helped us understand how we can work better together to achieve our company's goals," said Fowler.[174]

Reasonable and efficient operating procedures. Systems must be in place for how the work gets done and should be regularly reviewed to ensure that they are as efficient as possible.

Constructive external relationships. Employees need to be able to work well with people outside their department and organization. Regular meetings to discuss how to work more effectively with each other often improve these relationships.

Effective reinforcement systems. Holding employees accountable and rewarding positive outcomes encourages people to perform. However, employees must value the rewards they are given for them to be effective. See chapter 23 for more information on recognition and rewards.

Talented members. Dr. Huszczo says, "For a team to be effective, the necessary talent must be there, and it has to be utilized and continually developed and improved."[175] You must also have talented leadership. Most teams are not self-directed and cannot function without a good leader.

How do you get employees to work together as a team? Lee Iacocca summed it up nicely: "Start with good people, lay out the rules, communicate with your employees, motivate them and reward them. If you do all those things effectively, you can't miss."

---

[174]Asta Fowler, interview by Robin Paggi, April 16, 2018.
[175]Huszczo, Tools for Team Excellence.

Kat's Take

Gen Zers have done a lot of collaboration in school. They've worked in teams for various projects throughout elementary, junior high, and high school. Many college and graduate school courses emphasize teamwork and group work.

However, not all teams are created equal, as well you know. Although students have been encouraged to work in teams, too often they were never given much instruction on *how* to create excellent work in teams.

What makes a great team? How do you lead a team that doesn't want to do its work? These are only a few questions that don't get addressed in school. Often, one person ends up doing most if not all of the work for the project, because that person is the one who cares most about the grade.

So, even though Gen Z is used to collaboration, your new hires could still benefit from training or mentoring in teamwork. Teach them how to move projects forward and deal directly with problems that hinder team progress.

My best advice is to assign a good team mentor to your newest employees to guide their learning about effective teamwork. This might be as simple as providing a person to answer any Gen Z questions. Or it might be assigning a mentor to a group the Gen Z worker is leading and establishing a process so the mentor can give specific feedback about what went right or wrong and what needs to be addressed.

More Than Just a Day of Fun

Every once in a while, an employer asks me to facilitate a day or half day of team-building activities. The request usually comes because employees are squabbling over work issues or are having personality conflicts, and the employer thinks a day of bowling or scavenger hunting will help people get along better. I tell employers that a few hours of activities are not going to produce the results they want. If you want employees to work as a team, you need to give it a lot more attention and thought.

Team building needs to be an ongoing process, not something that happens once or twice a year. Expecting an annual day of game playing to make a group of people into a team is like expecting to get in good physical shape by exercising once a year. Make a goal of conducting team-building activities on a weekly or monthly basis.

My workplace conducts a weekly team-building activity to reinforce our core values of being open-minded, communicating well, practicing innovation and creativity, and providing "Wow!" customer service experiences. A trophy is awarded to a team member for demonstrating the core values on the job. That team member gets to keep the trophy on his or her desk for a week and then recognizes another team member who gets the trophy for a week. An email is sent to all employees explaining why the recipient of the week was chosen. This is a convenient, inexpensive, and effective team-building activity because it keeps a discussion going about our core values (most of us didn't even know the organization had core values before this was started), and it allows employees to get to know and celebrate each other, which boosts morale.

Team-building activities also need to have a purpose and address specific issues that employees are encountering. For example, if employees have a difficult time communicating with each other, your company could establish a monthly meeting to discuss how to improve communication throughout the organization. Each meeting could focus on a particular aspect of communication, such as listening. You could incorporate some fun into the discussion by having employees take a listening quiz and participate in listening activities to assess their listening skills (people, in general, are very poor listeners, and these activities tend to demonstrate that). The point of the team-building activities is to create personal and organizational strategies to improve listening (such as banning cell phones in meetings).

In addition, team-building activities should be accessible and enjoyable for everyone involved. A popular team-building activity is the "trust fall" in which employees fall backward into their coworkers' arms (we didn't let you fall to the floor, so you trust us now, right?). Don't do the trust fall or anything similar that has the slightest chance of hurting or humiliating an employee (oops, we didn't catch you!).

Make your team-building activities ongoing and purposeful if you want them to be effective. Building a great team doesn't happen in a day.

Know the Law!

If your team-building activities happen away from the workplace, be aware that some legal risks will probably be involved. For example, if your idea of team building is to take everyone to happy hour and pick up the tab, you might be liable if something goes wrong—especially if you allow an employee to drive away in an impaired state.

Also, if your team-building involves playing some kind of sport, ensure that employees know their participation is voluntary. Have them sign a waiver indicating so. Otherwise, you might face pay and workers' comp issues if someone gets hurt.

CHAPTER 25

HAVE SOME FUN!

I t's common knowledge that working without ceasing isn't good for the body or the soul. A growing trend in the workplace is to incorporate tactics and policies at work that enrich the body, soul, and mind of employees—who are then more likely to be more loyal and more productive. Gen Z employees are particularly interested in working in a place that allows for fun and friendships and life-enriching activities. Fostering a fun work environment can boost your employee morale, which in turn can boost your bottom line.

Having fun at work leads to creativity, productivity, better decision-making, and deeper camaraderie, says California State University, Long Beach, professor Dr. David Abramis in "Play in Work: Childish Hedonism or Adult Enthusiasm?" Employees who have fun at work are tardy less often and take fewer sick days than their dour counterparts. In sum, fun workplaces beget more loyal and productive employees who show up for work and show up on time.[176]

Evidently, many well-known companies believe in the power of fun. Google appears to be the champion of fun—its website displays pictures of indoor gardens with lounge chairs and rowboats, pub-style lounges, meeting rooms with foosball tables, and bowling alleys at its

---

[176]David Abramis, "Play in Work: Childish Hedonism or Adult Enthusiasm?," *American Behavioral Scientist* 33, no. 3 (1990, https://doi.org/10/1177/000276429003 3003010..

various office locations around the world. According to GOBankin-gRates, Google is worth just under $280 billion, so maybe a fun culture does inspire great work.

" Employers React to Gen Z

They love to make work fun. "

Of course, not many companies can afford to install a bowling alley or pub at the office, so Baudville, an employee recognition company, offers up some inexpensive ideas in its ebook *52 Ways to Have Fun at Work*.[177] Consider giving an Elastigirl figure to someone who has shown flexibility, a pair of cheap sunglasses for a bright idea, a rubber ball to someone who has bounced back from a challenge, or fun-size pieces of candy to sweeten someone's day.

Just be careful that you don't *require* employees to engage in frivolity and do set some guidelines so the fun doesn't go too far. An *Economist* article, "Down with Fun," pokes fun at this trend saying, "The most unpleasant thing about the fashion of fun is that it is mixed with a large dose of coercion. (Some workplaces) don't merely celebrate wackiness. They more or less require it. Compulsory fun is nearly always cringe-making."[178]

To keep from crossing the line, focus on innovative ways to create an atmosphere where employees feel comfortable and appreciated. They will have more fun and you may have more profits.

Encourage Friendships at Work

"Without friends, no one would want to live, even if he had all other goods." Aristotle wrote this sentiment, and I couldn't agree more.

For example, I recently met a friend for coffee, and my day was

[177]Baudville, *52 Ways to Have Fun at Work*, accessed June 26, 2020, https://whatsfor-funegypt.files.wordpress.com/2013/01/pdfs.pdf.
[178]*Economist*, "Down with Fun," September 16, 2010, https://www.economist.com/business/2010/09/16/down-with-fun.

brighter because my friend did what he always does: listened intently to my account of my recent mishaps, offered supportive comments, and made me feel better about life in general.

According to social psychologists, my mental and physical well-being can be enhanced by my friends in my life. Dr. Karen Dill-Shackleford, author, social psychologist, professor at the Fielding Graduate University, and blogger for *Psychology Today*, says such friendships are important because they "fill our need for belonging. Our friends give us someone with whom to discuss our ideas, beliefs, and problems. These are needs that we can't meet on our own."[179]

" Employers React to Gen Z

Once they became comfortable in their jobs, they began socializing more than I'd like. **"**

Obviously, friendships are important, and research indicates that having friends at work is vitally important. According to the study "Work-Based Predictors of Mortality," employees with "high levels of peer social support" tend to live longer.[180]

Work-based friendships are also beneficial to employers, according to Tom Rath, author of *Vital Friends: The People You Can't Afford to Live Without*. Based in part on research conducted by the Gallup organization, Rath's book indicates that employees who have a best friend at work are seven times more likely to be engaged with their work, which is good for business.[181]

Of course, there can be drawbacks to workplace friendships. Employers worry that employees will spend too much time socializing

---

[179]Karen Dill-Shackleford, "SocialJane: Hot Spot for Gal Pals," *Psychology Today*, April 27, 2010, https://www.psychologytoday.com/us/blog/how-fantasy-becomes-reality/201004/socialjane-hot-spot-gal-pals.

[180]Arie Shirom, Sharon Toker, Yasmin Alkaly, Orit Jacobson, and Ran Balicer, "Work-Based Predictors of Mortality: A 20-Year Follow-Up of Healthy Employees," *Health Psychology* 30, no. 3 (2011): 268–75, https://doi.org/10.1037/a0023138.

[181]Tom Rath, *Vital Friends: The People You Can't Afford to Live Without* (New York: Gallup Press, 2006).

instead of working or that friends will cover for inappropriate behavior (such as clocking in or out for the other). Supervisors who get too friendly with their subordinates are sometimes more lenient with them, which creates a sense of unfairness, and the end of a friendship can create tension in the office.

So, how should you approach friendships at work?

Recognize that a certain amount of office camaraderie is good for business and that you shouldn't put a damper on small doses of personal chitchat and benign jokes. However, you should let employees know when it appears that their personal relationships are interfering with productivity or professionalism and intervene if necessary.

Remember that most of your Gen Z employees have little workplace experience, so they may not realize when they are crossing those professional boundaries. Show them how to draw the lines between work and friendships.

Also be careful about becoming too friendly with your employees because it can lead to all kinds of problems, such as the perception of favoritism, a reluctance to hold your friends accountable or give honest feedback, and the possibility of sharing things you shouldn't. Even though the title of her article is "How to Be Friends with Your Employees (Without Crossing the Line)," Wanda Thibodeaux advises, "In most cases, you're better off if employees feel good around you but give the title of 'best buddy' to someone else."[182]

In short, friendships at work are good for everyone involved, as long as they don't interfere with work.

---

[182]Wanda Thibodeaux, "How to Be Friends with Your Employees (Without Crossing the Line)," *Inc.*, accessed June 26, 20, https://www.inc.com/wanda-thibodeaux/finding-balance-between-being-an-employees-friend-being-a-good-boss.html.

Kat's Take

Gen Zers, being extremely collaborative, may expect that they are going to be friends with most of their coworkers and even their supervisors. There is an expectation that everyone will get along, that everyone will be close, and that you'll have fun together.

Naturally, this attitude invites a blurring of lines between friendship and professionalism that might cause problems later. And your Gen Z workers might not know how to handle either personal or professional conflicts.

Provide simple training on what is professional behavior and what is not. And be especially careful not to be too friendly with your Gen Z employees, who may have a harder time discerning your intentions. Make sure you keep a clear line in place to avoid confusion.

Celebrate—But Be Wise about It

Some people feel their birthday is just another day and want no kind of recognition for simply staying alive another year. I'm not one of those people. I want everyone around me to celebrate the day I was born, and I like to be in the office on my birthday so I can get as much public recognition as possible. I want my coworkers to decorate my office, write something meaningful in a card chosen especially for me, and present me with a chocolate peanut-butter cheesecake with a lighted candle on top.

Fortunately, I work in an organization that has a birthday club, which ensures that I will get my office decorated, a signed card, and a cake. You're probably thinking that I received either way too much or way too little attention as a child. Perhaps, but lots of employees like to celebrate birthdays, personal milestones, such as getting married or having a baby, and holidays at work. And there are several business reasons you should get the party started.

First, celebrating special events tells employees that you care about them as people, and appropriate celebrations can add to an atmosphere of fun at work. When you celebrate only workplace accomplishments (such as a big sale), you imply that employees are valued only for what they produce. Employers who show they personally care about their employees are usually rewarded with employees who care about them, and that caring is demonstrated through increased productivity, morale, and loyalty.

Next, gathering employees together for a celebration helps to create a sense of camaraderie and encourage friendships. Employees are usually chatting during the event, which helps them get to know each other and connect. These personal connections usually help them work better together and lead to a decrease in workplace conflicts. Finally, allowing employees to take a break from the routine helps them to feel refreshed and alert when they return to work, creating energy and engagement.

Of course, when celebrating anything other than work at work, you should take some steps to ensure that these occasions don't become unhappy ones:

- **Ask if employees want to celebrate.** Some people don't celebrate their birthdays or holidays for personal or religious reasons. For birthday celebrations, don't announce ages or allow party paraphernalia that are derogatory toward aging people.
- **Ask about favorites.** If serving food, ask about food preferences or allergies. And it's best to steer clear of alcoholic beverages at work.
- **Be consistent.** Hurt feelings can result when you celebrate one employee's birthday with cake and candles in the conference room but drop off a card at another employee's desk. Also, allow all employees (not just some) to recognize their religious holidays.
- **Keep it clean.** Remind employees that cards, presents, entertainment, and holiday clothing should be appropriate for the workplace.
- **Allow employees to opt out.** Don't require anyone to participate in activities that make them uncomfortable or give them a hard time if they decide not to join in.

Employers aren't required to celebrate anything at work. However, those who share special occasions with their employees tend to be rewarded for their efforts. Perhaps that's worth the cost of a few decorations, a card, and a cake.

Pets at Work? Really?

I fell in love with Hazel the moment I saw her. It wasn't her beautiful brown eyes, silky black hair, or pretty face that did me in. It's just that puppies always have that effect on me. I'm certainly not unique in that respect, and most of my coworkers quickly fell for her too.

When my colleague Justin Thorn started bringing Hazel to work, he said people stopped by his office more often. "I know people were coming by just to see Hazel, but then they ended up talking to me. So, I got to know my coworkers a lot better, which was a good thing. She helped us bond."

Most of us visited Hazel when we were stressed. "People came to see her because they needed their puppy love," said Justin. It's true that just a few minutes of doggy kisses and tummy rubs made us feel better, and we returned to work in a happier mood. Hazel increased our morale, decreased our stress, and made our workplace a happier environment.

Lots of studies have shown dogs and other pets are generally good for the workplace because they have the same effect on most people that Hazel had on us. That's why about 7 percent of US employers allow pets at work, according to the Society for Human Resource Management.

Kat's Take

Lots of colleges and universities now bring puppies to campus during midterm and finals week to lower anxiety in students during the toughest part of the year. Often sponsored by the local SPCA, puppies are brought into a certain area on campus where any student can spend time playing and petting them. In fact, some places, like Stephens College in Missouri, allow pets on campus. If students don't have a pet to bring with them, they can foster one from the local SPCA.

Gen Zers have increasingly seen animals used as therapy and/or support animals for different medical or mental conditions. The thought of animals in the workplace probably won't be odd to them, as they have most likely seen friends or classmates with emotional support animals.

In fact, Gen Z employees may ask if they can bring their pets to work. Or they might have an emotional support animal that they will expect you to accommodate.

Potential Pet Problems

Before allowing employees to bring their pets to work, you do have some things to consider, as Jennifer Lonoff Schiff discusses in "14 Rules for Creating a Bring-Your-Dog-to-Work Policy":

- Not everyone is an animal lover, and some people are allergic to animals. Ensure that all your employees are on board with the pets-at-work idea before you allow a tail in the door.
- Accidents happen. I'm not just talking about puppies peeing on

the carpet. Scared animals sometimes bite and scratch. Be sure your insurance will cover these things or have pet owners commit to coverage.

- Pets can be distracting. I took Hazel into a workshop I was facilitating at our office, which was a big mistake because everyone was more interested in her than in my training. So, allowing pets into all work areas or to roam free might be unwise. Also, having them at work all day every day might be too much of a distraction for their owners, so consider having pet-free zones and pet-free days.

- We don't all get along. Allowing more than one pet at work at a time might lead to fighting among animals. Determining who gets to bring their pet to work and who doesn't might lead to fighting among employees. Try establishing a "one-pet-at-a-time" policy and allow employees to take turns.

- What's on the floor will be chewed or eaten. Just like baby-proofing a home, you'll need to pet-proof your business. Ensure that computer cables and the like do not turn into chew toys.

- Not everyone is a good pet owner. Pets might not have up-to-date shots, might have fleas, or might be ill. Also, just like some people don't clean up after themselves in the break room, not everyone cleans up after their pets. Before you allow pets in the workplace, create clear expectations for employees who bring their pets to work.[183]

To successfully integrate pets into the workplace, Schiff suggests creating a pet committee to address the issues above, create pet policies, and ensure accountability. This might sound a bit bureaucratic, but just winging it and hoping everything works out could lead to unpleasantness for the pets and their people.[184]

Many people consider their pets to be cherished members of their family. Done right, inviting employees to bring their pets to work could result in a happier, healthier work family.

---

[183]Jennifer Lonoff Schiff, "14 Rules for Creating a Bring-Your-Dog-to-Work Policy," CIO, November 2, 2015, https://www.cio.com/article/3000115/14-rules-for-creating-a-bring-your-dog-to-work-policy.html.

[184]Ibid.

CHAPTER 26

EQUIP YOUR LEADERS

When people discover that I provide leadership training, they often tell me that being a good leader just requires common sense. I typically reply that common sense is not so common (another tip of the hat to Voltaire) and what is common sense to one person is not necessarily common sense to others.

Furthermore, people are frequently promoted to leadership positions because they are technically competent. Then they (and others) discover that being a good leader requires a different skill set—one they often don't have. Most people need to be taught how to be good leaders. Unfortunately, few employers invest in providing their management picks with the knowledge and skills they need to be effective.

Kat's Take

Gen Zers, having worked in teams more than previous generations in school, have also been given more leadership training at school or through extracurricular activities than previous generations. But the leadership training they've been given is most likely different from the commonsense leadership training Baby Boomers or Gen X received in everyday life.

For example, you might have inadvertently learned leadership skills from your group of friends when you realized that no one wanted to play with you when you were constantly bossing them around. You realized you had to adjust your tactics. Or maybe you had to build your own team to avoid being left out or had other experiences that taught you practical skills.

Gen Zers have learned leadership more from school and books than previous generations. As such, they might have more knowledge about what makes a good leader but not a lot of practical application of that knowledge, unless they were in structured activities at school where they were planning projects or leading a club or team.

Leadership training should address the following areas.

Legal Knowledge

People in any kind of leadership position make decisions that can have legal consequences. Without training, they might make decisions that land their employer in court.

For example, during the pandemic lockdown, employees had a legal right to take time off work to care for a child whose school was closed. If a leader was unaware of that emergency legislation and denied an employee the time off, that would be a violation of that statute. Failure to provide statutory time off work for a variety of reasons often gets employers sued.

In addition to leave rights, legal training for leaders should include information about wage and hour issues (things for which employees must be paid); reasonable accommodations (for religion, disabilities, and medical conditions); employee privacy; lawful hiring, disciplining, and terminating; safety; and, of course, the big three: harassment, discrimination, and retaliation.

Interpersonal Skills

"Our supervisors can probably have more influence on our productivity, worker absenteeism, product quality, morale of our workforce, labor relations and cost reduction than any other group in the company," the vice president of personnel at a manufacturing company was quoted as saying in an article in *Harvard Business Review*.[185] Indeed, the way leaders communicate and interact with employees makes a huge difference in the results (or lack thereof) they get from them.

Leaders must possess a variety of interpersonal skills to inspire employees to perform. Because many of these skills do not come naturally to people, they need to be taught.

Managerial Skills

People in leadership positions often need to know how to plan, organize, direct, coordinate, and control the work being done. This requires a broad view of the organization and goes way beyond leaders just being able to do their jobs well. For example, an accountant might be promoted to a supervisory position because of excellent accounting skills; however, the promotion requires planning, directing, and controlling the work of others.

Being good at one's job is an important criterion for being promoted to a leadership position. However, being a good leader usually requires obtaining more knowledge and learning new skills.

Personality Styles

PDI Ninth House, a global leadership solutions group, has researched many aspects of leadership skills and determined the top three behaviors necessary for an employee to progress to leadership positions: influence

---

[185]W. Earl Sasser and Frank S. Leonard, "Let First-Level Supervisors Do Their Job," *Harvard Business Review*, March 1980, https://hbr.org/1980/03/let-first-level-supervisors-do-their-job.

over others, a high-energy level, and a take-charge approach.[186]

In my opinion, some of these behaviors come naturally to some people while others don't. For example, people who are naturally good team players often struggle with taking charge and telling others what to do. Therefore, to be effective, supervisors may need to learn to do what does not come naturally. One-on-one coaching can help with that.

"While personality traits are largely hard-wired, with proper coaching and focus, organizations can help current and future leaders accelerate positive behaviors," says Joy Hazucha, PhD, in the PDI Ninth House article.[187] I have also found this to be true.

The coach and the supervisor work together to

- identify specific behaviors that the supervisor needs to emphasize or avoid;
- create strategies to encourage appropriate behavior;
- implement the strategies; and
- debrief to report on results of implementing the strategies.

Employers and HR professionals can use this simple but effective coaching method to help supervisors engage in the behaviors necessary to be effective. Because just doing what comes naturally usually doesn't get the job done.

Managing Conflict

Helping to manage the conflict that inevitably arises in any organization is one way good leaders can have a huge impact in your organization.

Some business leaders find conflict essential. According to business professors and textbook authors David Whetten and Kim Cameron,

---

[186]PDI Ninth House, "PDI Ninth House Pulse on Leaders Research Reveals Surprising Differences in Key Personality Traits Necessary for Executive-Level Advancements," August 28, 2012, https://www.prnewswire.com/news-releases/pdi-ninth-house-pulse-on-leaders-research-reveals-surprising-differences-in-key-personality-traits-necessary-for-executive-level-advancement-167676855.html.

[187]Ibid.

"Conflict is the lifeblood of vibrant, progressive, stimulating organizations. It sparks creativity, stimulates innovation, and encourages personal improvement."[188]

Many other business authors and social science researchers believe most people dislike conflict and tend to avoid it. That includes many people in management and supervisory positions whose jobs usually require them to be involved in resolving conflicts.

People tend to avoid conflict for a variety of reasons, including their family backgrounds, cultural norms, personality styles, and personal experience. However, conflict in the workplace is inevitable, and managers and supervisors must know how to handle it effectively to get the best results from their employees.

Andrew Grove, former president of Intel, is quoted by Whetten and Cameron as saying,

> Many managers seem to think it is impossible to tackle anything or anyone head-on, even in business. By contrast, we at Intel believe that it is the essence of corporate health to bring a problem out into the open as soon as possible, even if this entails a confrontation. Dealing with conflicts lies at the heart of managing any business. As a result, confrontation—facing issues about which there is disagreement—can be avoided only at the manager's peril.[189]

" Employers React to Gen Z

Face-to-face interactions, difficult conversations, confrontation, and conflict are extra challenging for them and avoided whenever possible. Watching them navigate these situations is painful and presents ongoing coaching opportunities. "

---

[188]David Whetten and Kim Cameron *Developing Management Skills*, 10th ed. (Upper Saddle River, NJ: Pearson, 2020).
[189]Ibid.

How do employers, managers, and supervisors disagree without turning the office into a bloodbath? According to Kathleen Eisenhardt and her colleagues at Stanford University, "The challenge is to encourage members of management . . . to argue without destroying their ability to work together." [190] In their article in the *Harvard Business Review*, the authors say coworkers must adhere to several key "rules of engagement":

- Work with more, rather than less, information.
- Focus on the facts.
- Develop multiple alternatives.
- Share commonly agreed-upon goals.
- Inject humor into the decision process.
- Maintain a balanced power structure.
- Resolve issues without forcing consensus.[191]

Helping others resolve their conflicts involves many of the same rules of engagement, according to Whetten and Cameron. Follow these steps to mediate a conflict:

- Select the most appropriate setting for the meeting.
- Set ground rules (only one person talks at a time, etc.).
- Gather information on participants' perceptions of the problem causing the conflict.
- Maintain a neutral position.
- Have participants agree on the problem.
- Help participants brainstorm possible solutions.
- Ensure that participants make a plan to resolve the conflict.
- Check back later to ensure that the conflict has been resolved.[192]

This format is so easy that a fourth-grader could use it. In fact, many schools are teaching students how to mediate conflicts, and a fourth-grade mediator from Wilmette, Illinois, explained that "we help kids

---

[190]Kathleen Eisenhardt, Jean Kahwajy, and L. J. Bourgeois, "How Management Teams Can Have a Good Fight," *Harvard Business Review*, July-August 1997, https://hbr.org/1997/07/how-management-teams-can-have-a-good-fight.

[191]Ibid.

[192]Whetten and Cameron, *Developing Management Skills*.

who are fighting talk about their problems. Some people think kids can't help other kids solve their problems. But we can. It's real neat because we don't work out things for kids who are fighting. They solve their own problems, and we help."[193]

When leaders learn to effectively handle conflict in the workplace, conflict will not hurt the organization but can improve it by fostering open communication, innovation, and collaboration. Indeed, in his book *Good to Great*, Jim Collins agrees that conflict is part of the perfecting and exploratory process, used to confront and challenge ideas.[194] Or as psychoanalyst M. Esther Harding aptly put it, "Conflict is the beginning of consciousness."[195]

Kat's Take

Starting around 2016, we started noticing an odd trend among the high school students we were working with: students would suddenly stop responding to emails, texts, or phone calls. Every text was ignored. Every email was ignored. If their voicemail was set up, either it was full or messages went unanswered. Out of—seemingly—nowhere, students would go missing in action, and we would eventually have to call their parents to make sure the teens were okay. Parents would be puzzled and would push for their students to get in touch with us or might come to a meeting with their student.

We had not seen this kind of behavior in previous high school students, but we learned that it was becoming so normal that it had been given its own label: ghosting.

Ghosting is the slang term for simply disappearing off the face of the earth and never talking to someone again. I've talked to other employers, parents, and professionals to find that yes, it's an

---

[193]Ellen R. Delisio, "Responsive Classroom Practices Teach the Whole Child," Education World, 2011, accessed June 26, 2020, https://www.educationworld.com/a_issues/schools/schools016.shtml.

[194]Jim Collins, *Good to Great: Why Some Companies Make the Leap and Others Don't* (New York: Harper Business, 2001).

[195]BrainyQuote, "M. Esther Harding Quotes," raccessed October 3, 2020, https://www.brainyquote.com/quotes/m_esther_harding_178092.

odd trait that is, for the most part, confined to Gen Z.

Doing more investigation, reading a lot, and asking my own clients, I found that the answer to why students were ghosting me is a bit more complicated than they simply did not want to talk to me about their futures.

Gen Z grew up with technology, specifically smartphones, where picking up the phone and talking to someone or handling a conflict face-to-face is no longer necessary. You can end a relationship with a text (many in this generation do), a direct message on Instagram, or more cruelly, as a public announcement on social media. You are no longer required to confront people when you have a problem with them. And when you send them a message, you don't have to directly witness their anger, or frustration, or sadness. Technology can act as the buffer.

In addition, Gen Z has grown up with fewer opportunities for confrontations. If you have a bullying problem, it's probably online. Parents or other adults step in during school or sports to rectify conflicts. So, we are looking at an entire generation that has had little experience with conflict and rarely seen the impact of its words on someone else.

Because we could use parents as a conduit of communication, we eventually managed to get most of our "ghosting" students back in the office. When we did, we discovered that the students began ignoring us because they were afraid they had disappointed us. Or that we were mad at them. Or they didn't know what to do and didn't know how to ask. Anxiety played a big part of their lack of response. They simply did not know how to deal with the situation, so they stopped answering.

After we began to understand this behavior, we began reminding students that we're trying to help them plan their path and that it's normal to feel anxious about the process. We encouraged them to communicate their feelings and let us know about their struggles. We started teaching more about communication and how to have difficult conversations.

As a result, ghosting went down and communication went up.

Students began communicating more, reaching out more. They began telling us when they were scared or when they were confused and anxious.

Although I'm working primarily with teenagers who are still growing, I've had similar experiences with Gen Z employees as well. I had one employee simply disappear one day. She walked out and never came back. Through social media, I was able to determine that she was alive and well. But it's been more than two years now and I have never heard a word from this former employee. Not an email. Not a text. Not a phone call.

Prepare for this with your Gen Z employees. You will need to teach them how to manage conflict and how to improve communication lines. Let them know that it's okay to be honest about struggles or problems. When we started focusing on increasing communication among employees and between employees and management, we saw an increase in morale and communication.

Teach Leaders How to Communicate

When Jack Dorsey cofounded Twitter, he changed the way we communicate. Ironically, Dorsey admitted in a *60 Minutes* interview that one of his biggest weaknesses is communication, and he indicated he was even ousted from the company he cofounded because of his lack of communication skills.[196]

Dorsey is certainly not alone in being a boss with poor communication skills. In his study of really bad bosses, University of Toledo professor Clinton O. Longenecker identifies many characteristics that are related to poor communication skills, such as

- misrepresenting the truth and lying;
- failing to create clear direction and performance expectations;
- feedback and recognition issues; and

---

[196] *60 Minutes*, "The Innovator," March 17, 2013, https://www.cbsnews.com/news/the-innovator-jack-dorsey-17-03-2013/.

- bad communication skills and practices.[197]

"   Employers React to Gen Z

Everything from their body language to tone of voice says, "Please be gentle, for I am fragile." "

There are two primary problems when people in positions of power are poor communicators: they cause employees to leave and they cause lawsuits.

Your leaders must be trained to do the following:

- Tell the truth, especially in documentation. Sugarcoating the truth on a performance evaluation and then firing a person for poor performance has led to lawsuits.
- Be clear and direct yet tactful and respectful. Failure to do so causes people to leave. As the saying goes, people don't quit companies, they quit their supervisors.
- Avoid unpleasant surprises by speaking up. One of my favorite sayings is "Silence equals permission." If employees do something wrong, their supervisor needs to say something. Not saying anything until someone is fired causes unpleasant surprises and inspires revenge from the ousted employee.
- Think before hitting Send. They need to be aware that their emails could end up as trial exhibits.
- Always remember that their communication can and will be used against them. Attorney A. Kevin Troutman says it best: "Unguarded, inappropriate, or 'joking' comments can and do come back to haunt supervisors who forget this. When an employment relationship goes bad, seemingly innocuous comments often emerge. Comments made in jest rarely look good

---

[197]Business and Legal Resources, "Study Identifies 12 Characteristics of Really Bad Bosses," HR.BLR.com, April 19, 2012, https://hr.blr.com/HR-SBT/Study-Identifies-12-Characteristics-of-Really-Bad-.

in front of a jury."[198] (See appendix E for more information on bad word choices.)

Composer John Powell says, "Communication works for those who work at it."[199] Because communicating effectively requires time and energy, it is work. Is it worth the effort? Dorsey probably thinks so. He improved his, was invited back to Twitter, and is making an ungodly amount of money.

Improving the communication skills of your company's leaders might not make you rich, but it will certainly help you retain good employees and reduce the risk of spending your time and energy on lawsuits instead of on your business.

---

[198] A. Kevin Troutman, "Top 10 Supervisory Survival Tools for 2013," Fisher Phillips, accessed June 26, 2020, https://www.lexology.com/library/detail. aspx?g=ef28511a-9f3a-4cb5-9e3d-e005b812bc4d.

[199] John Powell, quotefancy, accessed October 3, 2020, https://quotefancy.com/ quote/1575455/John-Powell-Communication-works-for-those-who-work-at-it.

AVOID PROBLEMS

Section 6 Takeaways

- Identify harassment and discrimination.
- Create policies and training to prevent harassment and discrimination.
- Understand sexual harassment.
- Respect gender identity issues.
- Address office relationships.
- Be aware of racism and cultural differences.
- Combat implicit bias.
- Allow religious and political expression—within limits.
- Allow for complaints and know how to handle them.

CHAPTER 27

HARASSMENT AND DISCRIMINATION

A few years ago, I was a judge at a Virtual Enterprises competition in the human resources category. Teams of high school students were given various workplace scenarios to analyze and decide how they would handle those situations as HR personnel. When they presented their conclusions, almost every team concluded that its scenario involved harassment, even though few of those scenarios met the legal standards of harassment.

Gen Zers grew up with the term "harassment" in their vocabulary and, in my experience, tend to think they are being harassed whenever they don't like how they are being treated. Of course, they're not the only ones. I've spent a significant amount of time over the past decade conducting harassment prevention workshops, and I can tell you that a lot of employees—regardless of their age—feel any negative treatment is harassment.

That's why it's critical that employers provide annual harassment prevention training, even if it's not required in your state. Making sure all employees know exactly what behavior constitutes harassment helps them know what their rights and responsibilities are. And explaining what is *not* harassment can help prevent frivolous complaints, especially

for your new Gen Z employees who may have an overly broad definition of harassment.

Training material should include your organization's antiharass-
ment policy, examples of inappropriate behavior, and instructions for
filing a complaint. It should also make clear that it is illegal to retaliate
against someone who files a complaint.

" Employers React to Gen Z

When they are disciplined, they feel as though they are being
harassed.

"

Fortunately for employers, harassment is not measured by feelings but by standards set through federal and state agencies and the
courts. The gold standard is set by the Equal Employment Opportunity
Commission (EEOC), the federal agency that accepts, investigates, and
prosecutes harassment, discrimination, and retaliation complaints in the
workplace. And the EEOC says that harassment is unwelcome conduct
directed at someone or about someone because he's in a protected class,
because of the belief that he's in a protected class, or because he asso-
ciates with someone in a protected class. Discrimination comes in two
forms: adverse treatment and being adversely impacted because of one's
protected-class status.

Holding employees accountable for doing their jobs is not harassment. Micromanaging is not harassment. Even yelling at employees is
not harassment—unless they're being yelled at because of their status
in a protected class. In other words, a lot of things that might be bad
management techniques are not necessarily harassment.

Know the Law!

The original federal protected classes—race, color, religion, national origin, and sex—were created through the signing of the Civil Rights Act in 1964. Additional protected classes were established through subsequent legislation, such as the Americans with Disabilities Act.

States can have additional protected classes and many of them do. My home state of California currently has seventeen under the Fair Employment and Housing Act. It's critical that you know the protected classes in your state and, if you are in a position of authority, ensure that harassment and discrimination don't happen in your workplace.

Create a Policy

Federal law does not require employers to have a policy explicitly banning harassment and discrimination, and states vary as to whether such a policy is required or recommended. Regardless, it's a good idea to put in writing that harassment and discrimination are unacceptable at your workplace. In your policy, provide numerous examples of each, describe how to file a complaint, and explain that employees will not be retaliated against for complaining.

Talk to employees about the policy—explain why you're implementing it and answer any questions. Have them sign a form stating they understand the policy and will comply with it, and put the signed form in their personnel file. Consider discussing the policy and asking employees to indicate their intention to follow it on an annual basis.

You should provide examples of harassment and discrimination in your company policy. Because Gen Z likes to communicate electronically, be sure to include examples of how things like emails, instant messaging, texting, and sexting can lead to accusations of harassment.

In its decision on a textual harassment case, New York's Kings County Court noted that "along with their many benefits, [technological developments] bring with them ever greater potential for abuse."[200] Employees should be reminded that sending racy emails and texts can cause serious problems for them as well as their employer. They should pause to consider whether the thrill of sending the message is really worth the risk.

Provide Training

Few states require employers to provide harassment and discrimination training to their supervisors, much less their employees. Regardless, I encourage you to do it to protect your employees and your company. However, don't just have them watch a video and call it good.

Kat's Take

I think it's important for employers to realize that you can't just show old sexual harassment prevention videos to Gen Z and expect you've solved all problems. In a world of dirty emojis, Tinder, Snapchat, texting, and other avenues for harassment, it's better to have a full training and address a number of possible, modern scenarios.

Watching training videos from the 1990s where the harassment is way too obvious won't help your employees—especially the youngest ones. They need to know what to do if they receive a dirty emoji from a supervisor. Will they be retaliated against if they report it?

What should they do if no one in their department listens to them? Clearly addressing modern scenarios with a full training will help prevent problems later.

---

[200]Associated Press, "Stalkers Turn to 'Textual' Harassment to Antagonize Victims," *Daily News*, March 5, 2009, https://www.nydailynews.com/news/money/stalkers-turn-textual-harassment-antagonize-victims-article-1.369430.

When employers are accused of harassment or discrimination, their training to prevent both is usually scrutinized. (See appendix F for three court cases that emphasized the need for more than just video watching.)

Employers should know that courts often analyze the effectiveness of employers' training and the qualifications of trainers as key components of their prevention efforts of harassment and discrimination. Therefore, inadequate training or unqualified trainers can be a liability for employers. For more information on training and trainer requirements, contact the EEOC or your state's equal employment department.

I frequently provide workplace sexual harassment prevention training because California, where I live and work, has mandated such training. See appendix G for more information about California's training mandates.

How Long?

Employers sometimes want to know how long they need to continue providing training. My answer? You can stop providing training when harassment and discrimination are no longer an issue.

Several years ago, I wrote an article that was published in the *Bakersfield Californian* warning employers not to use videos as their primary tool for harassment prevention training. I was surprised when someone wrote a letter to the editor expressing his disdain about the article and harassment prevention training in general.

The writer said my article suggested "that businesses need to provide even more laborious and redundant training" and asked "when is it going to be enough?" He continued by saying "the majority of employees 'get it'" and the "laws aimed at preventing these workplace distractions (his term for harassment) had merit years ago, but now, more often than not, they are used by employees with personal agendas."[201]

In his defense, he wrote the letter before the #MeToo movement, when hundreds of women and dozens of men publicly came forward

---

[201]Letter to the editor, "Harassment Not Always Clear," *Bakersfield Californian*, March 23, 2016 https://www.bakersfield.com/opinion/harassment-not-always-clear/article_82258bf2-7095-513b-aa7e-e41875ebb45c.html 1.

after years of silence to tell their stories of being sexually harassed. Who could imagine that all these people had been subjected to sexual harassment and never said anything about it? Well, I've worked in human resources for almost twenty years, so I wasn't surprised.

I feel confident in saying that every woman has at least one story of being subjected to unwanted verbal, visual, or physical conduct of a sexual nature at work (which is the definition of sexual harassment). I've got a few stories myself, about both male and female supervisors and coworkers. None of my stories involve egregious conduct; however, they all involve behavior that made me uncomfortable and that should not have happened in the workplace. And like those who finally came forward to set off the #MeToo movement, I never said anything about the inappropriate behavior to the person subjecting me to it or to someone in a position of authority, mostly because the perpetrator was usually a person in a position of authority.

Perhaps, as the letter writer stated, the majority of employees understand that they shouldn't engage in verbal, visual, or physical conduct of a sexual nature at work. Unfortunately, many employees don't.

"The insidious complaints or accusations made by (system-playing) employees probably outnumber true violations," according to the letter writer.[202] As someone who constantly receives legal updates regarding harassment lawsuits from various organizations, I disagree.

The letter writer went on to say that because of harassment prevention training, "an employee is empowered by simply 'overhearing' something they feel is offensive. The system then begins to attack the unsuspecting violators, pushing the First Amendment aside in the process."[203]

Hopefully, harassment prevention training will help employees feel empowered to speak up when they overhear something they find offensive, instead of keeping quiet as I and so many others did. And, hopefully, there won't be unsuspecting violators because everyone will learn what they shouldn't say or do at work or around their coworkers. Finally, the First Amendment isn't pushed aside because the First Amendment

---

[202]Ibid.
[203]Ibid.

doesn't give us the right to say whatever we want to at work or away from it.

"What businesses, personnel professionals and the courts need to understand is that not everyone who cries wolf is a victim," the letter writer said.[204] That's true. That's also why employers and personnel professionals need to know how to conduct an investigation properly so those who are accused of wrongdoing have an opportunity to tell their side of the story.

The sad truth is that people are still being harassed at work (sexually and otherwise). Telling employers and employees what harassment is (and what it isn't), how to prevent it, and what to do if it happens should help to solve this problem.

The letter writer asked, "When is it going to be enough?"

Evidently, when harassment in the workplace is no longer—as he called it—a distraction.

The next several chapters examine various kinds of harassment and discrimination that can plague workplaces and cause all kinds of headaches for employers.

---

[204]Ibid.

CHAPTER 28

SEX AND GENDER ISSUES

Because of the #MeToo movement, most people are aware that sexual harassment has long been a problem in the workplace; however, researchers disagree over whether different generations tend to view it differently.

In her article "The #MeToo Generation Gap Is a Myth," Anna North points out several examples of those differences from writers of different ages who criticized each other for their definitions or descriptions of harassment or unacceptable behavior. Yet despite these examples, North cites a survey to conclude that "older and younger women generally agree on what behaviors constitute sexual harassment."[205]

North may be right, but my own experiences lead me to believe that women from different generations do define sexual harassment in different ways. And if women disagree on what behaviors can be called harassment, how can we expect women and men to have the same definition?

That's why it's so important to define harassment—sexual and otherwise—and determine how to handle it at work.

---

[205] Anna North, "The #MeToo Generation Gap Is a Myth," *Vox*, March 20, 2018, https://www.vox.com/2018/3/20/17115620/me-too-sexual-harassment-sex-abuse-poll.

Sexual Harassment

Employees who are subjected to unwanted verbal, visual, or physical conduct of a sexual nature that interferes with their ability to do their job are being sexually harassed. This conduct can take many forms and may come from supervisors, coworkers, or even clients and customers.

In her article "The 'New' Sexual Harassment," Kiri Blakely says, "Much of the problem is that newer technology—e-mail, IM, texting or posting on social-networking sites—makes it much easier for comments to be misconstrued on many levels." For example, "If you admire an employee's new haircut while she is in your office, she can read your tone and body language; and you can read hers. However, a late-night text message admiring your employee's new haircut can take on a lascivious tone, even if that is not the intention."[206]

Misunderstandings aside, lots of people are using technology to overtly express their desires for another, and such behavior can constitute harassment. A former Fort Lauderdale Hooters waitress sued the restaurant, claiming a manager sent her explicit text messages and photos, a practice known as "sexting."

As text messaging has become more prevalent, so has "textual harassment," in which senders use text messages to antagonize recipients. A study by the US Justice Department found that 25 percent of stalking or harassment victims were cyberstalked through email or texting.[207]

Your employees' emails, sexting, textual harassment, and cyberstalking may impact you because employers are responsible for providing a harassment-free environment; therefore, if this behavior takes place at work—and sometimes even outside work—an employer could be liable.

In addition to messages sent via company electronics, employees should know that an inappropriate email or text sent from a personal phone can be used against them. According to attorney Brian Lerner in

[206]Kiri Blakeley, "The 'New' Sexual Harassment," *Forbes*, August 9, 2009, https://www.forbes.com/2009/08/06/sexual-harassment-office-forbes-woman-leadership-affairs.html#1b3a389d7886.

[207]US Department of Justice, *Bureau of Justice Statistics*, "Stalking," accessed June 4, 2020, https://www.bjs.gov/index.cfm?ty=tp&tid=973.

the *Tampa Bay Times*, "Most employees realize now that emails don't go away. They also should know texts can be pulled from a phone number for documentation of a harassment case."[208]

Employees should be told that if they are subjected to inappropriate electronic messages, they should contact their supervisor or human resources personnel.

Gender Identity

You should provide training to everyone in your organization to help them avoid harassment or discrimination based on gender identity. Gen Z is typically familiar with the concept of gender identity and usually doesn't blink an eye about definitions and concepts that may make older workers highly uncomfortable. "Today's teens are more gender-nonconforming and gender-fluid than any previous generation, and it's serving them well," says Amelia Edelman in her article "It's Official: Gen Z Is Rejecting the Gender Binary & the World Needs to Follow Suit."[209]

For older workers, the concept of gender identity may be difficult to understand. So, I explain it to them by using a personal example:

I have different colored eyes—the right one is mostly brown and the left one is blue. This condition is called heterochromia iridum and is often genetic (in my case) or caused by injury. Although the condition has been noted for thousands of years (historical documents say Aristotle mentioned us and Alexander the Great was one of us), the California Department of Motor Vehicles (DMV) seems to think we don't exist.

The DMV gives everyone six eye colors to choose from—blue, green, hazel, gray, brown, or black—and you get to choose only one. But what if you have two eye colors, I once asked a DMV representative. Choose one, I was told. But my driver's license won't be correct if I choose only one, I argued. It really doesn't matter what eye color is on

---

[208]M. H. Pounds, "Technology Brings New Ways to Harass," *Tampa Bay Times*, September 1, 2009, https://www.tampabay.com/archive/2009/08/30/technology-brings-new-ways-to-harass/.

[209]Amelia Edelman, "It's Official: Gen Z Is Rejecting the Gender Binary & the World Needs to Follow Suit," SheKnows, October 18, 2019, https://www.sheknows.com/parenting/articles/2117014/gender-identity-gen-z/.

your license, the DMV rep said.

Well, here's a news flash for you—it matters to me.

Life is not easy when you're different from the majority of people and don't fit neatly into a category. I've been laughed at and teased ("You look like a Siberian husky!"), insulted ("Your eyes are weird!"), subjected to awkward questions ("What's wrong with your eyes?"), and given unwanted advice ("You should get colored contact lenses to make your eyes match"). Even so, I know my experiences pale in comparison to the treatment received by others who aren't easily slotted into our two gender categories.

Kat's Take

A number of colleges now ask students to provide more information about their identity and/or gender on their application. The University of California asks students to share more about their gender identity on its application, if they so choose. Many other college are following suit.

In addition, more student organizations in high schools and colleges encourage discussion on gender identity and sexual orientation, providing a safe space for those who are marginalized and a place for allies to learn and support students.

Most colleges now require students to take one or more courses that focus on diversity, encouraging students to further explore race, ethnicity, sexual identity, gender identity, and other elements that serve to educate and expand awareness.

Nonbinary Protections

People who are nonbinary do not identify as male or female or solely as one of those two genders. Like people with mismatched eyes, people who are nonbinary have always existed; there are references to a third gender among the earliest written records of Mesopotamia, and there are numerous examples of nonbinary genders throughout history. Although the concept may seem new to many Americans, according to a 2016 study by the Williams Institute (a think tank at UCLA Law School), approximately 1.4 million adults identify themselves as transgender and gender-nonbinary in the United States alone.[210]

When I mention at training classes that nonbinaries are protected from harassment and discrimination just as males and females are, someone usually expresses discomfort and/or disapproval with nonbinary persons. I then tell the participant about my mismatched eyes and how the government insists I choose a category that doesn't accurately reflect who I am. I explain that nonbinaries often face a similar situation—our government and society have made them choose a category (male or female) that doesn't accurately reflect who they are; however, this isn't a minor annoyance for them—they suffer greatly as a result.

For example, 56 percent of trans and gender-nonconforming teachers in an NPR Ed survey reported some form of workplace discrimination or harassment. Primarily this came from the administration or colleagues, not from their students. "I was horribly harassed by a coworker and very little was done about it," one nonbinary teacher said. "The focus was on making [the harasser] more comfortable."[211]

[210]Andrew R. Flores, Jody L. Herman, Gary J. Gates, Taylor N. T. Brown, "How Many Adults Identify as Transgender in the United States?," *UCLA School of Law Williams Institute*, June 2016, https://williamsinstitute.law.ucla.edu/publications/trans-adults-united-states/.

[211]Anya Kamenetz, "More Than Half of Transgender Teachers Surveyed Tell NPR They Are Harassed at Work," *National Public Radio*, March 8, 2018, https://www.npr.org/sections/ed/2018/03/08/575723226/more-than-half-of-transgender-teachers-face-workplace-harassment.

Gender Protections

The US Supreme Court ruled in 2020 that sexual orientation and gender identity are protected against discrimination, and the EEOC long ago stated that discrimination against individuals because of gender identity is in violation of Title VII of the Civil Rights Act of 1964.

The EEOC has also ruled on the following:

- Employers may not inquire about or require documentation or proof of an individual's sex, gender, gender identity, or gender expression as a condition of employment.
- Discrimination against applicants or employees based on any of the above is illegal.
- Employers must use an employee's preferred name and gender pronoun.
- Employers must permit employees to use the restroom that corresponds to the employee's gender identity or gender expression, regardless of the employee's sex at birth.
- Employees need comply only with the appearance, grooming, and dress standards of their gender identity.

In my trainings, I'm frequently asked, what if the above stipulations make other employees uncomfortable? I answer this way: Once upon a time, men didn't want to work with women because it made them uncomfortable. White people didn't want to work with people of color because it made them uncomfortable. Heterosexuals didn't want to work with gay people because it made them uncomfortable. Christians didn't want to work with non-Christians because it made them uncomfortable. We're usually uncomfortable when something is new to us. After a while, we usually figure out that people are people, regardless of what labels we put on them.

Categories are meant to simplify life, but sometimes they cause unnecessary damage by implying that something is wrong with people who don't fit neatly into them. If you identify strictly as male or female—good for you. However, lots of people don't, and they also have the right to live their lives as their true selves.

Interoffice Relationships

Although there is no law against employers or supervisors dating people who work for them, it can lead to a multitude of problems. (See appendix F for examples of lawsuits that have been filed when employers had—or attempted to have—sexual relationships with their subordinates.) A sexual relationship or the pursuit of one at work doesn't always lead to lawsuits. However, engaging in this type of behavior is risky business. Sexual harassment claims are often the result of an abuse of power by someone in a position of authority, but sometimes they are also the product of the ugly end of a consensual relationship.

Employers may implement a policy against supervisors having romantic relationships with the people they supervise in an attempt to prevent such lawsuits. I suggest implementing this kind of policy while also ensuring that supervisors understand the different kinds of sexual harassment and how they might find themselves paying a significant price for trying to mix pleasure with business.

Employers may *not* implement a policy that prevents coworkers from dating each other. However, they may require employees to sign a "love contract" that states they will not allow the relationship to interfere with their job or hold the employer liable if the relationship ends badly, making it difficult for the employees to work together. Feeling hostility from a former flame doesn't necessarily create a hostile work environment but can make the environment uncomfortable for many.

CHAPTER 29

RACE, CULTURE, AND BIAS

On May 31, 2020, George Floyd, a forty-six-year-old black man, was killed in Minneapolis when a white police officer pressed his knee into Floyd's neck for almost nine minutes while Floyd was handcuffed face down on the ground.

Also on May 31, 2020, Amy Cooper, a white woman, called the police in New York City, saying she was being threatened by Christian Cooper, a black man (no relation), who had asked her to leash her dog in Central Park.

On May 21, 2020, two white men were charged with killing Ahmaud Arbery, a black man, who had been jogging in their neighborhood in Georgia.

These are just a few examples of highly publicized incidents of black people being killed or harmed by white people in the United States that have set off massive protests and demands for change in the country. They have also sparked organizations and individuals around the country to embark on new examinations of racism and how to combat it.

"I'm not a racist. I did not mean to harm that man in any way," Amy Cooper said after the incident in Central Park.[212]

---

[212]Laura Ly, Amir Vera, and Brian Ries, "Dog Returned to White Woman Who Called Police on Black Man Bird-watching in Central Park, *CNN*, June 5, 2020, https://www.cnn.com/2020/06/05/us/amy-cooper-dog-returned-trnd/index.html.

Most of us like to think we are not racist; however, few of us are as innocent as we would like to be, and all of us harbor biases and blind spots. That's why it's so important for companies and organizations to go beyond legally sanctioned training on harassment and discrimination and seek to open people's eyes and minds.

Cultural Awareness

Be aware that race and culture are not the same thing. Therefore, cultural awareness workshops can be immensely useful in helping reduce friction in the workplace.

I participated in my first cultural awareness activity when I was in the fourth grade. Our teacher had all the students with brown or dark eyes stand on one side of the room and all the students with blue or light eyes stand on the other side. I stood in the middle of the two groups, not knowing where to go because of my different-colored eyes. Everyone stared at me, and the teacher, unprepared for this little snafu, fumbled around trying to figure out what to do. I don't remember what happened next, but I do remember learning that I didn't like cultural diversity activities.

Ironically, one of the things I do now is teach cultural awareness workshops. And I would venture to guess that most of the participants in those workshops are initially unhappy to be there. "Why do we have to listen to some lady drone on about respecting other cultures?" they probably wonder. "We already learned that in fourth grade!"

One reason such workshops are beneficial is that we often don't understand what culture is or what it does to us. Culture, according to Dictionary.com, is the sum total of ways of living built up by a group of human beings and transmitted from one generation to another. In other words, we are taught how to behave, what to value, and how to celebrate by the elders of our group.

I'm white and my culture taught me that it's okay to talk about money, that pets are valued family members who are welcome on the furniture, and that Christmas presents are to be opened on Christmas morning. My husband is also white, but his culture taught him that it is uncouth to talk about money, that pets are animals who live outside, and that Christmas presents are opened on Christmas Eve while eating pizza. Obviously, my husband was raised by heathens!

Of course I'm kidding about calling my husband's family heathens, but that's what our culture does to us—it teaches us that our way is the right way and people who do things differently are doing them wrong.

One workshop participant challenged me about that last statement a few years ago. She said she was very open-minded and so didn't think her way of doing things was always right and others were always wrong if they did things differently. I asked whether she thought everyone should be open-minded. She answered yes. I pointed out that thinking everyone should be open-minded like her was essentially a "my way is the right way" mentality too.

I ran into that participant about a year ago. She told me our conversation had been a mind-altering experience for her. That's what cultural awareness workshops can do.

Author Charles F. Glassman says, "In a few seconds, we judge another person and think we know them. When, the person we've lived with the longest, we still don't know very well—ourselves."[213]

We know that we're supposed to treat people of other cultures with respect—or at least not harass or discriminate against them. But do we realize the impact our own culture has had on our worldview? Do we realize how often we tend to disparage others (even when they're married to us) for doing things differently? The answer to those questions is usually no.

Very simply, cultural awareness workshops should mostly help us learn about

- the "rules" our culture taught us;
- the "rules" other people were taught;
- why our way is not always the best way;
- how we benefit from other ways; and
- the commonalities we share because of working together (mission, goals, etc.).

Becoming culturally aware begins with understanding that our rules are just that—ours—and that we see the world not as it is but as we are.

---

[213] Charles F. Glassman, Goodreads, accessed October 3, 2020, https://www.goodreads.com/quotes/7270046-in-a-few-seconds-we-judge-another-person-and-think.

Implicit Biases

I cannot tolerate intolerant people.

I'm probably biased against other people as well, I'm just not fully aware of it. That's something called implicit or unconscious bias. In 2019, employees at the more than eight thousand Starbucks in America learned something about it.

That's because Starbucks CEO Kevin Johnson decided to require all employees in the United States to receive training about implicit bias after a Philadelphia store manager called the police when two black men sat in her store for two minutes without making a purchase. The men were arrested for trespassing, and public outrage ensued. Training was scheduled with expertise provided by former US attorney general Eric Holder and Sherrilyn Ifill, president of the NAACP Legal Defense and Education Fund.[214] See appendix I for more information on that training.

According to Alexis McGill Johnson, "Implicit bias is our brains' automatic processing of negative stereotypes that have become embedded in our brains over time about particular groups of people oftentimes without our conscious awareness."[215] Johnson is the executive director of the Perception Institute, a group of social psychologists and strategists who study how our brains respond to physical differences such as race and sex.

A multitude of research studies have illuminated implicit bias in many groups of people:

- Faculty members respond to emails more often and more quickly when a stereotypically white name was used in the email.[216]

---

[214]Starbucks, "Starbucks Stories & News," July 2, 2018, https://stories.starbucks.com/stories/2018/beyond-may-29-lessons-from-starbucks-anti-bias-training-and-whats-next/.

[215]Ailsa Chang, "A Lesson in How to Overcome Implicit Bias," *All Things Considered*, National Public Radio, April 19, 2018, https://www.npr.org/sections/codeswitch/2018/04/19/604070231/a-lesson-in-how-to-overcome-implicit-bias.

[216]Katherine L. Milkman, Modupe Akinola, and Dolly Chugh, "What Happens Before? A Field Experiment Exploring How Pay and Representation Differentially Shape Bias on the Pathway into Organizations," *Journal of Applied Psychology 100*, no. 6 (2015):1678–1712, https://doi.org/10.1037/ap10000022.

- Doctors were less likely to recommend a helpful procedure to black patients even when their medical files were identical to those of white patients.[217]
- Car sales staff quote higher prices to black and female car buyers than they do for white male buyers.[218]
- Employers invite applicants to an interview more frequently when their resumes were sent from a person with a stereotypically white name like Greg rather than from a person with a stereotypically black name like Jamal.[219]

Even though it looks like the people involved in these studies were consciously biased, Sendhil Mullainathan, coauthor of the "Jamal" study, says that many of the human resources managers involved in his study were stunned by its results. "They prized creating diversity in their companies, yet here was evidence that they were doing anything but," Mullainathan says in his article "Racial Bias, Even When We Have Good Intentions."[220]

The authors of the article "How to Think about 'Implicit Bias'" say, "Our brain is constantly bombarded with data, so it notices patterns and makes generalizations trying to put order to the data. However, sometimes it overgeneralizes without us knowing about it, which could lead us to discriminate even when we think we're treating people equally."[221]

In other words, we tend to make a lot of snap judgments about people and things because of all the data rapidly coming at us. "Our snap

[217]Kevin A. Schulman, Jesse A. Berlin, William Harless et al., "The Effect of Race and Sex on Physicians' Recommendations for Cardiac Catheterization," *New England Journal of Medicine* 340, no. 8 (1999): 618–26, https://doi.org/10.1056/NEJM199902253400806 (published correction appears in *New England Journal of Medicine* 340, no. 14 (1999): 1130).

[218]Ian Ayres and Peter Siegelman, "Race and Gender Discrimination in Bargaining for a New Car," *American Economic Review* 85, no. 3 (1995): 304–21, https://econpapers.repec.org/article/aeaaecrev/v_3a85_3ay_3a1995_3ai_3a3_3ap_3a304-21.htm.

[219]Marianne Bertrand and Sendhil Mullainathan, "Are Emily and Greg More Employable Than Lakisha and Jamal? A Field Experiment on Labor Market Discrimination," *American Economic Review* 94, no. 4 (2004): 991–1013.

[220]Sendhil Mullainathan, "Racial Bias, Even When We Have Good Intentions," *New York Times*, January 3, 2015, https://www.nytimes.com/2015/01/04/upshot/the-measuring-sticks-of-racial-bias-.html.

[221]Keith Payne, Laura Niemi, and John M. Doris, "How to Think about 'Implicit Bias,'" *Scientific American*, March 27, 2018, https://www.scientificamerican.com/article/how-to-think-about-implicit-bias/.

judgments rely on all the associations we have—from fictional television shows to news reports. They use stereotypes, both the accurate and the inaccurate, both those we would want to use and ones we find repulsive," say Mullainathan.[222]

Are implicit biases all that bad? They are when your emails aren't answered, you're not prescribed a medical treatment, you have to pay more for a car, or you aren't invited to an interview because of them.

Kat's Take

Implicit bias is not limited to attitudes on race, as is shown in an accidental email experiment reported by Zlata Rodionova of the *Independent* in 2017.[223] A supervisor, Mr. Schneider, noticed one day that a client who was normally easy to work with was being particularly difficult. Trying to decipher why, he noticed that his email to the client had been sent with the signature of his coworker Nicole, who had been previously working on the same project.

After noticing the incorrect signature, Schneider reintroduced himself to the client, who demonstrated a complete turnaround in response, praising Schneider's ideas and expressing trust in his judgment. Schneider's advice had not changed. Only his name.

Schneider knew that Nicole often received pressure from their boss for working too slowly, but he had assumed it was because Nicole had less experience. But based on the inadvertent email experience, Schneider decided to trade in-boxes with Nicole for two weeks. He was shocked at how much more difficult clients became when they thought he was Nicole. Not only were his suggestions challenged, but clients began asking him out.

Immediately, his work slowed because he had to spend more time proving himself, while Nicole—writing under Schneider's name—suddenly could sail past him with clients and her work.

---

[222]Mullainathan, "Racial Bias."

[223]Zlata Rodionova, "Gender Inequality: What Happened When a Man and Woman Switched Names at Work for a Week," *Independent*, March 10, 2017, https://www.independent.co.uk/news/business/news/gender-inequality-man-woman-switch-names-week-martin-schneider-nicky-knacks-pay-gap-a7622201.html.

Did the client responses really have anything to do with expertise? No. Only the gender of the person responding.

Breaking the Biases

What can we do about implicit biases?

Patricia Devine and her colleagues at the Prejudice and Intergroup Relations Lab at the University of Wisconsin–Madison developed implicit bias training years ago that is considered to be effective in addressing the issue. The training presents bias as a bad habit that can be broken when people become aware of it, are motivated to do something about it, and create strategies to replace it.[224]

For organizations, creating policies that spell out how employees should handle various situations (such as people sitting in your store without making a purchase) can prevent individual snap judgments from causing company-wide chaos.

Creating a diverse workforce makes the biggest impact on lessening implicit biases. "We know that what works best is for workers to be put side by side with people from other groups and have them work together collaboratively as equals," says Harvard sociology professor Frank Dobbin.[225] Getting to know people as individuals helps to reduce biases.

Thanks to feedback from the Starbucks training and other sources, we have learned that to be more effective, unconscious bias training:

---

[224]Patricia Devine, Patrick Forscher, Anthony Austin, and William Cox, "Long-Term Reduction in Implicit Race Bias: A Prejudice Habit-Breaking Intervention," *Journal of Experimental Social Psychology* 48, no. 6 (2012): 1267–78, https://doi.org/10/1016/j.jesp.2012.06.003..

[225]Frank Dobbin and Alexandra Kalev, "Why Diversity Programs Fail," *Harvard Business Review*, July-August 2016, https://hbr.org/2016/07/why-diversity-programs-fail.

Should not	Should
Take a one-size-fits-all approach	Have more discussion/less instruction
Make white people the villains	Give information on how to implement the training
Focus on just one race	Be offered more than once

Gen Z is the most racially diverse generation in America. In their article "On the Cusp of Adulthood and Facing an Uncertain Future: What We Know About Gen Z So Far," Kim Parker and Ruth Igielnik provide these statistics: 52 percent are non-Hispanic white, 25 percent are Hispanic, 14 percent are black, 6 percent are Asian, and 5 percent are some other race or two or more races.[226] Even so, Gen Z workers will not all know how to seamlessly navigate issues of race, culture, and bias, so training is imperative.

---

[226]Kim Parker and Ruth Igielnik, "On the Cusp of Adulthood and Facing an Uncertain Future: What We Know About Gen Z So Far," *Pew Research Center*, May 14, 2020, https://www.pewsocialtrends.org/essay/on-the-cusp-of-adulthood-and-facing-an-uncertain-future-what-we-know-about-gen-z-so-far/.

CHAPTER 30

RELIGION AND POLITICS

W e are often cautioned against talking about religion and politics; however, a lack of knowledge about the legalities surrounding these issues could cause problems for you at work.

Gen Z is not very religious. In an article about Generation Z's religious practices, Kelsey Dallas says, "Around 42% of members of the generation were religiously unaffiliated in 2018."[227] Conversely, 59 percent of Baby Boomers are strongly affiliated with a religion, according to Pew Research Center.[228]

These generational differences could cause clashes at work, so give some thought to how you will accommodate religious beliefs and deal with any clashes between your employees.

When I was the HR manager of a law firm, I suggested to management that a hand scanner be installed to track employee time and attendance. At that time, employees clocked in and out with a card that they swiped through a scanner. Some employees frequently forgot

---

[227]Kelsey Dallas, "Want Some Good News about the Future of Faith? Look to Generation Z," *Deseret News*, March 1, 2020, https://www.deseret.com/indepth/2020/3/1/21156465/millennial-faith-religion-generation-z-research-trends-nones-church-attendance.

[228]Pew Research Center, "Religious Composition of Baby Boomers," accessed June 8, 2020, https://www.pewforum.org/religious-landscape-study/generational-cohort/baby-boomer/.

their cards, so the hand scanner was my solution to ensuring that their time was recorded properly. I thought it was very James Bond-ish; the employees thought it was a yucky hotbed of germs. To my knowledge, none of them thought it was giving them the mark of the beast and damning them to hell.

But Beverly R. Butcher Jr. apparently did when the Consolidation Coal Company installed a biometric hand scanner at the company's mine in Mannington, West Virginia, where Butcher had worked for over thirty-five years. An evangelical Christian, Butcher believed putting his hand in the scanner would give him the mark of the beast and refused to do it.

In case you're unfamiliar with the term, the mark of the beast is from the Book of Revelation in the New Testament of the Bible. The beast is the Antichrist, and a mark is placed on the hand or forehead of his followers in order to buy and sell anything at the end of time. Some evangelical organizations have warned their followers that technology such as hand scanners may eventually be used to imprint the mark of the beast, which dooms anyone who receives it.

Butcher repeatedly told company officials that he could not use the scanner because it violated his religious beliefs. He explained the relationship between the hand scanner and the mark of the beast and requested an accommodation. According to the EEOC, the company refused to consider any other way of tracking Butcher's time and told him he would be disciplined up to and including termination if he refused to use the hand scanner. So, Butcher retired and the EEOC sued.

A federal jury in Clarksburg, West Virginia, found that Consolidation Coal Company and its parent company had refused to grant a reasonable accommodation for Butcher's religious beliefs, which is a violation of Title VII of the Civil Rights Act of 1964. Butcher was awarded $586,860 in lost wages and benefits and compensatory damages.[229]

---

[229]Dawn Solowey, "The Antichrist at Work: 4thCircuit Affirms Judgment Against Employer for Failing to Accommodate Employee's Religious Belief Regarding 'Mark of the Beast,'" *Seyfarth*, June 16, 2017, https://www.laborandemploymentlawcounsel. com/2017/06/the-antichrist-at-work-4th-circuit-affirms-judgment-against-employer-for-failing-to-accommodate-employees-religious-belief-regarding-mark-of-the-beast/.

If you think it's crazy for anyone to believe that a hand scanner could imprint the mark of the beast and unjust that an employer would be required to accommodate that employee, you should know this: religious beliefs need not be seen as rational, doctrinally consistent, or accurate to be protected under Title VII. If employees ask for an accommodation because of religious beliefs, you need to work with them to determine whether a reasonable accommodation can be found—even when you don't believe in the employees' beliefs.

Religious Expression at Work

I'm not a football fan, but an incident in a game between the Kansas City Chiefs and New England Patriots in 2014 caught even my attention. Chiefs' safety Husain Abdullah intercepted a pass and returned it for a touchdown. When he dropped to his knees and lowered his head to the ground in prayer, a referee threw a flag and said it was unsportsmanlike behavior. Perhaps the referee did not know that Abdullah was engaging in an act of religious expression, which is allowed in the NFL and in just about every workplace in America.

Title VII of the Civil Rights Act (which applies to employers with fifteen or more employees) protects all aspects of religious observance and practice, which includes (among other things) prayer, proselytizing, and other forms of religious expression if these actions do not present an undue hardship for the employer.

For example, an employee who needs a quiet place to pray during lunch breaks and requests an available conference room to do so would probably not present an undue hardship. However, an employee who requests that an assembly line be shut down multiple times a day in order to pray probably would present an undue hardship.

Proselytizing may include engaging in one-on-one discussions about religious beliefs, distributing literature, or using a particular religious phrase (such as "God bless you"). According to the EEOC, employers must allow employees to engage in these types of activities unless doing so adversely affects coworkers, customers, or business operations.

Employees who spend an excessive amount of time talking about their religious beliefs may be told to limit that time (employees who spend too much time talking about *any* topic may be told the same thing). Employees who make certain coworkers uncomfortable with their religious talk may be told to stop talking to those coworkers about religion. Employees who express religious beliefs that could be perceived as harassing (e.g., telling homosexual coworkers that they are sinners) may be told to cease and desist. And employees who talk to customers about their religious beliefs may be told to stop if such talk disrupts business or if the customers would reasonably believe that the employee's message is on behalf of the employer.

NFL spokesman Michael Signora told the Associated Press that Abdullah should not have been penalized for his religious expression.[230] Likewise, you should not discipline your employees for their religious expression unless it unreasonably interferes with getting the work done.

Politics at Work

Although Gen Z is not overly religious, it is far more likely to be political. In a *Washington Post* article, Hannah Knowles writes, "Generation Z was already politically liberal, increasingly activist and fed up with the status quo. . . . Now the coronavirus crisis may solidify their political identity."[231] That was written before George Floyd was killed and many young people took to the streets night after night to protest.

According to Statista, 53 percent of survey respondents between eighteen and thirty-four strongly or somewhat strongly supported the protestors. That's not surprising since many of the protestors also fall into that age range. It might be because school is currently not in session or because a lot of people are unemployed with time on their hands. Whatever the reason, "thousands of college and high school students dot

---

[230]Dave Skretta, "NFL Says Abdullah Should Not Have Been Penalized," *AP News*, September 30, 2014, https://apnews.com/eccf2a5afcab4292a5c180bb90f8d52b.

[231]Hannah Knowles, "Gen Z Was Fed Up with the Status Quo. Coronavirus Could Affirm Their Beliefs," *Washington Post*, April 8, 2020, https://www.washingtonpost.com/nation/2020/04/08/gen-z-was-fed-up-with-status-quo-coronavirus-could-reinforce-their-liberal-politics/.

crowds across the nation in a groundswell of youth activism," according to Zane Razzaq of *the Milford Daily News*.[232]

Also according to Statista, as the age of the respondents increased, their support for the protestors decreased.[233] Once again, generations see things differently.

Even before the protests, Americans were deeply divided politically, and politicians and their supporters were regularly hurling nasty personal insults at each other.[234] If you're not an American history enthusiast, you might not know that's nothing new. In his article "Donald Trump and the Long History of American Politics Turning Violent," Matt Taylor recounts how prominent politicians such as Aaron Burr, Alexander Hamilton, and Andrew Jackson "were almost as notorious for their pistol duels as their politics" and how their followers often engaged in fisticuffs as well. Taylor quotes Noah Feldman, a Harvard legal historian, who said that our country's early political campaigns were "raucous and unruly" and "all of politics was just much, much wilder."[235]

That historical information might mean you no longer have to shake your head and wonder what our country is coming to; however, it doesn't mean you should allow people to be raucous and unruly at work.

Limits on Limits

Perhaps your workplace has not been subjected to such behavior yet, but it's good to be informed and ready in case it does. The primary thing

---

[232]Zane Razzaq, "'Like a Coming-of-Age Story': Meet Framingham's Young Black Lives Matter Protestors," *Milford Daily News*, June 6, 2020, https://www.milforddailynews.com/news/20200606/like-coming-of-age-story-meet-framinghams-young-black-lives-matter-protesters.

[233]Statista, "Support for the Protestors Responding to George Floyd's Death by Age U.S. 2020," June 5, 2020, https://www.statista.com/statistics/1122622/support-george-floyd-protesters-us-age/.

[234]Alan Greenblatt, "Talking Trash: Why Politics Has Gotten Nastier," *Governing*, May 1, 2018, https://www.governing.com/topics/politics/gov-why-politics-has-gotten-nastier.html.

[235]Matt Taylor, "Donald Trump and the Long History of American Politics Turning Violence," *Vice*, March 16, 2016, https://www.vice.com/en_us/article/8gkjwz/the-long-history-of-american-politics-turning-ugly-racist-and-violent.

that you need to know about politics at work is that the National Labor Relations Act gives employees the right to talk about politicians and political issues when those topics are work related.

Section 7 of the NLRA prohibits employers from preventing their employees from discussing the terms and conditions of their employment. Therefore, employees may not be prevented from discussing Candidate X when that discussion is really about the candidate's push for a higher minimum wage or some other policy that could affect employees' working conditions. But employees may be prevented from discussing Candidate X when that discussion is about the candidate's stance on abortion or some other topic that has nothing to do with work.

The same rules apply to clothing. For example, employees may be prevented from wearing a "Vote for Candidate X" shirt but may not be prevented from wearing a "Vote for Candidate X because he'll raise the minimum wage" shirt.

That said, you still have the right to put a stop to any communication or behavior that is negatively affecting productivity or causing distractions—whether that communication or behavior is protected or not.

Another thing you should know is that you can't prevent employees from participating in politics, control employees' political activities, coerce employees toward or away from any political action, discriminate against employees for their political activity or affiliation, and/or retaliate against employees for complaining that employers did any of the aforementioned things.

Social Media Troubles

Employees should know that publicly posting opinions about political or religious issues that are not work related might get them into trouble at work—even when the posting is done on their own time using their own electronic device.

For example, Curt Schilling, a former All-Star pitcher, was fired from his job as an ESPN baseball analyst because of a Facebook post about transgender men and public restrooms. The post shows a picture of a man dressed as a scantily clad woman with this message: "LET HIM IN! to the restroom with your daughter or else you're a narrow-minded, judgmental, unloving racist bigot who needs to die."

Schilling added: "A man is a man no matter what they call themselves. I don't care what they are, who they sleep with, men's room was designed for the penis, women's not so much. Now you need laws telling us differently? Pathetic."

Soon after, ESPN issued a statement that said, "ESPN is an inclusive company. Curt Schilling has been advised that his conduct was unacceptable and his employment with ESPN has been terminated."[236]

During the pandemic, an army social media manager was fired because he posted something on the army's official social media account that his superiors thought was derogatory toward Chinese people, according to the *Military Times*.[237] While there were lots of funny social media posts about the pandemic, joking about sanitizing, self-isolating, and toilet paper hoarding will probably be seen differently than racist jokes or snarky remarks about the death toll in the elderly population.

If you're in a position of authority, you should respond to social media jokes just as you would respond to office jokes that disparage people of a protected class. Your response should include the appropriate corrective action (verbal warning, written warning, suspension, or termination) based on the severity of the situation.

---

[236]Matt Fitzgerald, "Curt Schilling Fired by ESPN Following Anti-Transgender Comments," Bleacher Report, accessed June 6, 2020, https://bleacherreport.com/articles/2634131-curt-schilling-posts-anti-transgender-comments-on-facebook.

[237]Leo Shane, "Army Employee Fired for Insensitive Post about Coronavirus Outbreak," *Military Times*, March 21, 2020, https://www.militarytimes.com/news/pentagon-congress/2020/03/21/army-employee-fired-for-insensitive-post-about-coronavirus-outbreak/.

CHAPTER 31

HANDLING COMPLAINTS

One of the most important steps in handling complaints of harassment or discrimination is to make sure that you make it okay for victims to complain. And that your employees know they can feel safe if they complain.

Many of the women who initiated the firestorm that became the #MeToo movement complained of harassment that had happened years earlier. As a result, many people asked, "Why didn't they speak up years ago?"

One reason victims often don't speak up immediately is that the incident can be so traumatic. In her article "These Are All the Ways Sexual Harassment Can Make Your Life Miserable," Meera Jagannathan says that "unwanted sexual advances can wreak havoc on your mind, body and career."[238]

If unwanted sexual advances can cause such damage, imagine what sexual assault or rape can do to a person. Sexual harassment includes verbal, visual, or physical conduct of a sexual nature that is unwanted. Sexual assault includes touching breasts, genitals, or anus without

---

[238]Meera Jagannathan, "These Are All the Ways Sexual Harassment Can Make Your Life Miserable," *MarketWatch*, February 15, 2018, https://www.marketwatch.com/story/these-are-all-the-ways-sexual-harassment-can-make-your-life-miserable-2018-02-15.

permission. Sexual misconduct is an umbrella term that includes sexual harassment, sexual assault, and any conduct of a sexual nature that is without consent or has the effect of threatening or intimidating the person against whom such conduct is directed.

In his book *The Body Keeps the Score*, Dr. Bessel van der Kolk—founder and medical director of the Trauma Center in Massachusetts—explains that trauma can be so unbearable and intolerable that many who experience it simply try to push it out of their minds and pretend the incident(s) never happened. It's easy to understand that people who can't bear to think about such incidents can't bear to talk about them either.[239]

Fears of Retaliation

Another reason that victims of harassment or discrimination frequently don't speak up is that they are frequently retaliated against when they do make complaints. In the workplace, retaliation comes in many forms, including

- being fired, demoted, or having hours reduced;
- having working conditions changed or a job made more difficult;
- being more closely scrutinized;
- being transferred to a less desirable position or unfairly disciplined; and
- being threatened or verbally/physically abused.

The EEOC reported receiving 39,110 retaliation complaints in 2019, which accounted for more than half of the total complaints it received.[240]

Even though retaliation is illegal and employers who are found guilty of it are heavily fined, it still happens. For example, two female employees filed an internal complaint at an O'Reilly Auto Parts store in Orlando, Florida, about sexual misconduct, including groping, vulgar

---

[239]Bessel van der Kolk, *The Body Keeps the Score: Brain, Mind, and Body in the Healing of Trauma* (New York: Viking, 2014).

[240]US Equal Employment Opportunity Commission, "EEOC Releases Fiscal Year 2019 Enforcement and Litigation Data," January 24, 2020, https://www.eeoc.gov/newsroom/eeoc-releases-fiscal-year-2019-enforcement-and-litigation-data.

comments and gestures, and demands for sex. Both were retaliated against: one was sent out on deliveries with the wrong auto parts and had her hours reduced, and the other was fired after asking for a transfer.

The EEOC filed a lawsuit against the store on the employees' behalf seeking back pay with interest and compensation for past and future losses because of the emotional pain and humiliation the women suffered.[241]

Employers who fail to prevent retaliation from occurring exacerbate the effects of trauma, according to a study by psychologists Carly Parnitzke Smith and Jennifer Freyd. "These results suggest that institutions have the power to cause additional harm to assault survivors."[242]

What can employers do to protect their employees from retaliation? Mostly, resist the automatic urge to go into self-defense mode when employees make complaints about incidents involving the workplace. Additionally, don't let anyone—managers, supervisors, coworkers, or third parties—take any kind of adverse action against the complainants.

To protect themselves from retaliation complaints, employers should do the following:

- Create a policy against retaliation that is included in their harassment/discrimination policy.
- Have an open-door policy that identifies various people to whom employees can complain.
- Tell complainants about the retaliation policy and what to do if they feel they've been retaliated against.
- Tell employees who've been accused of wrongdoing about the policy and what they need to do to avoid an additional complaint of retaliation.
- Refrain from making any changes in the complainant's pay, benefits, duties, title, or working conditions following the complaint unless you have a defendable business reason for doing so.
- Follow up with the complainant to ensure that they haven't

[241]US Equal Employment Opportunity Commission, "EEOC Sues O'Reilly Automotive Stores for Sexual Harassment and Retaliation," press release, May 9, 2019, https://www.eeoc.gov/newsroom/eeoc-sues-oreilly-automotive-stores-sexual-harassment-and-retaliation.

[242]Carly Parnitzke Smith and Jennifer Freyd, "Institutional Betrayal," *American Psychologist 69*, no. 6 (2014): 575–87, https://doi.org/10.1037/a0037564.

experienced any retaliation.
- Document everything.

Being subjected to unwanted sexual behavior, being retaliated against, and being sued for retaliation are all traumatic events that can and should be prevented.

Because I spend a lot of my workweek conducting harassment prevention workshops, it's ironic that I was recently accused of harassment. Although it was a meritless complaint, I reacted the way I teach people to react in the workplace when they are accused of wrongdoing—I continued to do my job in a professional manner and didn't try to get back at the complainant in any way. Because I had done nothing wrong, the issue quickly went away.

But it definitely was not easy for me to react so calmly! When we feel threatened by things, such as people making complaints about us, our bodies are wired to go into self-defense mode—what is called the fight-or-flight response. According to Kendra Cherry's article on Verywellmind.com, "The term 'fight-or-flight' represents the choices that our ancient ancestors had when faced with danger in their environment. They could either fight or flee. In either case, the physiological and psychological response to stress prepares the body to react to danger."[243]

Someone complaining about us, especially when we've done nothing wrong, certainly triggers this response. Despite its organic origins, we can't seek revenge when people complain, even when it's a bogus complaint.

Whistleblowers

If you're an employer, manager, supervisor, or anyone else in a position of power, you can't fire, demote, transfer, or take some other employment action against employees for complaining about you, anyone else, or anything in the workplace. That would be retaliating against a whistleblower, and it's very much against the law.

In 2019, retaliating against whistleblowers became a hot topic

---

[243]Kendra Cherry, "How the Fight or Flight Response Works," *Verywell Mind*, August 18, 2019, https://www.verywellmind.com/what-is-the-fight-or-flight-response-2795194.

because Acting Director of National Intelligence Joseph Maguire spoke to the House Intelligence Committee about a federal employee who filed a complaint.

During the meeting, Rep. Terri Sewell told Maguire she was concerned that "what has happened with this whistleblower" will have a "chilling effect" on future whistleblowers coming forward.[244] What happened to this whistleblower is what happens to most people who file complaints—retaliation or the threat of it.

After the news of the complaint became public, the whistleblower's boss was recorded saying the whistleblower is "almost a spy" and the person who gave the whistleblower information is "close to a spy." The boss suggested they be treated as spies were in the old days, which could include execution.[245] That's an extreme version of retaliation.

The Whistleblower Protection Act protects federal employees and applicants for employment who lawfully report certain wrongdoing from personnel action being taken against them. Some states have whistleblowing laws that protect all employees from being retaliated against for reporting that their employer or its agents broke the law or violated the public's trust. The reporting can be done to a government official, the police, a supervisor within the organization, or "any public body" conducting a hearing or investigation.

Simply put, you can't punish employees for making complaints. It might be determined that the complaint is without merit; however, retaliating against an employee for making the complaint will still cost you in terms of repayment of lost wages to terminated employees, damages for injuries suffered, jail time, and so on.

Instead of retaliating, thank employees for coming forward when they make a complaint and fix whatever legitimate problem they bring to your attention—even when that problem is you.

---

[244]Rep. Terri Sewell, "Trump Administration's Withholding of Whistleblower Report Will Have 'Chilling Effect' on Intelligence Community," press release, September 26, 2019, https://sewell.house.gov/media-center/press-releases/rep-sewell-trump-administration-s-withholding-whistleblower-report-will.

[245]Rashaan Ayesh, "Trump Suggests Whistleblower Is 'Almost a Spy,'" *Axios*, September 26, 2019, https://www.axios.com/donald-trump-whistleblower-almost-spy-treason-2c4764dc-ea9c-4139-982a-8ebd3bf056bc.html.

Investigate Before You Terminate

Over the last several years, dozens of men in entertainment, business, and politics were accused of sexual harassment, assault, and rape. As a result, many lost their jobs and some were even convicted.

In 2018, Steve Wynn, CEO of Wynn Resorts in Las Vegas, was accused of sexual harassment and resigned his position as finance chair of the Republican National Committee even though he insisted the accusations against him were "preposterous." "We find ourselves in a world where people can make allegations, regardless of the truth, and a person is left with the choice of weathering insulting publicity or engaging in multi-year lawsuits," Wynn was quoted as saying in an NPR article by Khalon Richard.[246]

He has a point. Remember the TV show *The Wonder Years* that aired in the late 1980s and early 1990s and starred teenager Fred Savage? Actress Alley Mills, who played Savage's mom on the show, told Yahoo in 2018 that the show was canceled because of a sexual harassment lawsuit against then sixteen-year-old Savage and costar twenty-year-old Jason Hervey. Mills said that the suit, brought by a former costumer on the show, was "completely ridiculous" and that ABC settled out of court to avoid a scandal.

"It's a little bit like what's happening now—some innocent people can get caught up in this stuff; it's very tricky. It was so not true," Mills said in a *Vanity Fair* article by Laura Bradley.[247]

How do you know which allegations are true and which are not? As someone who investigates sexual harassment complaints, I know that the truth is often difficult to determine. However, when you're an employer, one thing is clear—it's important that you conduct an investigation before you terminate employees for sexual harassment.

---

[246]Khalon Richard, "After Sexual Misconduct Claims, Vegas Mogul Steve Wynn Fell Fast," National Public Radio, March 15, 2018, https://www.npr.org/2018/03/15/592318034/after-sexual-misconduct-claims-vegas-mogul-steve-wynn-fell-fast.

[247]Laura Bradley, "*Wonder Years* Actress Claims a Sexual Harassment Lawsuit Ended the Show," *Vanity Fair*, January 29, 2018, https://www.vanityfair.com/hollywood/2018/01/wonder-years-sexual-harassment-lawsuit-alley-mills.

Ask Before You Investigate

Before you begin an investigation, consider the following questions:

Do you have a policy that forbids sexual harassment in your workplace? Even though sexual harassment is against the law, it's easier for employers to determine when employees violate a policy rather than to determine whether they broke a law. Terminating an employee for violating policies is also easier to defend in court.

Do you have a plan in place for responding to sexual harassment complaints? Your plan should include items like determining when employees should be put on leave or transferred to another location during an investigation.

Is a formal investigation necessary? Many people tend to think that anything that bothers them is "harassment" and creates a "hostile work environment." Although it's important to take all complaints seriously, ask for specific examples of harassment from a complainant before launching into a full-scale investigation.

Who will conduct the investigation? In her article subtitled "Bad Investigations: A Plaintiff's Dream; Defendant's Nightmare," Maureen S. Binetti says, "A primary source of fodder for plaintiff's counsel in attacking investigations continues, remarkably, to be the complete inadequacy of the investigator." Investigators are often inadequate because of their lack of training and/or their relationship to the people being investigated, according to Binetti.[248] It's usually best to have a trained investigator outside the organization conduct investigations.

How will the investigation be conducted? Determine processes such as how evidence will be collected and whether witnesses will be questioned before taking action. "Mishandled employment investigations can be used by employees as offensive weapons," says Binetti.[249]

Have supervisors been trained on what to say and do during investigations? Confidentiality is critical during the process, and retaliating against employees for participating in investigations is against the

---

[248]Maureen S. Binetti, "California Dreamin' (Nightmarin') Bad Investigations: A Plaintiff's Dream; Defendant's Nightmare," *American Bar Association*, 2010, https://www.apps.americanbar.org.

[249]Ibid.

law. It's a good idea to share that information with people in positions of authority.

What will you do after the investigation? If you decide to discipline the accused, how will you determine the appropriate level of discipline? What should you tell the complainant? What kind of documentation should you keep and where should you keep it?

When people complain about sexual harassment, it's easy to believe the complainant and want to take swift action against the accused. However, employers must fully and effectively investigate harassment complaints to comply with Title VII of the Civil Rights Act, which requires employers to take all reasonable steps necessary to prevent discrimination and harassment from occurring.

Also, you don't want to fire someone who's done nothing wrong. Therefore, be sure to investigate before you terminate.

Know the Law!

Documenting investigations is critical as this court case demonstrates.

Arturo Martinez was a branch manager for W. W. Grainger, Inc. His supervisor, Jeff Timm, became concerned about Martinez's management style after having conversations with three of his subordinates while Martinez was on vacation. Even though none of the employees filed a formal complaint, Timm asked Grainger human resources specialist Joyce LePage to conduct an investigation into Martinez's treatment of his employees. LePage interviewed a number of employees who, according to court documents, reported that Martinez "created a fearful work environment and described instances when he yelled, swore, and was demeaning, volatile, and intimidating to employees."

LePage took extensive notes during the interviews with the employees, and then she and Timm met with Martinez to discuss how to move forward. When Martinez would not acknowledge that there was a problem with his management style, he was terminated. He then sued for racial and national origin discrimination.

The trial court dismissed the lawsuit and Martinez also lost on appeal. According to the appellate court, Martinez failed to establish that the reason for his termination was something other than his performance. Moreover, the court noted that "the deposition testimony of the branch employees confirmed that the notes LePage used to create the summary list for Martinez were accurate and that the specific examples she gave of his problematic managerial style were brought up during her investigation."[250]

Thus, an accurate, well-documented investigation helped this company defend itself against a discrimination lawsuit.

Write It Down

"I made a mistake in recalling the events of twelve years ago," said NBC news anchor Brian Williams.[251] In a tribute to a retiring soldier that aired on *NBC Nightly News*, Williams said that he had been aboard a helicopter that was hit by grenades while reporting on the American invasion of Iraq in 2003. Military personnel said that Williams was actually in a different helicopter, not the one fired upon.

Is it possible to misremember something like that? Some researchers say it is. Why should you care? Because misremembering could lead to problems for you in the workplace.

It happens like this: An employee calmly but firmly tells you he disagrees with a new policy that you've implemented. When you talk about the incident with your spouse that evening, you say the employee

---

[250]Martinez v. Grainger, *FindLaw*, 2011, https://caselaw.findlaw.com/us-8th-circuit/1589302.html.

[251]Ryan Parker, "Brian Williams Misremembers—and the Internet Won't Let Him Forget It," *Los Angeles Times*, February 4, 2015, https://www.latimes.com/entertainment/tv/showtracker/la-et-st-brian-williams-social-media-20150204-htmlstory.html.

raised his voice and said your policy was stupid. When you tell your business partner about it the next day, you say the employee yelled at you and called you an idiot. Why would you stretch the truth like this?

In their book *Mistakes Were Made (But Not by Me)*, psychologists Carol Tavris and Elliott Aronson say,

> Most of us, most of the time, are neither telling the whole truth nor intentionally deceiving. . . . All of us, as we tell our stories, add details and omit inconvenient facts; we give the tale a small, self-enhancing spin. That spin goes over so well that the next time we add a slightly more dramatic embellishment. . . . Eventually the way we remember the event may bring us a far distance from what actually happened.[252]

In her article "Neuroscience Suggests That Brian Williams May in Fact Be 'Misremembering'" on PBS.org, Allison Eck says, "The *New York Times* produced a video showing how Williams' story changed over the years. It's like witnessing a solo version of the classic game 'telephone': each time the story is told, it's slightly different."[253]

So, it's possible to misremember events from twelve years ago, but what about events from last week? Psychoanalyst Ken Eisold is quoted in an article in the *Pittsburgh Post-Gazette* as saying, "Each time we remember something, we are reconstructing the event, reassembling it from traces throughout the brain. As a result, memory is unreliable. We could also say it is adaptive, reshaping itself to accommodate the situations we find ourselves facing. Either way, we have to face the fact that it is 'flexible.'"[254]

What problems might misremembering present for you? Obviously, like Williams, it could make you look like you're lying. So, document

---

[252]Carol Tavris and Elliott Aronson, *Mistakes Were Made (But Not by Me): Why We Justify Foolish Beliefs, Bad Decisions*, and Hurtful Acts (San Diego: Harcourt, 2007).

[253]Allison Eck, A. "Neuroscience Suggests That Brian Williams May in Fact Be 'Misremembering,'" Public Broadcasting Service, February 9, 2015, https://www.pbs.org/wgbh/nova/article/brian-williams-may-fact-misremembering/.

[254]Bill Toland, "Brian Williams' 'Misremembering' Is More Complicated Than You Think," *Pittsburgh Post-Gazette*, February 6, 2015, https://www.post-gazette.com/news/nation/2015/02/07/On-Brian-Williams-Telling-the-truth-is-more-complicated-than-you-think/stories/201502060020.

important conversations and incidents immediately and accurately before you have the opportunity to think too long about them or talk about them over and over and embellish the story in the process.

And remember that when employees are telling their stories about conversations and incidents that they've had with coworkers and customers, they are probably misremembering too. Do some investigating and be sure to get others' side of the story before taking any action on what you've been told.

Williams lost his job as the anchor of *NBC Nightly News* because of his misremembering. Immediate documentation can help you circumvent misremembering and prevent you from facing a similar fate.

Kat's Take

Documentation will be an entirely new concept to anyone in Gen Z. Other than perhaps taking a screenshot of a text, Gen Zers have probably never documented conversations or incidents. So don't expect them to know this without teaching them.

I had a few difficulties with a previous employer. Fortunately, I had a mentor who had been with the company for twenty years tell me to print out or forward to myself any email or communication from a particular coworker about what was said and so on. She told me to document conversations, phone calls, and the like. "Date them, write down what happened, and keep that notebook with you at all times. Forward emails to your personal email, so you have a record of them. Print them out, if you have to." She also taught me how to take notes during conversations and how to reiterate what we talked about in an email to verify that everything had been understood correctly. She gave me other useful professional tips that considerably helped during my time there and in my future career.

At the time, I thought she was strangely paranoid. After all, the company would work in my best interest, right? I had a good memory, why did I have to go back and make sure that I was clear on what was said? Or someone else was clear on what we'd just agreed to? I already took great notes in college; did I really need to take notes during meetings?

Well, documentation really helped me out a year later when I encountered an incident that involved a coworker. When it boiled over, you can bet I was extremely glad I had followed my mentor's advice and documented every conversation, email, and agreement in a notebook I kept in my purse. I had emails printed out. I had a case.

As I was in my early twenties, I had no idea how to document anything. Luckily, I had a mentor who told me how. Gen Zers will be no different. Encourage them to document everything. Teach them how.

KEEP THEM HEALTHY, SAFE

Section 7 Takeaways

- Gen Z has suffered more mental illness issues than older generations.
- Gen Z is more comfortable talking about problems and more comfortable demanding accommodations.
- Securing your workplace can help workers feel safe and be more productive.
- Understand the legal landscape surrounding mental and physical disabilities.
- Encourage better physical fitness to help reduce work absences.
- Spell out policies regarding marijuana and alcohol use.

CHAPTER 32

ADDRESS MENTAL
HEALTH ISSUES

E ven before COVID-19 and the chaos that came with it—illness, death,
school closures, shelter-in-place orders, massive job losses, economic
downturn—Gen Z had been "beset by mental health issues such as
depression and suicide more than previous generations at this age."[255]

According to a study published in the *Journal of Abnormal Psychology* in 2019,

> More U.S. adolescents and young adults in the late 2010s (vs.
> the mid-2000s) experienced serious psychological distress, major
> depression, and suicidal thoughts, and more attempted suicide and
> took their own lives. These trends are weak or nonexistent among
> adults 26 years old and over, suggesting a generational shift in
> mood disorders and suicide-related outcomes rather than an over-
> all increase across all ages.[256]

[255]Emily Seymour, "Gen Z: Studies Show Higher Rates of Depression,"
Voice of America, August 25, 2019, https://www.voanews.com/student-union/
gen-z-studies-show-higher-rates-depression.

[256]Jean M. Twenge, Thomas E. Joiner, Mary E. Duffy, A. Bell Cooper, and Sarah G.
Binau, "Age, Period, and Cohort Trends in Mood Disorder Indicators and Suicide-Re-
lated Outcomes in a Nationally Representative Dataset, 2005–2017," *Journal of Abnormal Psychology* 128, no. 3 (2019): 185–99, https://www.apa.org/pubs/journals/releases/
abn-abn0000410.pdf.

What was causing this mental health distress prior to the pandemic? Global warming, mass shootings, sexual harassment and assault, family separations, work, finances, and health-related concerns were cited as sources in the study "Stress in America: Generation Z" by the American Psychological Association.[257]

Social media is another factor. "I think a lot of people in my generation struggle with (depression) due to the fact that we are so connected via the internet and social media, which brings a lot of pressure," says twenty-one-year-old Margo Joel in the article "Gen Z: Studies Show Higher Rates of Depression."[258] Although they have the ability to connect with people around the world, Gen Zers are still the loneliest generation, according to a 2018 study conducted by Cigna.[259]

Racism and racial injustice are another source of stress for some members of Gen Z. In her article "Black Kids and Suicide," Rheeda Walker says, "Black children had the highest rate of death by suicide" in 2016 and 2018 and "experiencing racism is associated with thoughts about suicide for black youth and adults."[260]

The stress of discovering that they were undocumented and faced possible deportation at any moment affected the mental health of the approximately eight hundred thousand children and young adults known as Dreamers. Before the 2012 executive order known as Deferred Action for Childhood Arrivals (DACA), which granted temporary reprieve from deportation for certain undocumented youth, some Dreamers admitted that hopelessness related to their undocumented status caused them to consider suicide.[261]

---

[257] American Psychological Association, "Stress in America: Generation Z," October 2018, https://www.apa.org/news/press/releases/stress/2018/stress-gen-z.pdf.

[258] Seymour, "Gen Z: Studies."

[259] Ellie Polack, "New Cigna Study Reveals Loneliness at Epidemic Levels in America," Cigna, May 1, 2018, https://www.cigna.com/newsroom/news-releases/2018/new-cigna-study-reveals-loneliness-at-epidemic-levels-in-america.

[260] Rheeda Walker, "Black Kids and Suicide: Why Are Rates So High, and So Ignored?," The Conversation, January 17, 2020, https://theconversation.com/black-kids-and-suicide-why-are-rates-so-high-and-so-ignored-127066.

[261] Elizabeth Arnada and Elizabeth Vaquera, "How DACA Affected the Mental Health of Undocumented Young Adults," The Conversation, September 5, 2017, https://theconversation.com/how-daca-affected-the-mental-health-of-undocumented-young-adults-83341.

The pandemic and everything it brought with it have increased mental health issues for many people of all ages, according to a 2020 article "The Mental Health Consequences of COVID-19 and Physical Distancing," which predicts an "overflow of mental illness."[262]

Unfortunately, a stigma about mental illness remains for many Boomers and Generation X, making them reluctant to talk about it—especially at work. However, younger people are far more open about mental health. In a 2019 poll conducted by the American Psychiatric Association, 62 percent of people age twenty to thirty-seven said they feel comfortable talking about their mental health at work, while only 32 percent of people over fifty said the same thing.[263]

If you're in a position of authority, you need to become comfortable with the topic—especially with your Gen Z employees because work can have a negative impact on employees' mental health, says Melissa Dittmann in her article "Building a Mentally Healthy Workforce." "Tedious job tasks, job insecurity or inflexible work schedules can demoralize some employees or lower their motivation." Lynne Casper, PhD, of the National Institute of Child Health and Human Development told Dittmann, "Workplace policies can have an effect on people's health, how they live their life and their ability to manage their work and family obligations."[264]

Even if work isn't the cause of mental illness, the workplace will increasingly be affected by lost productivity and employee absenteeism as mental illness grows. According to the World Health Organization, depression and anxiety cost $1 trillion each year in lost productivity globally.[265]

---

[262]Sandro Galea, Raina M. Merchant, and Nicole Lurie, "The Mental Health Consequences of COVID-19 and Physical Distancing: The Need for Prevention and Early Intervention," *JAMA Internal Medicine* 180, no. 6 (2020), https://jamanetwork.com/journals/jamainternalmedicine/fullarticle/2764404.

[263]American Psychiatric Association, "About Half of Workers Are Concerned about Discussing Mental Health Issues in the Workplace; A Third Worry about Consequences if They Seek Help," May 20, 2019, https://www.psychiatry.org/newsroom/news-releases/about-half-of-workers-are-concerned-about-discussing-mental-health-issues-in-the-workplace-a-third-worry-about-consequences-if-they-seek-help.

[264]Melissa Dittmann, "Building a Mentally Healthy Work Force," American Psychological Association, January 2005, https://www.apa.org/monitor/jan05/workforce.

[265]World Health Organization, "Mental Health in the Workplace," May 2019, https://www.who.int/mental_health/in_the_workplace/en/.

Take Steps to Create a Mentally Healthy Workplace

In her article "The Boss' Guide to Creating a Mentally Healthy Workplace," Amy Morin provides the following strategies to help reduce the risk of work contributing to mental illness:

- Promote a work-life balance—insist employees take vacations and encourage a life outside work.
- Discuss mental health in the workplace and train supervisors to spot signs of mental health problems and how to respond.
- Discuss free screening tools, such as those offered by Mental Health America, the National Suicide Prevention Lifeline, or many insurance programs.
- Contract with an employee assistance program and remind employees to use it.
- Make wellness a priority and offer wellness incentives.
- Provide in-service events, such as workshops on stress management.
- Support employees' efforts to get help; allow employees to take "mental health days" and offer flexible schedules.
- Reduce the stigma; don't punish employees for speaking up about their mental health issues by calling them "crazy" or disciplining them for taking time off for treatment.
- Make strides one step at a time.[266]

Many years ago, I was one of the oldest participants in a class with other HR professionals. The instructor asked whether we thought employees should be able to take off for a paid "mental health day." I and another woman about my age were the only students who said employers should not allow such a practice. As a Baby Boomer, I was taught that you go to work unless you're physically ill. I've since changed my mind.

---

[266]Amy Morin, "The Boss' Guide to Creating a Mentally Healthy Workplace," *Psychology Today,* December 10, 2018, https://www.psychologytoday.com/us/blog/what-mentally-strong-people-dont-do/201812/the-boss-guide-creating-mentally-healthy-workplace.

In addition to the statistics quoted above about the rise in anxiety, depression, and other mental illness, incidents of employees shooting their coworkers in the workplace have become more frequent in recent years. The US Bureau of Labor Statistics reported that 312 employees were killed on the job by a coworker between 2011 and 2015. A 2018 study conducted by the FBI said, "The shooters typically were experiencing multiple forms of stress."[267] If taking some paid time off will help reduce that stress and prevent such tragedies, I'm now all for it.

Talk to Employees When Issues Arise

According to the National Alliance on Mental Illness (NAMI), one in five adults and one in six from Generation Z in the United States experience a mental health disorder each year. These disorders include

- anxiety disorders (48 million people);
- major depressive episode (17.7 million people);
- posttraumatic stress disorder (9 million people);
- bipolar disorder (7 million people);
- borderline personality disorder (3.5 million people);
- obsessive compulsive disorder (3 million people); and
- schizophrenia (1.5 million people)[268]

Because of the prevalence of mental illness, it's critical you know what to do if employees reveal they have a disorder or if you suspect that they do.

Employees who reveal that they suffer from mental illness are probably doing so because they need time off work or other accommodations to manage their illness. The Americans with Disabilities Act requires employers with fifteen or more employees to provide a reasonable accommodation to employees (and applicants) with mental and

---

[267]John Woolfolk, "When Getting Fired Gets Violent: What Experts Say about Avoiding Workplace Tragedy," *San Jose Mercury News,* July 4, 2019, https://www.seattletimes.com/explore/careers/when-getting-fired-gets-violent-what-experts-say-about-avoiding-workplace-tragedy/.

[268]National Alliance on Mental Illness, "Mental Health by the Numbers," accessed June 10, 2020, https://www.nami.org/mhstats.

physical disabilities.[269] Some states also have their own laws regarding disabilities in the workplace; therefore, check with your state's equal employment department for more information.

Employers may request that employees provide medical certification when they ask for workplace accommodations. If you receive such certification, collaborate to determine what your employee needs to perform essential job duties. Although employee preferences should be considered, you should ensure that any accommodation is the best solution for the employee and the organization.

Know the Law!

The EEOC says providing a reasonable accommodation might include

- making existing facilities accessible;
- job restructuring;
- part-time or modified work schedules;
- acquiring or modifying equipment;
- changing tests, training materials, or policies;
- providing qualified readers or interpreters; and
- reassignment to a vacant position.

When employees say they need an accommodation because of a disability, you should

---

[269]US Equal Employment Opportunity Commission, "Disability Discrimination & Reasonable Accommodation," accessed June 10, 2020, https://www.eeoc.gov/disability-discrimination.

- analyze the essential duties of the job;
- identify any job-related limitations of the employee;
- identify possible reasonable accommodations;
- consider the preference of the employee;
- select and implement the accommodation most appropriate for both parties; and
- document all the above.[270]

Kat's Take

As mental health awareness rises and more students are being diagnosed with mental health issues, many Gen Zers are receiving accommodations in school and in college for any issues. Schools are working harder now to provide an environment where all children can learn, so such accommodations have become common.

Students with ADHD may be given extra time to complete their tests, which are administered in a quiet environment. Additional tools are provided for students who struggle with dyslexia.

Such accommodations seem routine for Gen Z, so prepare to be flexible in the workplace if employees come to you with requests for changes in their environment or work tools. Some employees might be assertive about what they need to better perform, while others may be less direct.

But they are likely to know what you are required to accommodate legally, so you should become familiar with all such laws and policies that govern your area and industry.

---

[270]US Equal Opportunity Commission, "Enforcement Guidance on Reasonable Accommodation and Undue Hardship under the ADA," accessed June 11, 2020, https://www.eeoc.gov/laws/guidance/enforcement-guidance-reasonable-accommodation-and-undue-hardship-under-ada.

Employees who need time off work because of mental illness might be eligible for federal family medical leave, and your state might also have policies granting time off work.

If you suspect that an employee has a mental illness because of a decline in performance or a change in the employee's behavior, such as lack of cooperation, absenteeism, irritability, or excessive crying, schedule a meeting with the employee and follow a format like the one set forth in "How to Talk to a Depressed Employee" by Joni E. Johnston.[271]

State your concern for the employee. "Robin, I want to talk to you because I'm concerned about you."

Talk about observable behavior. "You missed several important deadlines over the past two weeks."

Acknowledge the change in behavior. "That's just not like you."

Encourage action. "If things in your personal life are affecting you, we have a confidential employee assistance program that you can call." Or if your company doesn't have an EAP, you could say, "You might want to talk to a professional about it."

Be sympathetic. But limit the conversation if the employee begins to reveal personal information.

Reinforce your concern. "I really want to help you get back on track."

Reinforce the need for performance improvement. "It's up to you whether you seek professional help or not, but I still need for you to meet your deadlines."

Although the last line above might sound harsh, it is important that employees know that a mental illness does not excuse them from having to meet performance standards. It also might be the impetus they need to seek help.

Mental illness can be devastating. However, with the right treatment, it can be managed and most employees can continue to be productive workers. It's the employee's responsibility to get the right treatment. It's your responsibility to provide reasonable accommodations and performance discussions.

---

[271]Joni E. Johnston, "How to Talk to a Depressed Employee," *Psychology Today*, June 14, 2010, https://www.psychologytoday.com/us/blog/the-human-equation/201006/how-talk-depressed-employee.

Create a Safe Space

Helping your employees feel safe in your workplace can help ease some of the anxiety that your employees, especially the Gen Z ones, may be feeling. Because of the events they have experienced during their formative years, Gen Zers are reported to have a higher need for safety than other generations if they are going to perform at their best.

On February 14, 2018, seventeen students at Marjory Stoneman Douglas High School in Parkland, Florida, were killed by a gunman. That was the sixteenth multiple-victim shooting in US schools since 1996, the year the earliest of Generation Z was born.[272]

It's little wonder that 72 percent of the Gen Z respondents in the "2018 Stress in America" survey conducted by the Harris Poll said school shootings are a significant source of stress for them.[273] And mass shootings don't just happen in schools. According to Statista, there have been ninety-seven mass shootings in the United States since 1996, and Gen Z is very stressed about such shootings.[274]

And despite the cavalier attitude some Gen Zers expressed when COVID-19 first began affecting the United States, an April 2020 report shows Gen Z was more worried about the disease than were Baby Boomers and Millennials.[275]

When some businesses began to reopen following the shelter-in-place orders, the CDC released a sixty-page document containing guidelines that employers could implement to help keep employees safe at work.[276] However, because of differing attitudes toward those

---

[272]Allie Nicodemo and Lia Petronio, "Schools Are Safer Than They Were in the 90s, and School Shootings Are Not More Common Than They Used to Be, Researchers Say," News@Northeaster, February 26, 2018, https://news.northeastern.edu/2018/02/26/schools-are-still-one-of-the-safest-places-for-children-researcher-says/.

[273]American Psychological Association, "Stress in America: Generation Z," October 2018, https://www.apa.org/news/press/releases/stress/2018/stress-gen-z.pdf.

[274]Statista, "Mass Shootings in the U.S. 1982–2020," May 4, 2020, https://www.statista.com/statistics/811487/number-of-mass-shootings-in-the-us/.

[275]Philanthropy News Digest, "Gen Z More Stressed About COVID-19 Than Boomers, Millennials," April 25, 2020, https://philanthropynewsdigest.org/news/gen-z-more-stressed-about-covid-19-than-boomers-millennials.

[276]Centers for Disease Control and Prevention, "Coronavirus Disease 2019," accessed June 15, 2020, https://www.cdc.gov/coronavirus/2019-ncov/community/guidance-business-response.html.

guidelines and the virus itself, not all employers followed them.

Pandemic or not, employers are required by law to keep their employees safe at work. In addition to following federal- and state-mandated safety rules, take these steps to help meet the need for safety and help your employees feel safer at work.

Complete a risk assessment or safety audit to determine how your employees' safety might be compromised. For example, is your building in a high-crime area? Is the parking lot well lit? Are there places where people can hide around the building? Are there multiple entrances to the building that allow access for unmonitored visitors?

Create prevention strategies. Consider adding lighting and security cameras and requiring ID badges or access cards.

Create safety policies and protocol. Train employees on how to respond to emergencies. Taking steps to upgrade your security system not only helps employees feel safe, it demonstrates that you care about their well-being.[277] If you show you care about them, chances are they'll care about their performance.

---

[277]Edward Lowe Foundation, "Keeping Your Employees Safe at Work," accessed June 15, 2020, https://edwardlowe.org/keeping-your-employees-safe-at-work-2/.

CHAPTER 33

HEALTH AND THE LAW

There are many legal ramifications of dealing with employees' physical and mental issues in the workplace. This chapter offers a glimpse into some of them, but be prepared to get professional legal guidance if you encounter unusual or unfamiliar situations.

First, it's imperative that you know that discrimination against applicants or employees because of mental disabilities or perceived disabilities is unlawful. In addition, any information you learn about such disabilities must remain confidential.

The ADA restricts employers from disclosing medical information about their employees without written consent from the affected employee except in certain circumstances. Medical information includes

- physicians reports;
- lab results;
- family and medical leave request forms;
- return to work releases;
- workers' comp records;
- information on disabilities being accommodated;
- information on drug or alcohol rehabilitation; and
- other records that relate in any way to an employee's medical history.

Know the Law!

Employers and supervisors who do not safeguard medical records and keep medical information confidential risk being sued, as was the case in *Ignat v. Yum! Brands, Inc.*, the parent company of KFC, Taco Bell, and Pizza Hut.

According to court documents, Melissa Ignat, who worked in the real estate title department at the company, suffered from bipolar disorder. While she was absent from work because of the disorder, Ignat's supervisor told coworkers about her illness. Ignat said her coworkers subsequently "avoided and shunned her, and one of them asked [her supervisor] if Ignat was likely to 'go postal' at work." Ignat was terminated a few months later and filed suit alleging one cause of action for invasion of privacy by public disclosure of private facts.

The trial court dismissed the case because the disclosure was not in writing, which it determined was necessary based on previous court cases. However, the appellate court disagreed saying, "no one has come up with a good reason for restricting liability to written disclosures, and it has long been acknowledged that oral disclosures can be just as harmful."[278]

Federal law allows employers to disclose medical information without an employee's written consent in these situations:

- when employers are compelled by a court of law to disclose medical information or by a lawsuit filed by an employee;

---

[278]Ignat v. Yum! Brands, Inc., Court of Appeal, Fourth District, Division 3, California, May 18, 2013, https://casetext.com/case/ignat-v-yum-brands-1.

- when medical information is used for administering and maintaining employee benefits;
- when medical information is needed for a workers' comp claim or a request for medical leave;
- when an employee is unable to release medical information to a health care provider; and
- when supervisors need information about necessary restrictions or accommodations for work duties.

Otherwise, don't talk about your employees' health issues and ensure that others don't talk about them as well.

Genetic Information Is Protected

When I conduct harassment and discrimination prevention workshops, I include the fact that it is illegal to discriminate against applicants and employees because of genetic information obtained by the employer. Invariably participants give me a puzzled look—how could an employer obtain genetic information about someone and why would they want to? A lawsuit answers those questions and demonstrates what can happen to an employer as a result.

Title II of the Genetic Information Nondiscrimination Act (GINA) took effect in 2009. According to the EEOC, genetic information includes "information about an individual's genetic tests and the genetic tests of an individual's family members, as well as information about the manifestation of a disease or disorder in an individual's family members [i.e. family medical history]."

In other words, employers are not allowed to ask applicants and employees about their family medical history to find out what kinds of diseases or disorders they might inherit and then base employment decisions on that information. According to the EEOC, a company called Fabricut, Inc., did just that and was sued by the agency for doing so.

In a press release dated May 7, 2013, the EEOC said that when Rhonda Jones, a temporary employee at Fabricut, applied for a permanent position, she was sent to a medical examiner for a preemployment drug screen and physical after being offered the job. While there, "she was required to fill out a questionnaire and disclose the existence of numerous separately listed disorders in her family medical history."

After her medical testing, the examiner decided that Jones needed to be evaluated by her personal physician to determine whether she suffered from carpal tunnel syndrome (CTS). After a variety of tests, Jones's physician said she did not have CTS and Jones forwarded that information to Fabricut; however, the company rescinded the job offer because the lab it used said she did have CTS.

This is what the EEOC said: "Such alleged conduct violates GINA, which makes it illegal to discriminate against employees or applicants because of genetic information, which includes family medical history; and also restricts employers from requesting, requiring or purchasing such information." So, the EEOC sued Fabricut, and the company agreed to pay $50,000.

This was the first GINA-based employment discrimination lawsuit filed by the EEOC, but based on this statement in its May 7 press release, the lawsuit won't be EEOC's last: "One of the six national priorities identified by the EEOC's Strategic Enforcement Plan is for the agency to address emerging and developing issues in equal employment law, which includes genetic information."

Said EEOC regional attorney Barbara Seely, "Although GINA has been law since 2009, many employers still do not understand that requesting family medical history, even through a contract medical examiner, violates this law."[279]

Employers that require medical examinations would be wise to ensure that they are in compliance this law.

Handling Mental Disorders at Work

Most people with severe mental disorders do not work (NAMI reports that 70 to 90 percent are unemployed), but many people with milder cases do work. Two court cases—one finding in favor of the employee and one finding in favor of the employer—provide some insight into

---

[279]US Equal Employment Opportunity Commission, "Fabricut to Pay $50,000 to Settle EEOC Disability and Genetic Information Discrimination Lawsuit," May 7, 2013, https://www.eeoc.gov/newsroom/fabricut-pay-50000-settle-eeoc-disability-and-genetic-information-discrimination-lawsuit.

how to legally manage employees with mental disorders. (See appendix J for an in-depth look at the two cases.)

In both cases, employees suffering from bipolar disorder were terminated; one for "violent outbursts" and the other for threats made against coworkers. Both sued, claiming they had been discriminated against because of their condition. The courts eventually ruled for the employee who had been fired for her outbursts, saying the outbursts were a known symptom of her condition and firing her for that behavior violated the ADA.[280] In the other case, courts upheld the right for the employer to fire the employee who made threats, because it demonstrated that she was terminated for violating written policies prohibiting threats and violence in the workplace—a legitimate, nondiscriminatory reason.[281]

If you'd like to avoid lawsuits, you're encouraged to take the following steps:

- Create clear, written rules of conduct that are job related and consistent with business purposes.
- Engage in the interactive process with employees who disclose a mental disability to determine whether a reasonable accommodation can be arranged.
- Make employment decisions—such as terminating an employee— based on legitimate, nondiscriminatory, business-necessity reasons.

Fortunately, many mental disorders are manageable, allowing those who have them the ability to be successfully employed. Knowing the legalities of handling mental disorders at work helps employers be successful as well.

---

[280]Gambini v. Total Renal Care Inc., United States Court of Appeals, Ninth Circuit, March 8, 2007, https://caselaw.findlaw.com/us-9th-circuit/1100108.html.

[281]Wills v. The Superior Court of Orange County, Court of Appeals of California, Fourth District, Division Three, April 13, 2011, https://scholar.google.com/scholar_case?case=4676249712736054648&q=wills+v.+superior+court+of+orange+county&hl=en&as_sdt=2006&as_vis=1.

Physical Disabilities

The court case of *A. M. v. Albertsons LLC* demonstrates the need for employers to unfailingly accommodate employees with physical disabilities. The plaintiff in the case was employed as a checkout clerk at Albertsons. A previous treatment for cancer left her with a condition that made her mouth excessively dry. To counter this, she drank large volumes of water, which made it necessary for her to take frequent restroom breaks. On one occasion, her requests for a bathroom break were ignored and she urinated on herself at the check stand. She later sued, claiming Albertsons failed to accommodate her disability and failed to engage in the interactive process. A jury awarded her $200,000, which was upheld on appeal.[282]

Allowing for more restroom breaks should have been an easy accommodation, but other accommodations can be more difficult. Although the ADA might appear to impose an unfair burden on employers at times, many resources are available to help companies comply with the law and help people with disabilities enjoy an equal employment opportunity. These resources include

- Job Accommodation Network, which provides free consulting services about all aspects of job accommodations;
- Work Opportunity Tax Credit (WOTC), which allows employers to reduce their federal tax liability by as much as $2,400 per new hire; and
- Disabled Access Credit, which helps small businesses pay for the cost of making their businesses accessible (up to $5,000 in tax credits).

State and federal laws guarantee equal opportunity in employment for individuals with disabilities. Employing qualified individuals—people with skills, experience, and education—even though they might have a disability, benefits employers as well as those who want to work.

---

[282]A. M. v. Albertsons, LLC, The Court of Appeal of the State of California, First Appellate District, Division Four, September 18, 2009, https://law.justia.com/cases/california/court-of-appeal/2009/a122307/.

CHAPTER 34

ENCOURAGE PHYSICAL FITNESS

Not long after shelter-in-place orders went into effect in spring 2020, people started joking about the "Quarantine 15"—the fifteen pounds of weight people were gaining because of being home all day and stress eating.

That was not really good considering many of us were already fifteen or more pounds overweight. The US surgeon general has said that obesity has reached epidemic proportions in the country, and that includes members of Gen Z. According to the Centers for Disease Control (CDC), "Obesity now affects 1 in 5 children and adolescents in the United States."[283]

Scientific evidence demonstrates that obesity can lead to a variety of serious health conditions such as the following:

- high blood pressure (hypertension)
- high LDL (low-density lipoprotein) cholesterol, low HDL (high-density lipoprotein) cholesterol, or high levels of triglycerides

---

[283]Centers for Disease Control and Prevention, "Overweight & Obesity," accessed June 12, 2020, https://www.cdc.gov/obesity/childhood/index.html.

- type 2 diabetes
- coronary heart disease
- stroke
- gallbladder disease
- osteoarthritis (a breakdown of cartilage and bone within a joint)
- sleep apnea and breathing problems
- many types of cancer
- lower quality of life
- mental illness such as clinical depression, anxiety, and other mental disorders
- body pain and difficulty with physical functioning[284]

Obesity, poor nutrition, and a lack of physical inactivity can also lead to missed workdays. The authors of "State-Level Estimates of Obesity: Attributable Costs of Absenteeism" say obese employees miss almost twice as many workdays each year compared with employees of normal weight.[285] In addition to absenteeism, there is presenteeism, when employees work while struggling with physical and emotional health problems. According to the report *Weight Control and the Workplace*, obesity-related absenteeism and presenteeism cost US employers $73 billion annually.[286]

Obese employees can also cause higher health insurance costs for employers. According to the authors of "The Association Between Employee Obesity and Employer Costs," "Normal weight employees cost on average $3,830 per year in covered medical, sick day, short-term disability, and workers' compensation claims combined; morbidly obese employees cost more than twice that amount, or $8,067, in 2011 dollars."[287]

[284]Ibid.

[285]Tatiana Andreyeva, Joerg Luedicke, and Y. Claire Wang, "State-Level Estimates of Obesity: Attributable Costs of Absenteeism," *Journal of Occupational and Environmental Medicine* 56, no. 11 (2014): 1120–7, https://doi.org/10.1097/JOM.0000000000000298.

[286]Northeast Business Group on Health, *Weight Control and the Workplace*, accessed June 16, 2020, https://nebgh.org/wp-content/uploads/2016/04/NEBGH_SC_WeightControlFINAL10-31-13.pdf.

[287]Karen Van Nuys, Denise Globe, Daisy Ng-Mak, Hoiwan Cheung, Jeff Sullivan, and Dan Goldman, "The Association Between Employee Obesity and Employer Costs: Evidence From a Panel of U. S. Employers," *American Journal of Health Promotion* 28, no. 5 (2014) 277–85, https://doi.org/10.4278/ajhp.120905-QUAN-428.

If you're thinking about never hiring obese applicants, you should think again. Although there is no federal law providing protection from discrimination because of weight, people who are obese may qualify for protection under the ADA. Obesity can be linked to underlying medical conditions that substantially limit a major life activity, and that qualifies it as a disability.

Promote Health

Discriminating against applicants and employees who are obese is not the answer; a far better approach is to promote a healthy workplace. Although employees are ultimately responsible for their own health, employers can engage in a variety of low-cost activities to encourage healthy behavior. Consider the following ideas:

- Provide fruit instead of doughnuts at morning meetings and healthy food at business lunches.
- Work with vendors to ensure that company vending machines offer healthy food as well as cookies and candy.
- Make bottled or filtered water available and convenient.
- Encourage employees to walk during their rest and meal breaks.
- Invite nutritionists and other health care workers to speak at company meetings.
- Hold a weight loss competition.
- Work with local gyms to provide corporate discounts to employees.
- Sponsor health screenings.
- Encourage employees to get annual checkups.
- Incorporate fitness goals into workplace performance goals (if work related).
- Pay for a fitness instructor to lead exercise classes at work.
- Provide incentives and rewards for healthy behavior. Some legalities are associated with this, so employers should check with their legal counsel before doing so.

These kinds of activities can help employees become healthier, and healthy employees record fewer absences, greater productivity, and reduced health insurance costs. In sum, healthy workers lead to a healthier bottom line.

Chronic Absenteeism

What can you do about chronically absent employees?

First, determine what you are required to do. If you have at least fifty employees within a seventy-five-mile radius, you are required to provide Family Medical Leave Act leave to qualifying employees. This allows employees up to twelve weeks of unpaid leave because of a health condition that makes them unable to work or to perform one or more essential duties of their job. Your state might have a leave law as well.

Next, if you haven't done so already, create a policy that addresses the use of sick leave and other leaves of absence: how leave is accrued, qualifications for use, procedures for calling in sick, and possible disciplinary action if misused. Distribute the policy to employees, have an open discussion about its purpose, and have employees sign an acknowledgment form that they have received it.

Once the policy is in place, be sure to consistently enforce it. Monitor absences and talk to employees who frequently call in sick to determine whether a leave of absence or accommodation is necessary. If employees continue to be chronically absent despite taking state- or federal-mandated leaves or being reasonably accommodated, you may discipline them or even terminate them, but I recommend that you confer with an employment attorney first. Be sure to keep detailed records of employee absences, the reasons for them, and any disciplinary actions taken because of them.

According to the CDC, chronic illnesses are among the most preventable of all health problems. Talking to employees about their chronic absences could lead to better choices to prevent their chronic illnesses.

Employees Who Call in Sick When They're Not

Employers spend about 36 percent of their base payroll on employee absences. Direct costs include wages and benefits paid to the employee during the absence, overtime paid to other employees, and temporary staffing.

Employees have the statutory right to be absent from work for a number of reasons, including illness, injury, civic duty, and family obligations. It's the employees who call in sick when they're not that present a problem.

In the Harris Interactive survey "Working in America: Absent Workforce," nearly 40 percent of the respondents said they had called in sick for reasons other than being sick, such as taking a mental health day or running personal errands. Nine percent said they called in sick because they were too tired from staying up late watching a sporting event, awards show, or presidential election.[288]

Kat's Take

Gen Zers are more likely than older workers to take days off for their mental health. Instead of wondering if employees are *really* sick every time they call in sick, try designating a few "floater" or "mental health days."

A floater is a day an employee can take off for any reason—going to Disneyland or to just to get a breather. Floater days allow for more flexibility than "sick leave," and employees are less likely to lie about being sick if they know they have a few "any-reason" days. My previous companies allowed up to three floaters per year, which was the perfect amount, in my opinion.

For Gen Zers, this allows flexibility that gives them time for a mental health day. It also allows for some spur-of-the-moment trips, family emergencies, or other incidents that are a part of life. And your company will get credit from your employees for offering more flexibility and work-life balance for it.

---

[288]Kronos, "Working in America: Absent Workforce," accessed June 16, 2020, http://www.workforceinstitute.org/wp-content/themes/revolution/docs/Workingin-Amer-Survey.pdf.

"Culpable absenteeism" is the term used for employees who are absent without authorization for reasons that are within their control. These unplanned employee absences cost about 9 percent of the employer's base payroll. However, productivity, morale of coworkers who cover for employees playing hooky, and customer service may also suffer as a result of unplanned absences, meaning the indirect costs often exceed the direct costs.

Besides illness, injury, and obligations, why don't employees show up for work? According to the article "Attendance Management," reasons include low morale, poor working conditions, boredom on the job, lack of job satisfaction, inadequate leadership, poor supervision, stress, excessive workload, and discontent.[289]

Employers are often tempted to discipline employees who misuse sick leave. However, it's difficult to prove that employees have called in sick when they're not, and research has shown that traditional methods of absenteeism control that focus on disciplinary actions are ineffective.

Instead of trying to impose negative consequences, focus on making employees *want* to show up for work. They are more likely to show up when they

- identify with the goals of the organization and care what happens to it;
- find their jobs meaningful;
- like working for the organization;
- feel free to discuss their on-the-job problems with their immediate supervisor; and
- feel confident and have supportive relationships at work.

After you have addressed the factors that attract your employees to work, you can take the following steps to address any absenteeism problems:

- Create an attendance policy that clearly communicates the expectation of attendance.

---

[289]Benefits Interface, "Attendance Management," September 2013, https://benefits. org/optimize/optimize-risk-sharing/attendance-management.

- Monitor attendance and talk to employees about the purpose of sick leave and the impact an absence has on the organization and their coworkers.
- Provide supervisory training—management styles that are too authoritarian tend to promote high levels of absenteeism.
- Provide conflict resolution and team-building training—employees frequently say they do not go to work because they are angry with other employees.
- Provide personal time off (or "floater" days as mentioned in Kat's Take) in addition to vacation and sick leave, which gives employees a set amount of days off to be used at their discretion.
- Provide incentives such as cashing in unused sick leave and rewards for perfect attendance.
- Provide flexibility if possible, such as working from home.[290]

Employees who are committed to the company show up for work. Employers who foster that commitment end up paying people to work instead of paying them to stay home.

---

[290]Ibid.

CHAPTER 35

ALCOHOL AND DRUGS

Shortly after the pandemic shutdown in March 2020, memes started appearing on the internet about people drinking more alcohol, especially during the day. Perhaps people weren't joking because, according to a *Newsweek* article, alcohol sales increased 55 percent the first week people started staying home because of the shelter-in-place orders.[291]

Because the oldest members of Gen Z are in their mid-twenties, they probably didn't contribute much to the increase in alcohol sales. Besides, research indicates that members of Gen Z who are of legal drinking age don't drink that much alcohol. Instead, they tend to favor marijuana.

According to an *Ad Age* article, "It's always hard to generalize about an entire age group, but early signs suggest (Gen Z) will be a generation of marijuana consumers, embracing legal pot to unwind or treat ailments like insomnia and anxiety as perceptions of a drug once seen as a vice for lazy stoners get turned upside down."[292]

The perception of marijuana might have changed for many

---

[291]Jade Bremner, "U.S. Alcohol Sales Increase 55 Percent in One Week Amid Coronavirus Pandemic," *Newsweek*, April 1, 2020, https://www.newsweek.com/us-alcohol-sales-increase-55-percent-one-week-amid-coronavirus-pandemic-1495510.

[292]*Ad Age*, "Generation Z Americans Will Be the Ultimate Cannabis Consumers," April 22, 2019, https://adage.com/article/cmo-strategy/generation-z-americans-will-be-ultimate-cannabis-consumers/2165736.

Americans, and it is legal in a growing number of states. However, as of this writing, the federal government still declares it an illegal drug and requires some private employers to have drug-free workplaces.[293] Undoubtedly, the legalization of marijuana in many states has caused some people to believe they can smoke pot and work, but employers still have the right to insist on a drug-free workplace. Implementing a policy that addresses marijuana and other drugs helps your organization establish your standards, provide clarity to employees, and prevent lawsuits.

Attorneys J. Christopher Selman and Alexander G. Thrasher suggest your company drug policy should:

- define the terms "marijuana," "cannabis," or any other derivation of the drug. Simply prohibiting the use of "illegal drugs" can create ambiguity because of marijuana's legal status in various jurisdictions;
- indicate the use of marijuana, recreationally or on the job, is strictly prohibited;
- articulate drug-testing policies and procedures, including penalties for failing a drug test;
- educate employees on clinical issues relating to marijuana, such as its effects on the body, the length of time it can continue to impair cognitive and physiological functions, and the potential impacts on workplace safety and performance; and
- be included in recruiting and new-hire onboarding materials to ensure notice to the individual.[294]

Although medical marijuana is also legal in some states, employers in many of them may still prohibit card-carrying users from having it in their system while at work. It's important that you know your state's law and your company policy regarding medical marijuana before you take

---

[293]Substance Abuse and Mental Health Services Administration, "Drug-Free Workplace Programs," accessed June 12, 2020, https://www.samhsa.gov/workplace/legal/federal-laws.

[294]J. Christopher Selman and Alexander G. Thrasher, "Changing Marijuana Laws and Effective Drug Testing Policy," Labor & Employment Insights, February 7, 2019, https://www.employmentlawinsights.com/2019/02/changing-marijuana-laws-and-effective-drug-testing-policy/.

action against an employee for using it. See appendix K for discussion of a 2012 case involving medicinal marijuana in the workplace.

Alcohol Use and Abuse

Even though many employers are focused on marijuana use among their employees, there's a drug that's been legal for years that employers should really be concerned about—alcohol.

According to the federal Substance Abuse and Mental Health Services Administration, about 14 million Americans age twelve and up had an alcohol abuse problem in 2018.[295]

That's a problem for employers because, according to Robert J. Grossman, author of the article "What to Do about Substance Abuse," substance abusers are "three-and-a-half times more likely to cause accidents at work and in transit." Substance abusers also use more sick days than their coworkers (an average of 45 percent) and "their health care costs are double their peers."[296]

Despite those numbers, drinking at work has become somewhat in vogue again. In his article "3 Reasons Alcohol at Work Is No Biggie," Jared Shelly says employers "overcorrected" by banning alcohol at work when corporate America tried to clean up its act in the second half of the twentieth century. He cited several business owners who agreed that "drinking at work isn't a big deal" because it's common among companies like Twitter and Yelp, employees need a break, and it contributes to a "fun" atmosphere.[297]

Perhaps it's because alcohol is legal and more socially acceptable that employers tend to worry less about its negative impact at work. In a 2014 *Washington Post* article, Joyce Russell says, "In some cases,

---

[295]Substance Abuse and Mental Health Services Administration, "Key Substance Use and Mental Health Indicators in the United States: Results from the 2018 National Survey on Drug Use and Health," accessed June 16, 2020, https://www.samhsa.gov/data/sites/default/files/cbhsq-reports/NSDUHNationalFindingsReport2018/NSDUHNationalFindingsReport2018.pdf

[296]Robert J. Grossman, "What to Do About Substance Abuse," Society for Human Resource Management, November 1, 2010, https://www.shrm.org/hr-today/news/hr-magazine/pages/1110grossman.aspx.

[297]Jared Shelly, "3 Reasons Alcohol at Work Is No Biggie," BizPhilly, June 26, 2015, https://www.phillymag.com/business/2015/06/26/alcohol-office-mad-men/.

employees and even managers don't even know what the company's policies are for drinking at work. Or, if there are rules, they are not being enforced."[298] Such companies should know that one in five workers who participated in a George Washington University survey reported they had been "injured or put in danger on the job because of a colleague's drinking, or having to work harder, redo work or cover for a co-worker as a result of a fellow employee's drinking."[299]

John Pompe, manager of disability and behavioral health programs at Caterpillar Inc., told Grossman, "Alcohol—and substance-related problems—present a clear threat to employers in terms of productivity loss, safety, employee engagement, use of supervisory time and health care costs. The problem is that most employees with substance abuse problems go unrecognized and even more go untreated."[300]

Warning Signs

In her *Psychology Today* article "Warning Signs Your Co-Worker May Have an Alcohol Problem," Dr. Kristen Fuller says symptoms of alcohol abuse include employees who

- smell like alcohol;
- walk with an unsteady gait;
- exhibit hangover symptoms including headaches, sensitivity to light, and irritability;
- display unexplained changes in mood or behavior;
- have bloodshot eyes;
- sleep while at work;
- show a decline in overall appearance including bad breath, wrinkled clothes, and disheveled hair;
- repeatedly use mints or mouthwash;

---

[298]Joyce Russell, "Does Your Workplace Have a Drinking Culture (and Problem)?" *Washington Post*, March 9, 2014, https://www.washingtonpost.com/business/capitalbusiness/does-your-workplace-have-a-drinking-culture-and-problem/2014/03/07/094b8a3c-a55f-11e3-8466-d34c451760b9_story.html.

[299]George Washington University Medical Center, *Workplace Screening & Brief Intervention: What Employers Can and Should Do About Excessive Alcohol Use*, March 2008, https://bigsbirteducation.webs.com/Workplace_SBI_Report_Final.pdf.

[300]Grossman, "What to Do About Substance Abuse."

- avoid supervisors;
- are frequently late;
- frequently use sick leave;
- are often absent;
- bring alcohol in a concealed container to work;
- have difficulty concentrating;
- exhibit certain patterns of absenteeism (on Fridays, Mondays, or in the aftermath of payday);
- have unexplained disappearances while at work;
- withdraw from contact with other coworkers or employees;
- often have tense or strained interactions with others;
- need an unusual amount of time to complete a routine task;
- display outbursts of aggression or belligerence toward others;
- miss assignment deadlines;
- show an unexplained decline in work quality; or
- use multiple excuses to explain workplace deficiencies.[301]

Recommended Approach

The Occupational Safety and Health Administration suggests a comprehensive drug-free workforce approach that includes five components:

1. A policy
2. Supervisor training
3. Employee education
4. Employee assistance
5. Testing

According to OSHA, such programs, especially when testing is included, must be reasonable and take into consideration employee rights to privacy. In addition, some states, such as California, require employers to reasonably accommodate employees who wish to voluntarily participate in a drug or alcohol rehabilitation program.

---

[301]Kristen Fuller, "Warning Signs Your Co-Worker May Have an Alcohol Problem," *Psychology Today*, April 11, 2019, https://www.psychologytoday.com/us/blog/happiness-is-state-mind/201904/warning-signs-your-co-worker-may-have-alcohol-problem.

Know that if you employ fifteen or more employees, you cannot refuse to hire or promote or fire someone who is a recovering alcoholic because of ADA restrictions. (Your state discrimination law might have a different employee count.)

Also, if employees tell you (before you discover it) that they need to seek treatment for alcoholism, you are required to begin an interactive process to try to reasonably accommodate them. Such accommodations are usually time off without pay to seek treatment.

However, be aware that it is lawful to discipline all employees whose use of alcohol interferes with their job. See appendix L for discussion of one high-profile case involving an employee who was terminated because of alcohol use.

Employers do their employees and themselves a favor by addressing every kind of substance abuse in the workplace, because every kind of drug use is a threat to everyone involved, regardless of whether it is legal or not.

Be Careful How You Party

It's good to celebrate various events with employees, as discussed in chapter 25. However, because most celebrations usually involve alcohol, consider the following steps if you're the one throwing the shindig. See appendix M for discussion of one party that caused massive headaches for the company.

Have the event at a third-party location that has its own liquor license and crew. Parties at your workplace (or at your home) will more than likely make you the responsible party if there is any type of incident. Also, it's best not to make employees work at the party doing setup, serving, or cleanup because if they are hourly employees, you'll need to pay them for their time, including overtime pay if appropriate.

Emphasize that attendance is voluntary. If the party is mandatory, you could be liable for wages, third-party claims, and workers' compensation. If employees are even "expected" to attend, it will likely be deemed a mandatory function. Pay attention to employee communications (e.g., "We expect to see everyone at the company picnic on Saturday") and eliminate the expectation of compensation for attendance.

Allow employees to bring guests, as their presence usually encourages employees to be on their best behavior. Employees often act differently out of the traditional work environment, so clearly communicate expectations of behavior and attire for them as well as their guests.

Ensure that plenty of nonalcoholic beverages are available. Also have guests buy their own drinks from paid bartenders who can monitor their consumption (and refuse to serve them if they're underage or have had too much to drink). Consider having only beer and wine available and order plenty of food to help slow the absorption of alcohol.

Promptly deal with inappropriate behavior, such as excessive drinking, insubordination, employee disagreements, inappropriate discussions, and reports of unwanted sexual advances.

Following the above suggestions can help company parties result in fun instead of lawsuits.

CONCLUSION

Throughout this book, we have tried to show you how members of Gen Z may present some distinct challenges to employers and how these youngest employees may be different from older generations. However, it's important to remember that even though members of Gen Z have some shared experiences, each is a unique individual with unique strengths and weaknesses.

We have highlighted some of the experiences that have shaped this generation to help you understand this generation. But your best bet at understanding your Gen Z employees will be to get to know them personally. When you recognize their strengths and their weaknesses, you can better provide them the training and guidance that will inspire their best work.

Because Gen Zers have grown up in a fast-paced world where social media and technology are ever present, their strengths tend to lie in their adaptability, their positive outlook on life, and their ability to collaborate with others. Although they may lack the commonsense skills of prior generations, they are eager to learn, eager to make their mark in the world, and eager to take steps to make the world a better place. Overall, Gen Zers are likely to be politically involved and active in their communities, as they want to feel like they have purpose. Their intrinsic strengths can enhance your company culture and provide new perspectives that might open your firm up to a new audience, market, or direction.

Like every new generation, Gen Zers will shake everything up (as they already have) and move the world forward. They can also shake up your organization, your team, your unit for the better. Listen to them. Train them. Invite them to give input on projects, ideas, and the organization's plans. You'll be amazed at the dramatic difference you can see after you take these few extra steps.

PROVIDING REFERENCES

B e truthful when providing references for past employees.
Employers are commonly advised not to give any information
about former employees to prospective employers. Indeed, in his
book *Handling Employment for Bosses and Supervisors*, California labor
and employment attorney Geoffrey H. Hopper states, "It is recommended to my clients that they only confirm hiring and termination
dates. DO NOT address whether or not the individual is rehirable."[302]

Hopper is erring on the side of caution here as California Civil
Code Section 47 (c) "authorizes a current or former employer, or the
employer's agent, to answer whether or not the employer would rehire
a current or former employee," meaning that employers are protected
from claims of libel or slander when responding to the "rehirable-or-
not" question.

Being truthful also means *not* providing good references and letters
of recommendation for employees who don't deserve them. That could
lead to a lawsuit like this one.

---

[302]Geoffrey H. Hopper, *Handling Employment for Bosses and Supervisors* (Brandon, OR: Robert D. Reed Publishers, 2008).

A school district in the Midwest (referred to here as SD A) was sued by two students in another school district (referred to here as SD B) for failing to disclose information about a former teacher. According to news reports, the teacher was forced to resign from his teaching position with SD A because of "complaints of inappropriate behavior from parents of a fifth-grade girl. And [the teacher] previously had been disciplined for having pornography on his classroom computer."

Despite his forced resignation, the teacher was given a letter of recommendation by SD A, and he was subsequently hired by SD B, where he was working when he was arrested for molestation. The teacher was found guilty of molesting two girls in SD A and eight girls in SD B, and both school districts settled lawsuits with the victims.

However, a new lawsuit was filed by SD B students against SD A for passing the teacher to SD B with the knowledge that he had sexually abused students. Especially damaging to SD A was an email obtained by the plaintiffs' attorney written by a former assistant superintendent to a union representative: "Please keep this confidential, but I thought you would be interested in hearing that [the teacher] was arrested in [SD B] today. I don't know the specific charges, but it appears to be much worse than the issues he faced here. I'm glad we took the steps we did to get him out of the district. I believe it was you who said that he was on a path to further problems."

The lawsuit was originally dismissed; however, the Fourth District Appellate Court reversed the dismissal saying, "[SD A] and its administrators could have refused to prepare a letter of recommendation, warned [SD B] of the potential danger, and/or reported the abuse . . . as mandated by the Reporting Act."

Thus, sending off an employee who engaged in inappropriate behavior with a good reference can lead to a lawsuit.

The court also said that SD A could have warned SD B about the potential danger of hiring the teacher. Former employers are not legally required to provide information to an applicant's prospective employer about any wrongdoing the applicant committed while in their employ. However, employers who feel it is their moral obligation to do so are protected from claims of libel or slander if they can prove that the information is based on reasonable evidence and provided without malice.

What about providing a good reference for employees who *do* deserve it? I suggest giving a balanced account of their performance. Only providing information about their strengths and not their weaknesses could be misleading as well.

When asked by a potential employer to give information about a former employee, you should

- route all reference requests to one person, preferably the HR manager;
- create specific guidelines to be followed for anyone providing a reference; and
- have former employees sign a waiver to release information to prospective employers.

APPENDIX B

AT-WILL EMPLOYMENT PRECAUTIONS

At-will employment and probationary periods don't go together. I often find that at-will employers describe a ninety-day probationary period for new employees in their handbooks. It usually looks something like this:

During the probationary period, employees have the opportunity to evaluate the company as a place to work and management has the opportunity to evaluate the employee. During this period, both the employee and the company have the right to terminate employment without advance notice or reason. Completion of the probationary period does not guarantee continued employment.

I suggest at-will employers get rid of probationary periods because they're unnecessary and confusing and could make the at-will relationship null and void. At-will employers may terminate the employment relationship at any time for any legal reason, or no reason, without warning or prior notification. They aren't required to give employees ninety days to see if things work out.

In union organizations, employment is at-will during the probationary period, but after you pass probation, you can be terminated only for cause (except for layoffs). Using the term "probationary period" implies things will change once the period is over. Some courts have even ruled that the completion of a probationary period suggests an implied contract and that companies may fire only for good cause after the term is completed.

If an employee will receive benefits and/or an increase in pay after ninety days, make that plain without mentioning a "probationary period."

Also, refrain from calling your employees "permanent" employees as that implies they won't ever be fired. The more accurate term is "regular employees."

Something else to consider: Carefully word an at-will disclaimer. Choose your words wisely, lest they come back to bite you. That's the message the National Labor Relations Board (NLRB) sent with two rulings its representatives made on the wording of at-will disclaimers in employee handbooks.

The NLRB is an independent federal agency responsible for safeguarding employees' rights to organize and form unions. It also acts to prevent and remedy unfair labor practices committed by private sector employers and unions. In doing so, the NLRB investigates complaints of unfair labor practices, and its administrative law judges make decisions on those complaints.

Evidently, someone complained about the at-will disclaimer in a Hyatt Hotels employee handbook. According to the article "NLRB's Challenge of At-Will Language 'a Terrible Stretch,'" an NLRB regional director found fault with the company for having an "overly broad and discriminatory acknowledgment form in its employee handbooks," which seemed to violate the employees' right to organize.[303] Similar language was in a handbook of the American Red Cross in Arizona, and it was also ruled unlawful by an NLRB administrative law judge.

What's the problem with the disclaimers? NLRB acting general counsel Lafe Solomon explained that they seemed to encourage employees to believe nothing could change their at-will status, not even union representation, meaning union organization would be futile. Discouraging union organization is a violation of the National Labor Relations Act.

What language does the NLRB allow? The agency approved this

---

[303]S. Hill, "NLRB's Challenge of At-Will Language 'a Terrible Stretch,'" Society for Human Resource Management, August 14, 2012, http://www.*shrm*.org/legalissues/federalresources/.

disclaimer in Rocha Transportation's handbook:

Employment with Rocha Transportation is employment at-will. Employment at-will may be terminated with or without cause and with or without notice at any time by the employee or the Company. Nothing in this Handbook or in any document or statement shall limit the right to terminate employment at-will. No manager, supervisor, or employee of Rocha Transportation has any authority to enter into an agreement for employment for any specified period of time or to make an agreement for employment other than at-will. Only the president of the Company has the authority to make any such agreement and then only in writing.

Solomon concluded the Rocha disclaimer was lawful because it didn't require employees to agree that their at-will status could never be changed or to refrain from seeking to change it.[304]

So, a word to the wise: check your handbooks, applications, offer letters, and anything else that includes an at-will disclaimer to see if it differs greatly from the one above because this is now a potential area of concern.

---

[304]Ibid.

SOCIAL MEDIA
AND THE NLRA

Employers get into trouble when they have policies that could be construed as limiting their employees' rights under Section 7 of the National Labor Relations Act (NLRA), which protects an employee's right to engage in "concerted activity" to press for better "working conditions."[305] According to the National Labor Relations Board (NLRB), broad and ambiguous prohibitions on employee discussions are probably going to run afoul of the NLRA.

One employer's policy that prohibited "making disparaging comments about the company through any media, including online blogs, other electronic media or through the media" was deemed unlawful by the NLRB because "it would reasonably be construed to restrict Section 7 activity, such as statements that the Employer is, for example, not treating employees fairly or paying them sufficiently." Furthermore, according to the NLRB, the policy did not contain language that clarified to employees that the policy did not restrict their Section 7 rights.

Another employer's policy that employees should not identify

[305]National Labor Relations Board, "The NLRB and Social Media," accessed October 3, 2020, https://www.nlrb.gov/about-nlrb/rights-we-protect/your-rights/the-nlrb-and-social-media. All quotes in this appendix are from the same source.

themselves as working for the company unless they were discussing the terms and conditions of their employment in an appropriate manner was found to be unlawful by the NLRB because the policy implicitly prohibited "inappropriate" discussions of the terms and conditions of their employment without defining what an "appropriate" or "inappropriate" discussion would be.

The NLRB concluded that "employees would therefore reasonably interpret the rule to prohibit protected activity, including criticism of the Employer's labor policies, treatment of employees, and terms and conditions of employment." Even though this employer had a "savings clause" in its social media policy stating that the policy would not interfere with employees' rights to unionize, bargain collectively, or engage in other concerted activity, the NLRB found that the savings clause was insufficient because "an employee could not reasonably be expected to know that this language encompasses discussions the Employer deems 'inappropriate.'"

The "Team Member Conduct & Work Rules" of another employer were determined to be unlawful by the NLRB because the prohibitions on "disrespectful conduct" and "inappropriate conversations" were overly broad. According to the NLRB, "Employer policies should not be so sweeping that they prohibit the kinds of activity protected by federal labor law, such as the discussion of wages or working conditions among employees." Therefore, policies that generally prohibit "unprofessional" or "inappropriate" communication are viewed as being overly broad and unlawful.

The NLRB also frowns on policies that require employees to get permission to use the company's name or logo outside the course of business. Says the NLRB, "this provision of the policy could reasonably be construed to restrict employees' Section 7 rights to use the Employer's name and logo while engaging in protected concerted activity, such as in electronic or paper leaflets, cartoons, or picket signs in connection with a protest involving the terms and conditions of employment." And the board also dislikes policies that prohibit employee communications to the media (or require prior authorization).

FASHIONABLE PRECAUTIONS

When creating dress codes, you need to avoid your own fashion faux pas.

The NLRB has established its own list of fashion "don'ts" regarding employers' dress code policies. Why does the NLRB care about employers' dress code policies? Because it wants to ensure that employers do not establish policies that could be construed as limiting their employees' rights to engage in "concerted activity" to advocate for better "working conditions."

Thus, the NLRB frowns on policies that restrict employees from wearing clothing and accessories that express their feelings about their employment. Some fashion "don'ts" from the NLRB include the following:

- Telling employees they can only wear caps with the company logo. Quad/Graphics, Inc., implemented a policy prohibiting employees from wearing baseball caps without the company logo on them for safety reasons, to reduce gang activity and to facilitate employees' interactions with customers. The NLRB ruled that the policy was unlawful because it prevented employees from expressing pro-union sentiments.[306]

- Disciplining employees for questioning or complaining about dress code policies. Rumor had it that Wyndham Resort Development Corporation was going to require its male employees to tuck in their "resort casual" shirts. After an employee became agitated when questioning the VP of in-house sales about it in front of coworkers, he was given a written warning and then terminated. The NLRB ruled against the employer because the employee's complaining was tantamount to engaging in concerted protected activity.[307]

- Placing overly broad restrictions on what employees may wear at work. Alma Products Company ran afoul of the NLRB because it disciplined an employee for wearing the "slave shirt." Created in 1993 during union negotiations, the shirt had the word "slave," an image of a ball and chain, and employees' time clock numbers displayed on the back. Some employees wore the shirt with some regularity until 2005 when the company hired a new CEO. Considering the shirt to be racially offensive, he ordered the HR manager to draft a new dress code policy that stated that "clothing displaying vulgar/obscene phrases, remarks or images which may be racially, sexually or otherwise offensive and clothing displaying words or images derogatory to the Company will not be allowed in any facilities." An employee subsequently wore the slave shirt to work and was docked pay while he was sent home to change. The union then filed a complaint against the company for violating the employee's right to engage in a concerted protected activity, and the NLRB agreed

---

[306]Howard M. Bloom and Daniel D. Schudroff, "NLRB Judge Says Employers' Baseball Cap Logo Restriction Violates Employees' Section 7 Rights," JacksonLewis, August 8, 2013, https://www.laborandcollectivebargaining.com/2013/08/articles/nlra/nlrb-judge-says-employers-baseball-cap-logo-restriction-violates-employees-section-7-rights/.

[307]Joe Lustig, "Questioning Dress Code Was Protected Activity, NLRB Holds," *Joe's HR and Benefits Blog*, March 14, 2011, https://joelustig.wordpress.com/2011/03/14/firing-employee-who-questioned-dress-code-violated-law-nlrb-holds/.

with the charge.[308]

Although some of these examples involve unionized organizations, these fashion "don'ts" apply to nonunion businesses as well. The NLRB will get involved in any business that appears to be dissuading its employees in any way from expressing their opinions about the terms and conditions of their jobs, even with their clothing.

The NLRB is not the "final word" on dress code policies, and these cases might be "outliers"; however, employers need to be aware of the agency's positions.

So, here's a fashion "do": ensure that your dress code policy is as specific as possible, clearly states the legitimate business and safety reasons for its existence, and lets employees know that it is not intended to interfere with their right to engage in protected communications.

---

[308]Brian Murnaugh, "NLRB Judge Strikes Down Employer's Dress Code Following 'Slave' Shirt Discipline," Holland & Hart, August 2013, https://www.hollandhart.com/nlrb-judge-strikes-down-employers-dress-code-following-slave-shirt-discipline.

TROUBLESOME WORDS

H ere are some things supervisors have said to cause lawsuits:

"Because you have kids." This is what a supervisor who did not promote a qualified female sales manager allegedly told her when she asked why she had not received the promotion. The employee was awarded $301,500 (*Lust v. Sealy, Inc.*).[309]

"God decided only women can give birth." These words were said to have been spoken by the supervisor who denied family medical leave to a male state trooper when he requested time off to care for his wife and newborn child. The trooper claimed the supervisor told him that his wife would have to be "dead or in a coma" for the trooper to qualify for family medical leave. The trooper was awarded $375,000 in damages (*Knussman v. Maryland*).[310]

She has "an Ellen DeGeneres kind of look," said the supervisor who fired a female front-desk customer service representative, despite her favorable performance reviews. The supervisor went on to say that the employee lacked the "Midwestern girl look" and that women

---

[309] Lust v. Sealy Inc., *United States Court of Appeals, Seventh Circuit*, September 7, 2004, https://caselaw.findlaw.com/us-7th-circuit/1235855.html.

[310]American Civil Liberties Union, "ACLU Wins $375,000 Jury Award in Case of Dad Denied Leave to Care for First-Born Child," February 3, 1999, https://www.aclu.org/press-releases/aclu-wins-375000-jury-award-case-dad-denied-leave-care-first-born-child.

working at the front desk should be "pretty." The employee was awarded $1,800 in lost wages, $19,000 in emotional distress, $30,000 in punitive damages, $136,000 in attorney fees, and $13,350 in costs (*Lewis v. Heartland Inns of America*).[311]

"Disgusting." That's how the supervisor described the skin condition of an employee suffering side effects of medication taken for panic attacks. The supervisor also criticized the employee's body odor (also a side effect) and belittled her in front of other employees. After being terminated for excessive absences related to her condition, the employee sued for wrongful termination, harassment, disability discrimination, and failure of the employer to accommodate her condition. She was awarded $1,905,000 (*Roby v. McKesson*).[312]

The lesson here is not just a reminder that supervisors need to be careful about what they say to their employees. The more important lessons are that employers and supervisors

- may not discriminate against employees or applicants because of their family obligations;
- need to be knowledgeable about leave-of-absence laws and have HR personnel communicate with employees about their eligibility for such leaves;
- may not discriminate against employees or applicants because of their failure to comply with gender stereotypes; and
- must treat all employees with respect and make reasonable accommodations for their illnesses.

In addition to complying with employment law, supervisors would do well to adopt the philosophy that it is better to be silent and be considered a fool than to speak and remove all doubt.

---

[311]Dickinson Law, "Too Hot v. Not: The Rest of the Story," December 22, 2010, https://www.dickinsonlaw.com/blogs-articles/2010/12/22/too-hot-v-not-the-rest-of-the-story.

[312]Seyfarth Shaw, "California Supreme Court Expands Basis for Harassment Claims While Limiting Punitive Damages," December 2009, https://www.seyfarth.com/dir_docs/news_item/403e84bc-277b-4525-901c-43e3485f42bc_documentupload.pdf.

TRAINING CASES

When organizations are accused of harassment or discrimination, their training may be examined to see if it is adequate. These three cases show why companies should invest in sufficient training.

Equal Employment Opportunity Commission v. California Psychiatric Transitions, Inc. The EEOC reported that California Psychiatric Transitions, Inc., a mental health rehabilitation center, settled a sexual harassment and retaliation lawsuit with the EEOC, which alleged that a male supervisor subjected female employees to a sexually hostile work environment for several years. The sexual harassment training provided by the company to its supervisors in response to complaints by the women about the harassment consisted of showing a video (during which the alleged harasser was reportedly on the telephone). The EEOC deemed the training inadequate, and the company agreed to pay $145,000 in addition to retraining its entire workforce as part of the settlement.[313]

---

[313]US Equal Employment Opportunity Commission, "Mental Health Rehab Center to Pay $145,000 to Settle Sexual Harassment and Retaliation Suit," October 21, 2009, https://www.eeoc.gov/newsroom/mental-health-rehab-center-pay-145000-settle-sexual-harassment-and-retaliation-suit.

Wagner v. Dillard Department Stores, Inc. According to an article on HRhero.com, Dillard's was sued for sex discrimination for allegedly failing to hire Sarah Wagner because she was pregnant. The court reviewed the department store chain's antidiscrimination training and determined that it consisted of a ten-minute video and a few questionnaires and forms that gave examples of what questions are prohibited in job interviews. The court found that the chain's training was insufficient and "therefore reprehensible." Wagner was awarded $41,720 in back pay as well as punitive damages.[314]

Baty v. Willamette Industries, Inc. Employee Patricia Baty complained to Willamette Industries management that she was being subjected to a hostile work environment by her male coworkers. In response, a member of management conducted two forty-five-minute training sessions (one for management and one for nonmanagement employees) using a video. Baty was soon after terminated. The plaintiff argued that the training was an inadequate response by management, and the jury apparently agreed, awarding Baty over $1 million in compensatory and punitive damages (later reduced by an appeals court) in part because the response by management was perceived to be weak and insincere.[315]

---

[314]HR Hero, "Ignoring the Obvious: Turning a Blind Eye to an Applicant's Pregnancy," accessed June 8, 2020, http://www.hrhero.com/pregnancy/obvious.shtm.

[315]Baty v. Willamette Industries, Inc., *United States District Court, D. Kansas*, September 5, 1997, https://scholar.google.com/scholar_case?case=15606481542754091432&hl=en&as_sdt=2006&as_vis=1.

CALIFORNIA TRAINING MANDATES

The state of California mandates frequent sexual harassment prevention training. In 2004, Governor Arnold Schwarzenegger signed AB 1825 to require employers with fifty or more employees to provide two hours of sexual harassment prevention training to their supervisors every two years.

Governor Jerry Brown signed SB 1343 in 2018 to require employers with five or more employees to provide sexual harassment prevention training to all employees every two years. One hour is required for nonsupervisors and two hours for supervisors.

The state-mandated training must include information and practical guidance regarding federal and state law concerning the prohibition against, and the prevention and correction of, sexual harassment and the remedies available to victims of sexual harassment. The training must also include practical examples of harassment, discrimination, and retaliation, as well as information about preventing abusive conduct and harassment based on sexual orientation, gender expression, and gender identity.

In addition to sex, sexual orientation, gender expression, and gender identity, the training may include information about the other protected classes under California's Fair Employment and Housing Act (FEHA), which include race (including hair), color, national origin, ancestry, age (forty and over), marital status, pregnancy (including childbirth, breast-feeding, and/or related medical conditions), religion (including religious dress and grooming practices), military or veteran status, medical condition, mental and physical disability, and genetic information.

The training must be interactive and include questions that assess learning, skill-building activities to assess understanding and application of content, and hypothetical scenarios about harassment with discussion questions.

Qualified trainers include

- attorneys admitted for two or more years to the bar whose practice includes employment law under the FEHA and/or Title VII of the federal Civil Rights Act of 1964;
- human resources professionals with a minimum of two or more years in designing or conducting harassment prevention training, responding to harassment or discrimination complaints, conducting harassment or discrimination investigations, advising employers or employees regarding harassment or discrimination, or who have completed a train-the-trainer course; and
- professors or instructors in law schools, colleges, or universities who have a postgraduate degree or California teaching credential and either twenty instruction hours or two years of experience teaching about employment law under the FEHA or Civil Rights Act.[316]

---

[316]California Department of Fair Employment and Housing, https://www.dfeh.ca.gov/wp-content/uploads/sites/32/2017/08/AttachB-ChangesWithout RegEffecT02CCR-11024-SexualHarassmentTraining-andEd.pdf.

SUPERVISOR PROBLEMS

Organizations are advised to create policies against managers or supervisors or anyone in power dating or trying to date their subordinates. Many examples exist in US history that demonstrate the kinds of legal troubles that can develop when people in positions of power ignore these guidelines.

One of the most famous examples is former president Bill Clinton, who was accused of propositioning Arkansas state employee Paula Jones and exposing himself to her in a Little Rock hotel room when he was governor of Arkansas. According to Peter Baker in the *Washington Post*, Clinton denied the allegation while giving Jones $850,000 to drop her lawsuit against him.[317]

Quid pro quo ("this for that"). In this type of sexual harassment, a person in a position of power seeks a sexual favor from a subordinate in return for job continuance, benefits, promotions, and the like or punishes the subordinate for not complying. A lawsuit filed in federal court by former Chrysler auto worker Janet Burney against the United Auto

---

[317]Peter Baker, "Clinton Settles Paula Jones Lawsuit for $850,000," *Washington Post*, November 14, 1998, https://www.washingtonpost.com/wp-srv/politics/special/clinton/stories/jones111498.htm.

Workers (UAW) accused the union of, among other things, quid pro quo. Soon after Burney began dating Pat Byers, a union official and the son of a union leader, she was given a new position and significant raise. According to court documents, "Pat Byers had told [Burney] repeatedly that as long as she was with him her job . . . was secure." Soon after Burney ended the relationship, she was terminated. Court documents state that the order to fire Burney came from the UAW's headquarters in Detroit.[318]

Hostile work environment. In its decision in *Miller v. Department of Corrections*, the California Supreme Court found a supervisor who had numerous simultaneous relationships with employees was guilty of creating a hostile work environment for the other employees. Prison warden Lewis Kuykendall was sexually involved with three female staff members, who allegedly received favorable treatment including promotions, protection, and other perks. According to an article on Laboremploymentblog.com, "there were no unwelcome requests for sexual favors, leering, or lewd conduct—it was the warden's favoritism toward (the) three other women . . . that the plaintiffs claim(ed) created the hostile work environment . . ."

The court agreed, citing an EEOC policy that states, "If favoritism based upon the granting of sexual favors is widespread in a workplace . . . colleagues who do not welcome this conduct can establish a hostile work environment . . . regardless of whether any objectionable conduct is directed at them and regardless of whether those who were granted favorable treatment willingly bestowed the sexual favors. In these circumstances, a message is implicitly conveyed that the managers view women as 'sexual playthings,' thereby creating an atmosphere that is demeaning to women."[319]

Retaliation. Complaining about the sexual advances of her supervisor allegedly led to the firing of a teenage farmworker, according

[318]Leftlane News, "UAW Named in Sexual Harassment Lawsuit," February 16, 2011, https://leftlanenews.com/2011/02/16/uaw-named-in-sexual-harassment-lawsuit/.

[319]Sheppard Mullin, "California Supreme Court Concludes Widespread Sexual Favoritism May Create a Hostile Work Environment," July 26, 2005, https://www.laboremploymentlawblog.com/2005/07/articles/sexual-harassment/california-supreme-court-concludes-widespread-sexual-favoritism-may-create-a-hostile-work-environment/.

to a lawsuit filed by the EEOC against Adam Brothers, a California farming company. According to the EEOC, the teen complained that her supervisor made lewd gestures with his tongue, brushed up against her and grabbed her private areas, and asked her to perform a sex act. Following her complaint to a farm foreman, she was transferred, disciplined, and then fired two weeks later. Adam Brothers agreed to pay the former employee $20,000 as well as $7,500 to Proteus, Inc., a nonprofit organization that provides job training and employment procurement assistance to farmworkers.[320]

[320]US Equal Employment Opportunity Commission, "Adams Brothers Farming Settles EEOC Sexual Harassment and Retaliation Suit," April 7, 2011, https://www.eeoc.gov/newsroom/adam-brothers-farming-settles-eeoc-sexual-harassment-and-retaliation-suit.

STARBUCKS TRAINING

The Starbucks unconscious bias training included a four-hour workshop, guidebook, video and audio clips played on an iPad, and a speech from Chairman Howard Schultz about his vision for a more inclusive company and country.

During the training, employees:

- discussed differences between themselves and others;
- reflected on the meaning of a place of belonging;
- examined their own biases;
- proposed suggestions for corporate policy;
- offered input on the obstacles they face in making all customers feel welcome; and
- determined what steps they would take to make customers and each other feel more welcome.

The employees reported mixed reactions, including the following quotes:

"I do think Starbucks has good intentions with what they're trying to do, and I think the training will combat bias."

"The literature and media provided by the company for the program was decently informative, but what I thought was the most effective was that the program allowed for an environment that felt comfortable to discuss our differences. . . . Hearing testimony from some of my coworkers that are people of color was essential to the program."

"In my opinion, the training was a waste of four hours."

"Starbucks' training was blanketed to every store, instead of being tailored to different demographics. That people of color had to sit through a four-hour training on 'how not to be racist' is kind of ridiculous."

"The training materials focused a lot on police brutality, which had nothing to do with the incident that happened. . . . At one point, a girl at my table actually had to get up and leave because video after video they showed black people being assaulted by police or black people being verbally assaulted and white people being racially biased toward people of color."

"The Nelson video actually provided some good discussion. It was the first one of the materials that actually got everyone to talk about their own experiences."

"I think the training is an appropriate response/solution to what happened in Philadelphia."

"They told us we need to be 'color brave' instead of color blind and it was the whitest thing I've ever heard."[321]

Unfortunately, employees also said they didn't quite know what to do after the training, which was demonstrated by a Philadelphia employee who was fired when he made fun of a customer with a stutter.[322]

---

[321]Jennifer Calfas, "Was Starbucks' Racial Bias Training Effective? Here's What These Employees Thought," *Time*, May 30, 2018, https://time.com/5294343/starbucks-employees-racial-bias-training/.

[322]David Chang, "Philly Starbucks Worker Accused of Mocking Man's Stutter," *NBC Philadelphia*, July 4, 2018, https://www.nbcphiladelphia.com/news/national-international/philadelphia-starbucks-worker-accused-man-stutter-mockery-cup-controversy/2065148/.

TWO CASE EXAMPLES

I n the case of *Gambini v. Total Renal Care*, employee Stephanie Gambini suffered an emotional breakdown at work and was diagnosed with bipolar disorder. She revealed her illness to her employer and coworkers and asked that they not be offended by the mood swings she experienced because of the disorder. Her symptoms gradually grew more severe, which negatively affected her job performance, and she was subsequently summoned to a meeting with her supervisor and given a performance improvement plan.

According to court documents, Gambini "threw the performance plan across the desk and in a flourish of several profanities expressed her opinion that it was both unfair and unwarranted. Before slamming the door on her way out, (she) hurled several profanities at her supervisor," then kicked and threw things at her cubicle following the meeting. Gambini entered the hospital the next day and was approved for a medical leave of absence.

The following day she was fired for what her employer called "violent outbursts." The district court that heard the case found in favor of the employer; however, the verdict was reversed by the Ninth Circuit Court of Appeals who reasoned that because Gambini's "violent outbursts" were symptomatic of her disorder, she was terminated because of it, which violated the Americans with Disabilities Act.[323]

---

[323]Gambini v. Total Renal Care.

In the case of *Wills v. The Superior Court of Orange County*, employee Linda Wills also suffered from bipolar disorder. During her employment, she took numerous medical leaves to treat the disorder but never revealed to her employer the reason for the leaves. She did tell some of her supervisors she suffered from depression. One day Wills became enraged at some coworkers and said she had added them to her "Kill Bill" list (a reference to the *Kill Bill* movie in which the main character made a list of people she intended to kill). The threat was reported to her superiors, and Wills was removed from her position and placed on medical leave by her doctor a few days later.

While on leave, Wills sent strange emails and ringtones to her coworkers that seemed to express anger toward them for supposedly betraying her. After a few weeks, Wills was released to work; however, the Orange County court put her on administrative leave and conducted an investigation into her actions. Following the investigation, Wills was terminated for threatening her coworkers (among other things). In its termination notice to Wills, the court explained that her conduct violated its employee handbook provisions prohibiting verbal threats, threatening behavior, and violence. Wills sued, claiming she was discriminated against because of her mental disability. In this case, the trial court found in favor of the employer because it demonstrated that Wills was terminated for a legitimate, nondiscriminatory reason.[324]

Why did Gambini win her case and Wills lose hers? The answer is a lesson for employers about the definition of the term "violent" and of making employment decisions based on established business policies.

In the Gambini case, court documents demonstrate that the Ninth Circuit Court of Appeals reversed the district court's verdict for the employer because of a technicality—the district court failed to instruct the jury that "conduct resulting from a disability is part of the disability and not a separate basis for termination." More importantly, the court claimed that a jury could reasonably find the "requisite causal link" between Gambini's disability (which she informed her employer about) and her "violent outbursts" (such as kicking her cubicle), which resulted in her termination. Thus, the court determined that she was fired for her disability.

---

[324]Wills v. The Superior Court of Orange County.

In the Wills case, court documents demonstrate that the trial court determined that her discrimination claim was invalid because Wills was terminated for a legitimate, nondiscriminatory reason—she violated written policies prohibiting threats and violence in the workplace. Upon appeal, the California Appellate Court upheld an employer's right to terminate an employee for making violent threats or committing violent acts even if they are caused by a disability. In addition, the court distinguished the Gambini case, in which the employee's "violent outbursts" merely frightened her coworkers, from the Wills case, in which the employee actually threatened her coworkers with violence.

MEDICINAL MARIJUANA AT WORK

Kohl's Department Stores created a policy in 2012 that stated employees in certain states (including California) would not be discriminated against for being registered medical marijuana card holders or for testing positive for marijuana components or metabolites. However, Kohl's retained the right to discipline and terminate employees who used, possessed, or were impaired at work.

Justin Shepherd went to work at the Kohl's in Patterson, California, in 2006. Like many California employers, Kohl's had Shepherd sign a written agreement upon his hiring that stated he was an at-will employee.

According to court documents, Shepherd had worked at Kohl's for five years when he was diagnosed with acute and chronic anxiety and began using medicinal marijuana based on his doctor's recommendation. He did not disclose this information to his employer. Kohl's updated its drug policy a year later so he was under the impression that he would not be discriminated against or terminated for his drug use.

Two years after that, Shepherd was injured at work. He submitted to a standard drug test, tested positive for trace amounts of marijuana metabolites (which did not surprise him), and explained he had a prescription for pot and had used it while off duty. He thought that explanation would suffice; however, a corporate HR director told Shepherd he "should have chosen a different medication" and terminated him for being under the influence, violating safety rules, and acting in conflict with the interest of Kohl's.

Shepherd sued for (1) disability discrimination, (2) failure to engage in the interactive process, (3) failure to reasonably accommodate him, (4) invasion of privacy, (5) wrongful termination in violation of public policy, (6) breach of contract and the implied covenant of good faith and fair dealing, and (7) defamation.

The judge dismissed the first five complaints but said a reasonable jury could find that Kohl's policy saying it would not discriminate against medical marijuana users created an employment agreement that Shepherd claimed was violated (breach of contract). And because the drug test was the only evidence that marijuana was in his system, a reasonable jury could find that Shepherd was not under the influence and that statements by Kohl's management that he was were made with a "reckless or wanton disregard for the truth" (defamation). So, the judge allowed him to move forward with those claims.[325]

If you'd like to avoid a defamation claim by a former employee, it's a good idea to stick to the facts if you're going to provide a reason for the termination. In this case, Kohl's management should have said Shepherd was fired for a positive drug test, not because he was under the influence while at work.

---

[325]Shepherd v. Kohl's Dep't Stores, Inc., United States District Court for the Eastern District of California, April 25, 2016, https://casetext.com/case/shepherd-v-kohls-dept-stores-inc.

A COACH AND
A PROBLEM

I n 2015, the University of Southern California (USC) fired its head football coach, which sparked some controversy about whether his termination was lawful since his firing apparently was related to the coach's drinking problem.

Steve Sarkisian was put on an "indefinite" leave of absence after reportedly showing up to a team meeting intoxicated. According to numerous sources, Sarkisian had previously attended a variety of school events where he appeared to be drunk. One day after his leave began, he was fired.

Those who said his termination might not be legal did so because they knew alcoholism qualifies as a disability according to the ADA and employers are required to reasonably accommodate employees who are or become disabled.

In his article "Alcoholism and How USC May Have Violated ADA by Firing Steve Sarkisian," David Kim says,

One common form of accommodation with respect to alcohol dependency is an unpaid leave of absence while the employee seeks treatment or other counseling. Frankly, it would be a red flag if an employer that grants an individual a leave of absence (for any reason, let alone a disability) then decides to terminate that same individual shortly after the leave was given. But that's exactly what USC did.[326]

All of that's true but, as the saying goes, there's more to the story. After being clearly intoxicated at a USC pep rally, Sarkisian denied he had a drinking problem but agreed to go into treatment, according to ESPN staff writer Kyle Bonagura.[327]

Evidently, the coach did not seek treatment and he definitely continued to drink. According to the US Commission on Civil Rights, an employer generally has no duty to provide an accommodation to an employee who has not asked for an accommodation and who denies having a drinking problem. The ADA also allows an employer to discipline, discharge, or deny employment to an alcoholic whose use of alcohol adversely affects job performance or conduct.

---

[326]David Kim, "Alcoholism and How USC May Have Violated ADA by Firing Steve Sarkisian," HR Daily Advisor, October 19, 2015, https://hrdailyadvisor.blr.com/2015/10/19/alcoholism-and-how-usc-may-have-violated-the-ada-by-firing-steve-sarkisian/.

[327]Kyle Bonagura, "Apologetic USC Coach Steve Sarkisian Said He Mixed Alcohol, Medicine at Event," ESPN, August 25, 2015, https://www.espn.com/los-angeles/college-football/story/_/id/13508272/usc-trojans-coach-steve-sarkisian-seek-treatment-mixing-alcohol-medication.

NIGHTMARE SCENARIO

Because serving alcohol at company parties is risky, the Marriott Del Mar Hotel in San Diego, California, gave employees two drink tickets and served only beer and wine at its holiday party in 2009.

Michael Landri was employed as a bartender at the hotel when he attended the party. Landri drank a beer and a shot of whiskey at his house before the party and then took a mostly filled flask of whiskey to the party. Even though only beer and wine were supposed to be served, the bartender on duty brought in a bottle of whiskey from the hotel's liquor supply, and Landri filled his flask at least one more time before he left for home.

After arriving safely at his home, Landri decided to drive an intoxicated coworker home. He was driving more than 100 miles per hour when he hit another vehicle, killing its driver, Dr. Jared Purton. Landri pleaded guilty to gross vehicular manslaughter while under the influence of alcohol (he had a .16 blood alcohol level) and received a six-year prison sentence.

Dr. Purton's parents filed a wrongful-death action against Landri, the hotel, and others. They alleged that the hotel "held the party for its benefit, including to improve relations between employees, improve relations between it and employees, and increase the continuity of employment by providing a fringe benefit." Further, although Landri became "extremely" intoxicated at the party, he was allowed to leave the hotel and drive home. The hotel argued it was not liable because "the accident did not occur within the scope of Landri's employment." The trial court agreed; however, the appellate court did not.

According to the Court of Appeal:

- The party and drinking of alcoholic beverages benefited the hotel by improving employee morale and furthering employer–employee relations.
- The drinking of alcoholic beverages by employees was a customary incident to the employment relationship.
- Evidence that hotel managers consumed hard alcohol with employees at the party and that a hotel manager served hard alcohol to employees suggests that employees had the employer's implied permission to consume hard alcohol at the party.
- Furthermore, an employee testified that "historically there has been a lot of drinking and not a lot of control at these types of (employee) parties."

Thus, the court concluded that "a reasonable trier of fact could conclude that Landri was acting within the scope of his employment while ingesting alcoholic beverages at the party." Furthermore, the court found that the ingesting of alcoholic beverages at the party caused the accident; therefore, the fact that the accident happened after Landri had left the party, arrived home, and then drove after that didn't matter ("We focus on the act on which vicarious liability is based and not on *when* the act results in injury.")

The court said that the hotel created the risk of harm by allowing an employee to become intoxicated and that it could have lessened this risk by

- having a policy prohibiting smuggled alcohol;
- enforcing its drink ticket policy;
- serving drinks for only a limited time;
- serving food; or
- forbidding alcohol altogether.[328]

If you'd like to avoid a similar fate, it would be wise to follow the court's suggestions.

---

[328]Purton v. Marriott International, Inc., Court of Appeals of California, Fourth District, Division One, July 31, 2013, https://scholar.google.com/scholar_case?-case=4290977229330224801&q=Purton+v.+Marriott&hl=en&as_sdt=2006.

ACKNOWLEDGMENTS

Thank you to Jay Rosenlieb and David Blaine for employing me and teaching me about human resources—this book would not have been possible without their guidance (although any inaccuracies in content are my own). Thanks also to Tammy Rutledge and Lorraine Souder for their invaluable feedback on my first drafts; to Jeff Thorn and Alex Campos for allowing me to work on this book while isolating at home during the COVID-19 pandemic; to my husband, Pat, for being such a good quarantine partner; and especially to Kat Clowes, for the invitation to coauthor this book.

INDEX

R
racism, 221, 252
Rasmussen, Frederick N., 142–143
Rath, Tom, 187
Razzaq, Zane, 233
"real-world" testing, 41–42
recognition, 163, 170, 172–175
recognition, name, 12
references, 49–52
relationships, 107, 180–181, 220
religion, 229, 230–232
reputation, 6
research training, 94–95
responsibilities, clarity of, 180
retaliation, 237–240
rewards, 170, 172–175, 181
Richard, Khalon, 241
Rodionova, Zlata, 226
roles, clarity of, 180
Rosa, Anthony De, 108
rules of engagement, 199
Russell, Joyce, 276–277
Rutledge, Tammy, 59, 78

S
safety, 113, 259–260
sales goals, 70
Sarkozy, Nicolas, 114
Sasic, Ema, 92
Savage, Fred, 241
schedule, flexibility of, 171–172, 271
Schiff, Jennifer Lonoff, 192–193
Schilling, Curt, 234–235
schools, 9–10, 92, 259. See also
    colleges; education
Schultz, Howard, 93
security, 127, 148
Seely, Barbara, 264
Seitz, Dan, 127
Selman, J. Christopher, 275

service, acts of, 177
Sewell, Terri, 240
sexting, 215
sexual advances, 236
sexual assault, 236–237
sexual harassment, 210–213, 215–
    216, 220, 236, 241, 242
sexual misconduct, 237
Shakespeare, 48
Shechtman, Morris R., 38, 40, 43
Shelly, Jared, 276
shootings, 255, 259
sick leave, 270, 272
Signora, Michael, 232
Singer, Rick, 18
Skerrett, Patrick J., 107
skills, 29–30, 35–36, 40–42, 102, 196
SMART goals, 69–70, 180
smartphones. See cell phones
Smith, Carly Parnitzke, 238
Smith, Zane, 19
Snapchat, 12
snowplow parents, 17–18
social media
    hiring through, 7–8
    importance of, 8
    incivility and, 104–105
    job openings and, 7–8, 12
    legal considerations for, 118–119
    mental health and, 252
    monitoring of, 122–124
    overview of, 117–118
    policies for, 118, 121–122
    politics and, 234–235
    potential within, 3–4
SSPS (Striving Styles Personality
    System), 32–33
standard operating procedures, 65–66
Stark, John, 153, 154–155
Steinmetz, Katy, 150

ABOUT THE AUTHORS

ROBIN PAGGI is the training and development specialist at Worklogic HR, a human resources outsourcing company. She is also a certified professional coach and provides individual counseling to supervisors and employees who need to improve their supervisory and communication skills. Paggi has a BA in communications, an MA in communication studies, and an MA in interdisciplinary studies with a concentration in human resource development. She has professional certifications in human resources, training, coaching, industrial and organizational psychology, conflict resolution, investigations, emotional intelligence, and administering the Myers-Briggs and DiSC personality assessments.

KAT CLOWES is the founder and CEO of March Consulting, a company that helps students with the college application process and planning out their career path. She has a BA in communications with an emphasis in television and film from Santa Clara University, an MBA with an emphasis in Entrepreneurship from Mt. St. Mary's University, and holds a certificate in Educational Consulting from University of California, Irvine. Clowes is the author of *Put College to Work: How to Use College to the Fullest to Discover Your Strengths and Find a Job You Love Before You Graduate*.

Printed in the USA
CPSIA information can be obtained
at www.ICGtesting.com
JSHW012117040923
47807JS00014B/106

9 781610 354004